Music Psychology in Education

The Bedford Way Papers Series

6 *Men as Workers in Services for Young Children: Issues of a mixed gender workforce*
   Edited by Charlie Owen, Claire Cameron and Peter Moss
7 *Convergence and Divergence in European Education and Training Systems*
   Andy Green, Alison Wolf and Tom Leney
8 *FE and Lifelong Learning: Realigning the sector for the twenty-first century*
   Edited by Andy Green and Norman Lucas
9 *Values and Educational Research*
   Edited by David Scott
10 *The Culture of Change: Case studies of improving schools in Singapore and London*
   Peter Mortimore, Saravanan Gopinathan, Elizabeth Leo, Kate Myers, Leslie
   Sharpe, Loise Stoll and Jo Mortimore
11 *Education and Employment: The DfEE and its place in history*
   Edited by Richard Aldrich, David Crook and David Watson
12 *The Maths We Need Now: Demands, deficits and remedies*
   Edited by Clare Tickly and Alison Wolf
13 *Why Learn Maths?*
   Edited by Steve Bramall and John White
14 *History of Education for the Twenty-First Century*
   Edited by David Crooks and Richard Aldrich
15 *The Children of London: Attendance and welfare at school 1870–1990*
   Susan Williams, Patrick Irvin and Caroline Morse
16 *Developing Inclusive Schooling: Perspectives, policies and practice*
   Edited by Carol Campbell
17 *School Textbook Research: The case of geography 1800–2000*
   Norman Graves
18 *Changing Britain, Changing Lives: Three generations at the turn of the century*
   Edited by Elsa Ferri, John Bynner and Michael Wadsworth
19 *Teacher Pay and Performance*
   Peter Dolton, Steve McIntosh and Arnaud Chevalier
20 *Childhood in Generational Perspective*
   Edited by Berry Mayall and Hela Zeiher
21 *Homework: The evidence*
   Susan Hallam
22 *Teaching in Further Education: New perspectives for a changing context*
   Norman Lucas
23 *Legalised Leadership: Law-based educational reform in England and what it does to
   school leadership and headteachers*
   Dan Gibton
24 *Theorising Quality in Higher Education*
   Louise Morley

Music Psychology in Education

Susan Hallam

Bedford Way Papers

INSTITUTE OF
EDUCATION
UNIVERSITY OF LONDON

First published in 2006 by the Institute of Education, University of London,
20 Bedford Way, London WC1H 0AL
www.ioe.ac.uk/publications

Over 100 years of excellence in education

© Institute of Education, University of London 2006

British Library Cataloguing in Publication Data:
A catalogue record for this publication is available from the British Library

ISBN 0 85473 716 2

Text design by Joan Rose
Cover design by Andrew Chapman

Printed by Alden Group Ltd, Oxford

Contents

Preface   vii

1 Introduction   1

2 Music, the brain and learning   11

3 Early development   29

4 Musical ability   44

5 Listening, appraising and responding to music   57

6 Composing and improvising   70

7 Learning to play an instrument and develop vocal skills   91

8 Learning through practice   118

9 Motivation and musical identity   142

10 Assessment   155

11 Teachers and teaching   165

12 The impact of music through life   179

References   194

Index   277

Preface

The psychological study of music has a long history, which parallels the development of psychology as a discipline. The first simple test of musical ability was developed in 1883 by Stumpf. This marked the beginning of a long tradition of psychometric testing in music. Other early work focused on learning and memory; the perception and cognition of music; and practical issues, for instance, the impact of background music on studying. The field is now well established, with research being undertaken in relation to every aspect of human musical behaviour. Although much of the research is of direct concern to music educators, it has not been presented in an easily accessible, single volume. This book attempts to address that issue, reviewing research that has relevance to education and making explicit its implications.

1 Introduction

The nature of musical sound

Music is a human construct. While sound may exist as an objective reality, for that sound to be defined as music requires human beings to acknowledge it as such. As Radocy and Boyle put it:

> If sounds are created or combined by a human being, recognised as music by some group of people and serve some function which music has come to serve for mankind, then those sounds are music. (1988:19)

What is acknowledged as 'music' varies between cultures, groups and individuals. For instance, the Igbo of Nigeria have no specific term for music; their term *nkwa* denotes 'singing, playing instruments and dancing' (Gourlay, 1984). *The Oxford Dictionary* defines music as:

> The art of combining sounds of voice(s) or instrument(s) to achieve beauty of form and expression of emotion.

To define music in these terms depends on subjective judgements of what constitutes beauty of form and expression of emotion. This may vary from individual to individual. Indeed, some may argue that what constitutes 'music' for them is neither beautiful nor expressive of emotion. Their definition of 'music' may be based on different criteria. The proliferation of musical genres in Western cultures in recent years, and group identification with them, has led some to challenge whether genres appreciated by other groups are indeed 'music'. Despite the variability in what might constitute 'music', there is general agreement that musicality is a universal trait of humankind (Blacking, 1995; Merriam, 1964). However, what may be music to the ears of one individual may not be to the ears of others.

The origins of music

However music is defined, it is universal and found in all cultures. Some have suggested that it is at the very essence of humanity. Along with language, it distinguishes us from other species. Does it therefore have evolutionary significance? Answers to this question are inevitably speculative. Miller (2000) argues that music exemplifies many of the classic criteria for a complex human evolutionary adaptation. He points out that no culture has ever been without music (universality); musical development in children is orderly; musicality is widespread (all adults can appreciate music and remember tunes); there is specialist memory for music; specialised cortical mechanisms are involved; there are parallels in the signals of other species – for example, birds, gibbons and whales – so evolution may be convergent; and music can evoke strong emotions, which implies receptive as well as productive adaptations.

Further support for an evolutionary basis for music comes from evidence of its existence many thousands of years ago. The earliest musical instrument so far discovered, a bone flute, is estimated to be about 50,000 years old. Even this may have been predated by singing. Found in a Neanderthal burial site, it indicates the existence of music before *Homo sapiens* (Anon., 1997; Turk, 1997). In China there is evidence of the use of bone flutes as early as 6000 BC, stone flutes from 1200 BC, and a system of classification of instruments according to the materials that they were made of from 500 BC (Zhenxiong *et al.*, 1995). There is similar evidence of the early use of instruments in several cultures (see Carterette and Kendall, 1999).

If music does have an evolutionary origin, what might it be? Huron (2003) provides an overview of the main theoretical positions:

- mate selection – music performance may have arisen as a courtship behaviour;
- social cohesion – music may create or maintain social cohesion through the promotion of group solidarity and altruism;

- group effort – music may contribute to the co-ordination of group work;
- perceptual development – music may contribute towards the more general development of sound perception;
- motor skill development – singing with movement and other music-making provides opportunities for refining motor skills;
- conflict reduction – music may reduce interpersonal conflict within groups through shared activities unlikely to provoke argument or dispute;
- safe time passing – music may provide a way of passing time which avoids engagement with possible dangerous situations;
- trans-generational communication – music may have originated as a useful mnemonic device for passing on information from generation to generation.

Those supporting a sexual selection theory (e.g. Miller, 2000) argue that male musical performance influenced female choice of mate. This may be why music is so important during adolescence. While this is an attractive proposal, it does not explain female interest in music, although musical performance might equally contribute to male mate selection. Other theories propose that music evolved from emotional or impassioned speech or indeed was an imitation of bird song (for reviews see Cross, 2003; Huron, 2003). Several authors have proposed that music developed as a result of the mother–child relationship, in particular soothing and comforting behaviour that led to the development of lullabies. This theory is supported by evidence that the human brain has systems for music perception which operate from birth, enabling 'significant nonverbal communication in the form of music' (Gaston, 1968:15). Dissanayake (1988) further suggests that the musicality of the mother–infant interaction might lay the foundations for a grammar of the emotions.

Several theories focus on music's importance in relation to social cohesion. Sloboda (1985) speculates that music making is 'rewarding' because participating in it generates social bonding and cultural coherence. Its role in a range of ceremonies supports this view (Roederer, 1984). Its survival value lies in synchronising the mood of many individuals who can then collectively take action to strengthen their means of protection and defend themselves from attack (Dowling and Harwood, 1986). Moving together rhythmically in music and dance may reinforce this process (Kogan, 1997). Overall, this approach suggests that music reinforces 'groupishness', the formation and maintenance of group identity, collective thinking, synchronisation and catharsis (the collective expression and experience of emotion) (Brown, D., 1991), assisting in the forming of coalitions, the promotion of co-operative behaviour and the creating of potential for hostility towards outgroups.

Cross (2003) takes these arguments further. Drawing on the work of Smith and Szathmary (1995), who maintain that human culture constitutes one of the main transitions in evolution; and the work of Mithen (1996) that suggests that the appearance of *Homo sapiens sapiens* is marked by the emergence of a flexible cross-domain cognitive capacity, he argues that

> music is uniquely fitted to have played a significant role in facilitating the acquisition and maintenance of the skill of being a member of a culture – of interacting socially with others – as well as providing a vehicle for integrating our domain-specific competences so as to endow us with the multi-purpose and adaptive cognitive capacities which make us human. (2003:52)

Cross suggests that because music intrinsically has a 'transposable aboutness' (2003:51), many meanings which can change from situation to situation, this may be exploited in infancy and childhood as a means of forming connections and interrelations between different domains, social, biological and mechanical. Musical activity may simultaneously be about movement, mood, emotion and mastery, embodied in sound affording the opportunity to explore cross-domain mappings.

Not all authors agree that music has evolutionary purpose. Some suggest that music, along with the other arts, has no evolutionary significance and no practical function (Barrow, 1995; Pinker, 1997). Sperber (1996) condemns music as an evolutionary parasite. Pinker argues that music is bound to the domain of language, auditory scene analysis, habitat selection, emotion and motor control, and merely exploits the capacities that have evolved to subserve these areas. Music is 'exaptive', an evolutionary by-product of the emergence of other capacities that have direct adaptive value. From this perspective music exists simply because of the pleasure that it affords, its basis is purely hedonic. Whatever the origins of music, there is no doubt that engagement with it is rewarding for human beings as a species. If this were not the case, individuals would not spend so much time involved in musical activity (see Chapter 12).

The functions of music in society today

Music has a multiplicity of functions which operate at several levels: that of the individual, the social group and society in general (Radocy and Boyle; 1988; Gregory, 1997). Merriam (1964) distinguishes between the uses and functions of music. Uses refer to the ways in which people use music; functions are concerned with the reasons or broad purposes for which it is used. Merriam recognises ten major musical functions: emotional expression, aesthetic enjoyment, entertainment, communication, symbolic representation, physical response, enforcing conformity to social norms, validation of social institutions and religious rituals, contributions to the continuity and stability of culture, and contributions to the integration of society (Merriam, 1964). These functions can be seen as operating at different levels within society (Hallam, 2001d).

The functions of music at the individual level
At the individual level music has been seen as a vehicle for emotional expression. Ideas and emotions that might be difficult to convey in ordinary verbal interchanges can be expressed through music. Music elicits physical responses. It can aid relaxation or stimulate activity.

It is particularly effective in changing our moods (Thayer, 1996). Music therapy can also be a particularly valuable medium through which individuals who have lost touch with reality might regain it. Involvement in music provides opportunities for individuals to experience aesthetic enjoyment and be entertained. For those involved in making music it can be seen as a source of reward and intellectual stimulation. It provides interesting and challenging activities at the rehearsal stage, where technical and musical mastery are the aim. Performance itself provides opportunities for the demonstration of expertise and musicianship, while successful performance can lead to an increase in self-esteem for the individual concerned. Individuals may derive considerable pleasure from playing to themselves, satisfying a range of personal needs. In addition musical activities may improve a range of transferable skills, including concentration, self-discipline, physical co-ordination and literacy skills (for a review see Hallam, 2001d).

The functions of music at the group level
In addition to the functions that music serves at the individual level, it also serves important functions for groups. Music can be viewed as a means of communication. It is a social activity in that creating, interpreting, performing and hearing music depend on shared social meanings. Music can serve to provide shared experiences and understandings which assist in binding together social groups, supporting their identity. This is apparent in its use in children's games and also in adolescence – music becomes one of the central aspects of young people's chosen youth culture. Music is also used in work contexts. It can facilitate the appropriate level of stimulation for mental or physical activity and may also serve to ensure that individuals literally work in time together. Emotional expression can also be important at the group level; for instance in protest songs. It provides a means of expressing feelings towards subjects that are taboo or where there are inhibitions regarding the expression of emotions – for example, love. Instances of this can be found not

only in relation to romantic love but to love of God, country, school or institution.

The functions of music in society

In society as a whole music provides a means of symbolic representation for other things, ideas and behaviours. It can, for instance, represent the state, patriotism, religion, bravery, heroism or rebellion. It can encourage conformity to social norms, for instance through songs, which can play a major part in indicating appropriate behaviour and providing warnings to others. It may also play a major role in inciting challenges to those social norms and define groups in conflict. It provides validation of social institutions and religious rituals, and plays a major part in all major ceremonial occasions – for example, weddings, military functions, funerals and sporting events. In some societies it contributes to inducing trance in individuals involved in particular ceremonies. Music also contributes towards the continuity and stability of culture and perhaps most importantly to the integration of society. Individuals within society respond in similar ways to the music of their own culture, providing cohesion; while the social nature of musical activity invites and encourages individuals to participate in group activities reducing social isolation – for example, dancing and singing.

The power of music is reflected in the way that the state often attempts to exert control over it. In Nazi Germany music was carefully selected for use at mass rallies to generate appropriate patriotic emotions. In the USSR, the music of Shostakovich was censured by the Soviet government. During the Cultural Revolution in China, Western music was denounced as decadent and forbidden. In Iran, when Ayatollah Khomeni was in power, tight restrictions were placed on particular types of music. In white-dominated South Africa, centres of African music were demolished, while musicians living in exile continued with their music to influence the attitudes of the world against the prevailing political system. In the Western world, criticism of rock music and its purported effects by the 'establishment' have been well documented (Martin and Segrave, 1988).

Music not only serves a range of functions in societies, but its nature reflects the values, attitudes and characteristics of a society. For instance, Weber (1958) suggests that the Western classical tradition reflects a drive to rationalise and understand the environment. Technological advances impact on the way that music making develops, as do the extent of contact with and influence of other musical cultures (Nettl, 1975), and the development of musical literacy. The latter extends what can be passed on to future generations. Oral cultures restrict what can be remembered (Sloboda, 1985).

Music in education

The extent to which music education is provided through state education systems internationally varies, as does the means by which it is offered. Provision depends on the nature of the education system, economic wealth, political factors and the perceived role and value placed on music in society. Given the importance of music at the individual, group and societal levels, it is important that music has a place within education systems. However, from time to time governments have seen fit to control music in education, either removing it from the school curriculum or taking central control of it through the implementation of a national curriculum. Recently, because of threats to the place of music in the curriculum of some developed countries, the benefits of music education – beyond those for its own sake – including the development of a range of personal and social skills in children have been stressed. These issues will be returned to in Chapter 12.

Formal music education can be approached in a range of ways. At different times and in different cultures, it has focused on listening, understanding and appreciation of music; performance; creativity; combinations of these; or has developed within a more general arts education. Depending on the focus adopted, children may learn to read musical notation; develop critical listening skills; acquire knowledge about the history of music, instruments, world musics, acoustics and the contribution of music to other art forms; learn to compose or improvise using a range of instruments or computer technology; develop technical skills in playing an instrument or singing; and develop performing and communication skills. Within general music education, there are ongoing debates as to which of these should be included, and whether the curriculum should focus on traditional national musics and cultures or Western popular culture, the latter being increasingly a worldwide phenomenon. While the issue of what should be taught in schools is a philosophical matter, the way in which children develop skills in each of these areas, are assessed on their performance, and are taught has been a focus of music psychology and will be considered in Chapters 5, 6, 7, 10 and 11. Learning of any kind requires time and opportunity. The considerable amount of time needed to acquire high levels of musical expertise also requires dedication on the part of the learner. Issues relating to time spent in learning and motivation will be considered in Chapters 8 and 9, while the early development of musical skills and the way the brain develops in response to these will be considered in Chapters 2 and 3.

There are also debates as to whether music education should be available for all children or whether it should be available only for those who show particular interest in or aptitude for music. In many cultures provision is made at both levels. For instance, music may become optional as pupils progress through school; specialist selective schools may offer a full-time education with music at its core; extra-curricular music schools may operate out of school hours, providing tuition and ensemble opportunities; centrally or locally funded music services may provide instrumental music tuition in schools during the school day in addition to a range of out-of-school music activities. The balance between general and specialised state provision of music education rests to some extent on conceptions of musical ability which will be considered in Chapter 4 and the value placed on music in society. Complementary to state-funded provision, private teachers and local community groups may offer further opportunities to develop musical skills. In some cultures music is learnt informally within the community through everyday activities where it is a natural part of work, play, rituals, ceremonies, and religious and family occasions. Such informal music making occurs, to some extent, in all societies, forming an essential part of musical culture. The way that music plays a role throughout our lives will be considered in Chapter 12.

Further Reading

Cross, I. (2003) 'Music, cognition, culture and evolution'. In I. Peretz and R.J.A. Zatorre (eds) *The Cognitive Neuroscience of Music.* Oxford: Oxford University Press (pp. 42–56).

Hargreaves, D.J. and North, A.C. (eds) (2001) *Musical Development and Learning: An international perspective.* London: Continuum.

Huron, D. (2003) 'Is music an evolutionary adaptation?' In I. Peretz and R.J.A. Zatorre (eds) *The Cognitive Neuroscience of Music.* Oxford: Oxford University Press (pp. 57–77).

Pierce, J.R. (1999) 'The nature of musical sound'. In D. Deutsch (ed.) *The Psychology of Music.* (2nd edition) London: Academic Press (pp. 1–24).

Wallin, N.L., Merker, B. and Brown, S. (eds) (2000) *The Origins of Music.* Cambridge, MA: The MIT Press.

2 Music, the brain and learning

In the recent past, there has been a substantial increase in research exploring the representation of music-related functions in the brain. This is in part attributable to advances in techniques for studying the brain. While these technological developments have furthered our knowledge of brain structures and processes, the musical materials used in many studies have continued to be oversimplified, with little resemblance to 'real' music. Despite these difficulties, considerable progress has been made in developing our understanding of the brain structures and functions involved in processing and learning music.

Brain structures for processing music

The traditional view of a left–right dichotomy of brain organisation which assumed that music was processed in the right hemisphere and language in the left was challenged many years ago by Bever and Chiarello (1974), who demonstrated the influence of professional training on hemispheric lateralisation during music processing. Non-musicians exhibited right and professional musicians left hemispheric preponderance. Since then improved methodology has allowed much more precise exploration of brain structures and processes, highlighting the adaptability and plasticity of the brain. The neural systems underlying music appear to be distributed through the left and right cerebral and cerebellar hemispheres, with different aspects of music processed by distinct neural circuits (Altenmuller, 2003). The most recent research indicates that processing depends on each individual's personal biography of musical learning and that the majority of relevant sound information is neurally encoded, even if we are not consciously aware of it. The first stages of processing are the least and the latest stages the most dependent on the attentional processes of the listener (Tervaniemi, 2003). This has important implications for the different ways in which we listen to and respond to music.

Evidence from individuals with brain damage

Early evidence that musical processing is multi-modal and widely distributed in both cerebral hemispheres came from studies of individuals with neurological disorders. The selective impact of brain damage on musical functions was first reported by Bouillaud in 1865. He gave an account of a patient who was able to continue composing and writing music when he had lost the ability to speak or write text. Since that time further evidence has emerged that musical functions can be spared or impaired depending on the nature of the brain damage. Loss of musical function, amusia, is often accompanied by aphasia (loss of language functions), but each can occur in the absence of the other. Benton (1977) categorised the amusias into oral-expressive or vocal amusia, instrumental apraxia (dysfunction in playing an instrument), musical agraphia (inability to make notes of heard tones or to copy notes from a paper), musical amnesia (inability to identify or sing generally well-known melodies), musical alexia (inability to read musical notation), perturbations of rhythm, and receptive amusia (inability to discriminate pitch loudness, duration, timbre and rhythm) (for reviews see Brust, 2003; Weiser, 2003). This diversity illustrates the wide range of different types of music-related behaviours which can be impaired through brain damage and the extent of their distribution across both cerebral hemispheres.

Some disorders exist from birth. Musical savants are individuals with severe congenital difficulties in normal cognitive functioning who exhibit exceptional musical skills (Young and Nettelbeck, 1995; Sloboda *et al.*, 1985). There are also individuals who self-identify themselves as deficient in musical processing or productive skills, tests confirming their difficulties in a range of musical skills including musical pitch recognition, rhythmic discrimination (Peretz *et al.*, 2003), and rhythmic synchronisation (Dalla Bella and Peretz, 2003). Their difficulties were not consistent across all musical skills (Peretz *et al.*, 2003), confirming the presence of different forms of congenital amusias.

Processing of pitch, melody and harmony
Several authors have suggested that there are two key elements to music processing, one related to pitch, another to timing; although others have argued that melody and rhythm are treated as a unified dimension (for a review see Peretz and Zatorre, 2005). The right auditory cortex has generally been seen as playing an important role in the processing of pitch, while temporal information has been seen as being processed in the left auditory cortex (Zatorre *et al.*, 1992; Liegeois-Chauvel *et al.*, 1998, 2003; Peretz, 2003). However, not all the data are consistent with this (Langner, 1992). There is evidence that while right-hemisphere dominance is often found for pitch-based musical tasks, laterality can be changed by instruction and degree of musical training (Peretz and Morais, 1987; Peretz *et al.*, 1987). The left hemisphere may also co-operate if contour cues are not available and interval information is required (Peretz, 1990).

Pitch stimuli seem to be processed through the ascending auditory pathway to the primary auditory cortex. Experiments where pitch strength is manipulated in different ways suggest that there may be a pitch centre in the lateral part of the Heschl's gyrus, adjacent to the primary auditory area. However, the analysis of patterns of pitch such as melodies, as opposed to the pitch of individual notes, involves much more distributed processing in the superior temporal lobes and frontal lobes. Processing may occur at three levels: simple, including the encoding of simple temporal, spectral and spatial information; complex, providing a stable representation of that information; and semantic, where symbolic use is made of the auditory information (Griffiths, 2003).

A further key element of musical processing relates to harmony. There seem to be basic physiological and anatomical properties of auditory and cognitive systems which determine why some combinations of notes sound more harmonious than others. Implicit knowledge of a particular tonal system may inform this process. Bilateral lesions of primary auditory cortex and auditory association cortex can lead to severe impairments in consonance perception. These seem to be closely associated with severely impaired pitch perception (Tramo *et al.*, 2003). Non-musicians and children respond to authentic cadences and inappropriate endings in similar ways to musicians, suggesting that the acquisition of implicit knowledge about harmony and the processing of music according to that knowledge are general abilities of the human brain (Koelsch and Friederici, 2003).

Pulse, metre and rhythm

Music, like language, consists of a succession of auditory events in time which require elaborate temporal processing. Relatively little is known about the cerebral substrates underlying auditory temporal processes in music, and findings to date have been mixed. In processing terms, metre is the most complex because its perception and production require information on sound intensity (accented and unaccented events) and on periodicity of rhythmic events. The cerebral mechanisms underlying pulse, metre and rhythm are not yet clear, although it has been suggested that auditory neurons in the left hemisphere are more selective for temporal pattern than pitch (Liegeous-Chauvel *et al.*, 1999; Platel *et al.*, 1997; Samson and Ehrle, 2003). Lerdhal and Jackendoff (1983) suggest two components, one requiring a left-hemispheric, local-level, serial, cognitive operation; while the other, processing metre, requires a right-hemispheric global-level holistic strategy. The evidence to support this is mixed (Sakai *et al.*, 1999; Kuck *et al.*, 2003). Different mechanisms for processing rhythm and metre have been found in a study of epileptic patients (Liegeous-Chauvel *et al.*, 1998) and, irrespective of hemisphere, in studies of patients with brain damage (Peretz, 1990). Schuppert *et al.* (2000) revealed a hierarchical organisation with an initial right-hemisphere recognition of metre followed by identification of rhythm via left-hemisphere subsystems. Consistent engagement of the distinct neural circuits in the cerebellum across musical-rhythmical tasks suggests its central role in the temporal organisation of cognitive and perceptual processes in music (Schmahmann, 1997), indicating a strong motor component to the mental representation of musical rhythm. Overall, the evidence indicates a widely distributed cortical and subcortical network subserving the motor, sensory and cognitive aspects of rhythm processing (Penhune *et al.*, 1998; Platel *et al.*, 1997; Schlaug, 2001; Thaut, 2003) with distinct processing of metre and rhythm (for a review see Peretz and Zatorre, 2005).

The perception of timbre

Timbre is defined as a combination of various acoustical parameters involving stationary and dynamic features of tone. Non-musicians are more sensitive to changes in timbre than in pitch (Pitt, 1994) and differences in timbre are very effective initiators of stream segregation (Cusack and Roberts, 2000; Singh and Bregman, 1997). Right hemisphere superiority has been reported in several studies of timbre using natural instruments and synthetic sounds, and most studies of patients with brain lesions have indicated that processing of timbre occurs in the right hemisphere (see Samson, 2003), although there are exceptions to this (Tramo and Gazzanigga, 1989). Overall, the findings obtained in lesion and brain-imaging studies support involvement of the right auditory temporal areas in processing musical timbre (Samson, 2003), although left-temporal lobe structures may make a contribution.

Cultural influences on neurological responses to music

As education increasingly embraces world musics, it is important to understand how music from different cultures is processed. There has been little research in this area. Such as there is suggests that the brain is sensitive to music of specific genre (Genc *et al.*, 2001) and to familiar rather than unfamiliar instruments (Arikan *et al.*, 1999). However, Western listeners, while making different behavioural responses to Western and Chinese music, showed no differences in functional magnetic resonance imaging (fMRI) mapping results (Demorest and Morrison, 2003), suggesting a cultural impact on the way that we understand music but not on the basic processes involved in its perception.

Musical memory

Currently, we are far from understanding how lengthy sequences of music are stored in our brains, although it is clear that music activates large parts of auditory cortex in both hemispheres. We know that complex sounds are first broken down in their frequency components in the periphery of the auditory system and in the primary auditory cortex. At later stages this information is integrated into more complex responses, and single units respond to more and more complex contents (Rauschecker, 1998; Wessinger *et al.*, 2001). Memories of familiar tunes seem to be stored in a relatively abstract way as they can be recognised when they are played at different pitches and tempos or by different instruments, although stored representations do preserve some surface features like absolute pitch and tempo (Levitin, 1994; Levitin and Cook, 1996). Most listeners appear to remember the 'gist' (Dowling and Harwood, 1986), although memory for particular interpretations requires surface characteristics to be recalled (Raffman, 1993). It is clear that the multi-modal components of musical processing cannot be sharply localised to one part of the brain or even to one cerebral hemisphere. The psychological whole that emerges from their interaction is very widely distributed (Brust, 2003).

The impact of learning on brain functions

The cerebral cortex has the ability to self-organise in response to external stimuli. That is how learning occurs. Hebb (1949) proposed that learning and memory were based on changes in synaptic efficacy in the brain. He suggested that effective connections between neurons were formed dependent on their firing together. Several interrelated mechanisms appear to contribute towards cortical remodelling, including changes in the efficacy of existing connections, the modification of excitatory synapses based on early gene expression and the sprouting of new connections. These different changes are likely to take place over different time scales (Pantev *et al.*, 2003). The study of the development of musical skills has proved a useful vehicle for exploring the impact of learning on brain functions.

Changes as a result of deprivation in one sensory modality
Deprivation in one sensory modality can lead to dramatic reorganisation of cortical processing in other modalities; for instance, compensatory improvement of hearing or touch in the blind which may include musical abilities (Rauschecker, 1995). The brain network is not fixed but is subject to short- and long-term plastic changes allowing, at early processing stages, for adaptations and compensations in the case of damage to certain brain substrates. Learning a musical instrument is easier during childhood because our motor abilities are more malleable and because the auditory cortex has sensitive periods for self-organisation. However, this does not preclude learning at later ages; it merely means that more effort is required.

Changes in the brain as the result of training
In order to explore change in brain structures and functions, some research has focused on comparing the brains of musicians and non-musicians. Differences that have been found include a larger

corpus callosum (the part of the brain connecting the right and left hemispheres), greater symmetry and size of left and right hemispheres in the motor cortex, some gender-mediated differences in the size of the cerebellum, and regional differences in grey-matter volume (Schlaug, 2003). These differences may reflect an increasing need for inter-hemisphere communication; the development of motor skills utilising both hands; and the need to integrate and initiate complex motor, cognitive and emotional skills. Playing a musical instrument, which demands extensive procedural and motor learning, results in plastic reorganisation of the human brain, including the rapid enhancing of existing connections and the establishment of new ones. Of course, it is possible that the differences found between musicians and non-musicians are a reflection of structures in place in the brains of musicians prior to their training. Special anatomy or brain function may be a prerequisite for musical skill acquisition rather than its consequence, although evidence from the study of skill acquisition in a range of domains suggests that this is unlikely.

Aural skills

The brain substrates for aural perception are able to adapt quickly to incoming stimuli, including music, in both the long and short term. In one study, participants listened to some of their favourite music, from which one specific spectral frequency was removed. Initially, this produced a change in reported perception, but participants quickly adapted to this and their appreciation of the music during the three-hour listening time was unchanged, demonstrating the speed at which reorganisation of representations in the adult human auditory cortex can occur (Pantev *et al.*, 2003).

In the longer term, the brain substrates underlying auditory processing remain adaptive and subject to plastic changes (Pantev *et al.*, 1999). With training and practice, additional mental representations of music that rely on different brain substrates develop. Professional musicians use larger and more complex neuronal networks during music processing than non-professionals (Altenmuller, 1989). Long years of instrumental practice are associated with an increase in neuronal representation specific to the processing of the tones of the musical scale, the largest cortical representations being found in musicians who started playing before they were 9 years old (Pantev *et al.*, 2003). Attentive auditory processing is related to the instrument played (Munte *et al.*, 2003). Processing of pitch in string players was characterised by longer duration surveillance and more frontally distributed event-related brain potentials (ERP) attention, drummers generated more complex memory traces of the temporal organisation of stimulus sequences, and conductors demonstrated pre-attentive surveillance of auditory space. These differences in the quality of processing demonstrate that the brain responds to behavioural needs but, once developed, enhanced brain functions operate in processing under passive listening conditions, suggesting that they are deeply engrained processing strategies shaped by years of musical experience.

Absolute pitch

The phenomenon of absolute pitch has also been studied. Those individuals who possess absolute pitch can identify or produce isolated pitches in the absence of a reference pitch. Musicians with absolute pitch have an increased left sided asymmetry of the planum temporale (Schlaug *et al.*, 1995a, 1995b; Keenan *et al.*, 2001). Zatorre *et al.* (1998) showed that in a pitch discrimination task possessors of absolute pitch demonstrated significant brain activity in the frontal cortex while listening to tones without any explicit instructions being given, whereas non-possessors did not. When asked to judge interval patterns (relative pitch), both groups showed a similar pattern. Activity in this area may be related to labelling of either absolute or relative pitch as it is known to be concerned with establishing and maintaining conditional associations in memory – the ability to make a specific response in relation to a specific stimulus.

Although we do not know the precise mechanisms that distinguish people with absolute pitch, the picture emerging from several studies is that there may be a genetic component relating to the degree of lateral asymmetry of cortical structures concerned with auditory processing (in the posterior portion of the superior temporal gyrus). Persons with absolute pitch tend to show a greater degree of anatomical hemispheric asymmetry of this area of the brain compared with non-musicians and musicians without absolute pitch (Zatorre *et al.*, 1998; Schlaug *et al.*, 1995a, 1995b). Whether this reflects greater growth of the left-hemisphere auditory cortical structure or a reduced volume of the right-hemisphere auditory structure is not known.

Support for the genetic hypothesis comes from research which has identified an individual who can perform as well as musicians with absolute pitch but who has had no musical training (Ross, D. *et al.*, 2003). Other research has demonstrated that over half of those asked to sing a popular tune that they knew well from previous knowledge of a recording were within a semitone of the actual key and 25 per cent were within a quarter tone (Levitin, 1994), suggesting that we may all have some capability for recalling exact pitch. Even if there is a genetic component, early and prolonged musical training is usually necessary (Schlaug *et al.*, 1995a, 1995b), the age of commencement being particularly important (Miyazaki, 1988). Baharaloo *et al.* (1998) found that 40 per cent of musicians who began lessons before the age of 4 had absolute pitch, in contrast to 26 per cent who began training at 4–6 years and 8 per cent who began at 6–9 years. It may be that training in note identification needs to precede the acquisition of relative pitch skills (Ward, 1999). At the moment it is not possible to say with any certainty whether the cortical differences identified in those with absolute pitch are a consequence of its development, its cause, or a combination of both.

Motor skills

The development of the motor skills required for playing a musical instrument leads to changes in the motor cortex. Compared with non-musicians, string players have greater somatosensory representations of finger activity, the amount of increase depending on the age of starting to play rather than the amount of practice per se (Pantev *et al.*, 2003; Elbert *et al.*, 1995; Karni *et al.*, 1995). Musicians also tend to exhibit greater symmetry in the left and right hemispheres, mainly due to the increased size of the right hemisphere which controls the left hand, which is frequently required to develop a wide range of motor skills in advanced performance on an instrument. The age of commencement of playing is important in the size of the effect (Amunts *et al.*, 1997).

The start of such changes has been demonstrated over short periods of time. Learning five-finger exercises on the piano over the course of five days produced enlargement of the cortical representation area targeting the long-finger flexor and extensor muscles (Pascuel-Leone *et al.*, 1994). The size of the cortical representation for muscle groups increased significantly after each session but returned to baseline when practice ceased. For one group that continued to practise for a further four weeks, the cortical maps obtained on Mondays after the weekend rest showed a small change from baseline with a tendency to increase in size over the course of the study. This short-term flexible modulation may represent a first and necessary step leading to long-term structural change as the skill becomes overlearnt and automatic (Pascuel-Leone, 2003).

Neuroplasticity can be maladaptive – for example, focal hand dystonia (hand cramp where there is disorganisation of control of the fingers such that the movements of some fingers on a hand become involuntarily linked to those of others). This is particularly incapacitating to professional instrumental musicians. Therapy involving immobilisation by splints of one of more of the fingers other than the focal systonic finger, and that finger being required to practise repetitive exercises in co-ordination with one or more of the other digits, can restore functioning to near normality. As this proceeds, neuroimaging results indicate normalisation of the cortical representation maps (Pantev *et al.*, 2003), further highlighting the plasticity of the human brain.

Imagery and rehearsal

Musical imagery refers to the experience of replaying music by imagining it inside the head (Halpern, 2003). Imagery seems to depend on a partially shared neural substrate that forms part of perceptual analysis mechanisms (Zatorre *et al.*, 1996; Zatorre, 2003). This means that in thinking through a musical work in real time, similar processes are activated as when we listen to it. This has important implications for the ways in which music is learnt, suggesting that further reinforcement leading to overlearning can occur in the absence of the original stimulus.

Most commonly, the phenomenon of mental rehearsal has been applied to practising. For instance, Pascuel-Leone (2003) showed that when a group carried out mental rehearsal of five-finger piano exercises, sitting at the piano but not physically undertaking the movements, this resulted in reorganisation of the motor outputs to the finger flexor and extensor muscles in a similar manner to a group who practised the movements physically. Mental simulation of movements activates some of the central neural structures required for performance of the actual movements and seems to be sufficient to promote the modulation of neural circuits involved in the early stages of motor skill development. This results in marked improvement in performance and reduces the risk of damage through overphysical practice. The cerebellum and anterior cingulated cortex are active during anticipatory imagery of music, justifying the idea that mental rehearsal by activating some of the same brain regions as occurs during a real performance supports learning without physically playing (Rauschecker, 2003).

Learning biographies

As we have seen, the brain develops in response to the particular musical activities which each individual undertakes. Individuals seem to vary in the brain regions which are necessary to ensure complex auditory functions (Schuppert *et al.*, 2000). Widespread and individually developed neuronal networks underlie music processing. To explore the direct impact of particular learning strategies, Altenmuller *et al.* (1997) asked students aged 13–15 to judge symmetrically structured phrases as balanced or unbalanced. A declarative group received traditional instructions about the differences, including verbal explanations, visual aids, notation, verbal rules, and some musical examples which were played for them. A procedural group participated in musical experiences which established genuine musical representations through singing, playing, improvising or performing examples from the musical literature. A control group did not receive any instruction. The music processing of the verbally trained declarative group produced increased activation of the left fronto-temporal brain regions, probably reflecting inner speech and analytical, step-by-step processing. The musically trained procedural group showed increased activation of the right frontal and bilateral parieto-occipital lobes, indicating a more global way of processing and visuo-spatial associations. In the control group overall, activity decreased slightly. These findings indicate that the way that musical processing is taught influences brain activation patterns. The brain substrates of music processing reflect the auditory 'learning biography' of each individual (Altenmuller, 2003:349).

Emotion and music

There is wide variability in individual emotional responses to music. These depend on a variety of complex socio-cultural, historical, educational and contextual variables. Music seems able to activate phylo-genetically old parts of the nervous system that are strongly implicated in the induction and learning of fear responses (LeDoux, 1996) and which can operate subconsciously. Current thinking suggests that when we hear music or other sounds, our emotional responses to them are controlled by the amygdala. This evaluates sensory input for its emotional meaning. It receives input about sensory information directly and quickly from the thalamus, a relay station for incoming information, before it has been processed by the conscious thinking part of the brain, the cortex. Information is received from the cortex, but more slowly. This explains those immediate responses to music which occur automatically, for instance tapping our feet and responding tearfully to children singing. Cortical pathways take longer to react to incoming information, but provide a more complete cognitive assessment of the situation. In musical terms, they invoke memories relating to the particular music being heard. These may also influence our emotional responses to music, but because we are consciously aware of them our responses are more likely to be within our control (LeDoux, 1993).

The amygdala has close connections with the hypothalamus, the part of the brain which instigates emotional behaviour. This ensures that we can respond quickly to incoming stimuli, particularly when such reactions are important for our survival. One of the major neurological components of emotion is the autonomic nervous system (ANS). This has two divisions: the sympathetic division, which prepares the body for fight or flight; and the parasympathetic division, which works to conserve energy. The sympathetic division energises the body by speeding up the heart rate, stimulating the production of adrenalin and other neurotransmitters and stimulating the conversion of glycogen to create energy. The parasympathetic division slows down the heart rate and stimulates digestion and the secretion of saliva. The evidence suggests that different types of music stimulate aspects of each division.

In the same way that we might respond to a loud noise, we can respond immediately to the sound of music without conscious thought. As the music changes in tempo, dynamics, pitch and timbre, the changes will be monitored and our ANS will respond. Changes are also monitored at a higher level and meaning is attached to them. Here, our expectations about the nature of the music are important. If the music does not match our expectations, we are likely to experience an emotional response. Music sets up expectations and tensions in listeners who are familiar with particular styles. Depending on how these are realised or resolved, they can create different emotional responses (Meyer, 1956).

Exploration of experiences of positive emotional responses to music, 'shivers down the spine' and measured brain activity has demonstrated that the brain areas implicated are those which are activated in response to highly rewarding or motivationally important stimuli. The pattern of activity is similar to that observed in brain imaging studies of euphoria and pleasant emotions. Activity in relation to these reward processes is known to involve dopamine and opioid systems as well as other neurotransmitters. The amygdala, implicated in fear and negative emotions, also shows a decrease in activity as emotional responses become more intense (Blood and Zatorre, 2001). The powerful impact of music may be because it evokes particular emotions while simultaneously inhibiting incompatible ones (Blood *et al.*, 1999).

Implications for education
Recently, educationalists have demonstrated considerable interest in brain research as a means of informing their practice. Indeed, curricula and teaching methods have been developed which purport to reflect particular right- or left-brain processes. The literature reviewed above demonstrates the futility of such an approach. The brain is able to adapt rapidly to environmental demands in the short and long term, and over time develops appropriate neurological structures to meet individual needs, whatever they may be. The way the brain functions, in terms of structures and processes, differs depending on what we have learnt and how we have learnt it. It is very flexible and adapts to what is required, responding to each

individual's learning biography. The way pupils are taught influences the ways in which they approach particular tasks. If they are taught about cadences through verbal, logical explanations accompanied by musical examples, then they will approach the task from that perspective; if they are taught implicitly through active engagement with making music, then they will approach any subsequent task from that perspective. What educationalists need to focus on is the content and skills which they wish learners to acquire. Providing sufficient time is spent in learning, the brain will develop the appropriate neurological networks to retain the knowledge and skills learnt.

The evidence demonstrates the importance of time in learning. While brain structures adapt quickly to new musical experiences in the short term, this learning is lost unless it is revisited on a regular basis. Substantial neurological change takes a long time. The brain appears to exhibit greater ease of adaptation in childhood. Adult brains retain plasticity but the process appears to take longer. Interestingly, it is time spent learning over a long period of time rather than specific hours practising which is most predictive of neurological change. This supports findings from the literature on practising (Hallam, 1998c). There are clear implications here for music education in the early years and in primary schools. To develop complex musical skills requires time and practice. These skills develop more easily in the early years. If children are to develop high-level, complex musical skills, they need to be provided with high-quality opportunities for learning in pre-school and primary settings.

For teachers, there is a clear indication that engagement in mental rehearsal or imagery can be a powerful supplement to active engagement with music. This is particularly important where music has to be memorised and also to avoid some of the medical conditions that can ensue for musicians through overpractice. In relation to musical perception, the research indicates how the use of different timbres can support non-musicians in identifying separate melodic strands. Knowledge of the sounds made by different instruments would seem to be a key element of this, as is teachers finding appropriate musical stimuli to develop this skill in their students.

Debates about the genetic nature of musical ability abound in the literature. While it has been generally accepted that humans as a species are predisposed to process musical stimuli, there is still controversy regarding the nature of differences between individuals. The existence of musical savants, who exhibit general cognitive deficiencies but who have enhanced musical skills, is clear evidence that musical skills are not necessarily related to other cognitive functions. There are implications here for the education of children with special educational needs who may have the potential to func-tion at or above normative levels in relation to music and should be given the opportunity to do so. The existence of individuals with specific deficiencies in musical processing also has implications for education. As these deficiencies affect only some areas of musical processing, teachers need to identify areas of strength and weakness and build on the former to support the development of the latter. Overall, it would seem that all children can achieve in at least some aspect of musical education.

Finally, educators need to acknowledge the power that music has to influence moods, emotions and arousal levels. Music stimulates reward systems in the brain and engagement with it is naturally enjoyable. It is only as individuals are encultured into particular musical genres that they develop antagonistic feelings towards other genres. The more familiar we are with particular types of music, the more we enjoy listening to them. To facilitate the benefits of listening to different kinds of music in relation to mood, emotion and arousal, it is important that children have extensive experience of hearing and becoming encultured to a wide range of musical genres. This does not need to be in formal lessons but can be through more informal engagement with music in a range of social occasions.

Further reading

Avanzini, G., Faienza, C., Minciacchi, D., Lopez, L. and Majno, M. (eds) (2003) *The Neurosciences and Music*. New York: New York Academy of Sciences.

Peretz, I. and Zatorre, R.J.A. (eds) (2003) *The Cognitive Neuroscience of Music*. Oxford: Oxford University Press.

Peretz, I. and Zatorre, R.J.A. (2005) 'Brain organization for music processing'. *Annual Review of Psychology*, 56 (pp. 89–114).

3 Early development

The implicit musical knowledge which adults acquire over time is built on structures present in infancy. These provide the basis for perceptual learning and enculturation, the process by which the child develops internal schemata of the music of its culture. This process is mediated by the learning environment and begins when the foetus is in the womb.

Prenatal auditory experiences of music

The human auditory system is functional three to four months before birth. The process of musical enculturation begins from that point. After 28 to 30 weeks of gestation, foetuses reliably react to external sounds, their heart rates varying as a result of exposure to music (Woodward, 1992). Infants show recognition responses to music that they have heard in the womb both before and immediately after birth (Hykin *et al.*, 1999; Shahidullah and Hepper, 1994) and are significantly more soothed and attentive to music that their mothers have listened to daily in the last three months of pregnancy (Feijoo, 1981; Hepper, 1988). They also prefer lullabies to which they have been repeatedly exposed in the latter part of their development to unfamiliar melodies (Satt, 1984; Panneton, 1985). Trevarthen (1999) has argued that the rhythm of the mother's body and hearing external sounds provide the foetus with early musical experiences which may impact on the structures and functions of the auditory system nervous pathways. Familiarisation with specific sounds contributes to sensitivity to them and to subsequent infant preferences for given voices (particularly that of the mother), the maternal language, music sung by the mother or particular musical sequences (Lecanuet, 1996).

The role of the mother or caregiver

In early infancy, parents and the family play a crucial role in musical enculturation. 'Motherese', the non-verbal communication that takes place between parents and infants, plays an important role in musical development. This pre-verbal quasi-musical interaction constitutes the beginnings of musical competences. Traditionally, mothers have sung to infants as they take care of them (Trehub and Schellenberg, 1995; Trehub and Trainor, 1998). They sing lullabies (Trehub *et al.*, 1993a; Unyk *et al.*, 1992), play songs (Rock *et al.*, 1999; Trehub *et al.*, 1993b; Trehub *et al.*, 1997a) or songs adapted from the adult repertoire (Trehub *et al.*, 1997c). Infants have special sensitivities to lullabies sung by caregivers. Lullabies have smooth pitch contours, a strong tonal centre, repetitive rhythms and a distinct vocal style. Infants prefer lullabies to adult or play songs and enjoy mothers' singing more than that of fathers (Trehub and Henderson, 1994; Unyk *et al.*, 1992; Shenfield *et al.*, 2003). When singing to infants, adults tend to sing at a higher pitch than normal and at a slower tempo, and exaggerate the emotional aspects of the song (Papousek, 1996; Trainor *et al.*, 1997; Trehub *et al.*, 1993b; Unyk *et al.*, 1992). This maternal style of singing is found in childcare contexts across cultures (Trehub and Schellenberg, 1995; Trehub and Trainor, 1998). Newborns and infants listen more attentively to singing which is in this infant-directed style (Masataka, 1999; Trainor, 1996). Infants pay particular attention to recordings of their own mother, particularly when she is singing rather than speaking (Bacher and Robertson, 2001; Trehub and Nakata, 2002). Maternal singing seems to have a very powerful effect on infants' arousal levels, lullabies soothing and encouraging sleep, play songs leading to alert attention. How mothers instinctively adapt their behaviour to the child's needs is illustrated by the way in which, as the child becomes older, mothers adapt their singing style, lowering the pitch and more clearly articulating the lyrics as language skills develop (Bergeson and Trehub, 1999).

The development of musical perception in infancy and early childhood

From birth the infant has very well-developed systems for processing music. Infants are predisposed to attend to melodic contour, rhythmic patterning and consonant sounds, and are similar to adults in their sensitivity to the pitch and rhythmic grouping of sounds. However, the complex skills required for understanding and analysing music within any particular culture take time to develop, and depend on the type and extent of exposure to music of any particular child.

Pitch and melody

Infants have the same capacity to process pitch as adults. They categorise sound into pitches (Demany, 1982) and can identify sounds of the same pitch with different harmonic structure (Clarkson and Clifton, 1985). At 6–9 months old they can match the pitches of vowels that are sung to them (Kessen *et al.*, 1979), and by 7–10 months old they can discriminate the direction of pitch change for intervals as small as one semitone. They are able to distinguish easily between a pair of tones an octave apart and a pair not quite an octave apart (Demany and Armand, 1984) and, like adults, detect small interval changes more easily than large ones (Schellenberg and Trehub, 1994, 1996a, 1996b). Infants show recognition of contour patterns from about 6 months onwards, easily noticing differences in melodic contour. The main difference between adults and infants is in their recognition of the tonal scale of a particular culture. Scale patterns are not innately known and have to be learnt (Trehub *et al.*, 1984, 1985, 1987, 1990; Trehub and Trainor, 1990).

The way that infants group sounds in relation to pitch and time follows the same rules as for adults. Perceptual grouping principles relevant to music are operative in infancy (Bregman, 1990; Deutsch, 1999). Infants group tone sequences on the basis of similarities in pitch, loudness, and timbre (Thorpe and Trehub, 1989; Thorpe *et al.*, 1988; Demany, 1982), although infants require greater differences to notice change (Krumhansl and Jusczyk, 1990; Thorpe and Trehub, 1989). They categorise complex tones on the basis of pitch (Clarkson and Clifton, 1985); recognise multi-tone patterns across variations in tempo (Trehub and Thorpe, 1989) and pitch level (Trehub *et al.*, 1987); and perceive the timbral similarity of complex tones across variations in pitch, loudness and duration (Trehub *et al.*, 1990). Those factors that promote the connectedness of auditory sequences for adult listeners do likewise for infant listeners (Trehub, 1990). Just as adults segregate a sequence of notes alternating rapidly between two pitch ranges into two perceptual streams (Bregman and Campbell, 1971; Dowling, 1973), so do infants. Infants 4–6 months old hearing contrasting renditions of simple piano minuets that Mozart composed as a child, one with a pause between phrases, the other with a pause within phrases, showed a preference for the version with the pause between phrases, suggesting recognition of phrase structures (Jusczyk and Krumhansl, 1993; Krumhansl and Jusczyk, 1990). Thorpe and Trehub (1989) also showed that infants noticed changes within groups but not between them in a manner similar to adults. Children aged 4–12 are able to break sequences of notes into two phrases well above chance level, even at the age of 4, although there is slight improvement with age and musical experience (Drake and Bertrand, 2003).

Tonality
Over time infants acquire knowledge of the melodic schemata of their culture (Dowling, 1982, 1986, 1988), gradually moving from recognising clearly distinctive features through to being aware of more subtle ones (Morrongiello *et al.*, 1985; Pick *et al.*, 1988). Tonality does not seem to be innate. Infants need to learn the particular tonal systems of their culture and this process takes time. In Western cultures by 1 year old, infants respond differently to diatonic and non-diatonic patterns and by the age of 3 or 4 display

the ability to respond to the degree of tonality of the stimuli (Dowling, 1988). This process may be aided by the tonal construction of nursery songs, which usually emphasise the pitch content of basic scales and tend not to have key changes. Depending on their musical environment, by the age of 5 children can generally organise songs around stable tonal keys but do not have a stable tonal scale system that can be used to transpose melodies. This develops later (Lamont and Cross, 1994).

Rhythm

Infants have a predisposition for processing rhythm. Babies sway and bounce rhythmically in response to music up to the age of about 6 months, the co-ordination between these movements and the timing of the music gradually increasing with age (Moog, 1976). Infants can differentiate tone sequences with identical pitches but contrasting rhythms (Demany *et al.*, 1977; Trehub and Thorpe, 1989; Chang and Trehub, 1977), and can impose rhythmic group-ings on tone sequences on the basis of pitch or timbre similarities (Thorpe and Trehub, 1989; Thorpe *et al.*, 1988). They are sensitive to changes in the relative temporal patterns of rhythms (Trehub and Thorpe, 1989) and at 2 months can detect a small change in tempo, are able to habituate to a particular tempo, and react if there is a change of tempo (Baruch and Drake, 1997). Under some circumstances they can adapt their spontaneous sucking rate to the rate of an auditory sequence (Drake *et al.*, 2000).

Multi-level rhythmic structures appear early. The spontaneous songs of 2-year-olds show evidence of a beat and rhythmic subdivisions overlaid on it. From the age of 4 years children are able to detect small changes in tempo and can synchronise with music (Drake, 2000). By the age of 5 the child has quite sophisticated structures (Drake, 1991) and can reproduce a steady beat and varying binary subdivisions of the beat. There is some development during the school years but there is little difference between 7-year-olds and adult non-musicians (Drake, 1993). When 5–7-year-old children reproduce complex rhythms, they simplify them and their performance is better for regular rather than irregular rhythms (Drake and Gerard, 1989). There seems to be a temporal zone of optimal processing. Two-month-old infants demonstrate a reaction to novelty only for sequences at 600 ms interonset interval (Baruch and Drake, 1997), while children aged 4–10 seem to demonstrate the same zone of optimal tempos, although the range increases with age (Drake *et al.*, 2000).

Harmony and timbre

Infants are more attentive to and affected by music based on consonant rather than dissonant intervals (Trainor and Heinmiller, 1998; Zentner and Kagan, 1998). This may reflect species preferences that have influenced the types of musics which have developed over time. Indeed, some have argued that avant-garde composers by abandoning the tonal system have created forms which are inherently difficult for human listeners. Not everyone agrees with this, some suggesting that the principal barrier facing atonal music is its lack of cultural acceptance. Infants can discriminate differences in timbre (Clarkson *et al.*, 1988). They first discriminate stimuli with the same fundamental frequency but different harmonics, then learn to discriminate less salient stimuli from which the fundamentals have been removed, suggesting similar processing to adults.

Musical memory in infancy

Memory for music is crucial to its reproduction. Implicit knowledge of particular tonal systems provides a framework which may facilitate the memorisation of particular songs or pieces of music. Six- to ten-month-old infants do not have implicit knowledge of Western musical conventions (Schellenberg and Trehub, 1999; Trainor and Trehub, 1992; Trehub *et al.*, 1999) but they quickly become accustomed to the particular structure of the music that surrounds them, preferring patterns that conform to that structure by around 12 months (Trehub *et al.*, 1997b).

Six-month-old infants remember the specific tempo and timbre of music with which they are familiar, failing to recognise pieces when they are played at new tempos or with new timbres (Halpern, 1989). Ten-month-olds represent acoustic patterns specific to the particular performances with which they were previously familiarised (Saffran and Griepentrog, 2001). Early infant representations seem to be extremely specific, but this changes over time. The first changes relate to the recognition of highly familiar melodies when they are played in a new key (Halpern, 1989; Trehub *et al.*, 1987; Chang and Trehub, 1977) and a tone sequence when the tempo is altered, as long as the relative durations remain the same (Trehub and Thorpe, 1989). Initially, the ability to transform representations seems to depend on how well the infant knows them (Schellenberg and Trehub, 1996a, 1999). As skills develop, the structure of the task and familiarity with the stimulus domain influence which levels of representation are prioritised, enabling infants to switch from relying on absolute pitch cues to using relative pitch cues when necessary. Pre-school children can recognise familiar tunes across many different types of transformations, so more flexible musical representations do develop.

Overall, the evidence suggests that infants are sophisticated listeners to music. They seem to prefer music which is not taken out of context (the beginning rather than the middle of sonatas) (Saffran, 2003), they can represent complex pieces of music in long-term memory (Trehub *et al.*, 1997), and their representations of music in long-term memory are not an undifferentiated series of notes. Passages are linked together to form a coherent musical whole.

Singing in the early years

From 9 months old infants begin to make spontaneous babbling or singing sounds which are distinguishable from speech in terms of patterns of pitch and rhythm. Dowling (1994) suggests that there are at least two early forms of babbling: patterns of proto-syllables and vocal play. Between 9 and 12 months the proto-syllable babbling patterns lead to speech while both patterns lead to spontaneous singing. After 18 months infants spontaneously begin to generate music which has systematic form, uses discrete pitch levels and repetition of rhythmic and melodic contours, and is recognisable as song (Ostwald, 1973). However, they lack a stable pitch framework and in any single song a very limited set of phrase contours is used (Dowling, 1984). By the age of 3, typically the child relies on the words of the song and can produce distinct pitches, but has no interval stability or tonal coherence. At 4, the child still relies on the text of the song, but the reproduction of its melodic contour is improving in accuracy, although the whole still lacks coherence. By the age of 5, individual contours and intervals are produced accurately and children can produce recognisable songs with stable tonality (Davidson, J.W., 1994). They also improvise and invent (Stadler-Elmer, 1994). There are wide individual differences in the extent to which pre-school children engage in singing, for some it is a part of almost all activity, while others sing only occasionally (Sundin, 1997). Home background may play a crucial role in this (Kelley and Sutton-Smith, 1987).

Absolute pitch

Absolute pitch is generally defined as the ability to identify or produce isolated pitches in the absence of a reference pitch. There has been considerable debate as to whether the possession of absolute pitch has a basis in an individual's genetic make-up or is a learnt skill. Absolute pitch is rare in the general population, and infrequent amongst professional musicians (Dowling, 1999). Typically only between 4 and 8 per cent of musicians have absolute pitch. Stumpf first noted the existence of absolute pitch in his review of the talents of great composers in 1883, and for many years it was seen as genetically determined and indicating musical giftedness (Ward and Burns, 1982). Ward (1999) has shown that absolute pitch can be traced back through families, and genealogical research has attempted to establish the type of genetic relationships involved in its inheritance

(Revesz, 1953). The arguments for its genetic origins rely on four key elements (Bahr *et al.*, 2005): that it is present very early in life (before the age of 5); that it is acquired very quickly (Burns and Campbell, 1994); that it is acquired without effort (Takeuchi and Hulse, 1993); and that it runs in families (Revesz, 1953).

Some authors have argued that as a species we are predisposed to attend to absolute rather than relative pitch (Saffran, 2003; Saffran and Griepentrog, 2001). Some support for this comes from evidence that adults can typically approximate the pitch levels of familiar songs (Levitin, 1994). Takeuchi and Hulse (1993) call this 'residual absolute pitch'. We may all be predisposed to develop absolute pitch but require an appropriate environment for it to develop. Support for this comes from a range of sources. For instance, there is a high incidence of absolute pitch in the blind (Bachem, 1940; Welch, 1988; Hamilton *et al.*, 2000). Early training appears to be important, and where this training occurs the incidence of absolute pitch is high, near 50 per cent (Miyazaki, 1993). Takeuchi and Hulse (1993) argue that absolute pitch can be acquired by anyone but only during a critical period ending in the fifth or sixth year. There are certainly high correlations between age at commencement of musical training and the percentage of musicians possessing absolute pitch (Sergeant, 1969). Experiences between the ages of 3 and 6 have been identified as important in some studies (Baharaloo *et al.*, 1998, 2000; Cohen and Baird, 1990; Lenhoff *et al.*, 2001; Takeuchi and Hulse, 1993). One large survey found that the mean age at which absolute pitch possessors began musical activities was 5.4 years as opposed to 7.9 years for non-possessors (Gregersen *et al.*, 1999). Sergeant (1969) indicated that those who started studying before the age of 7 were most likely to have absolute pitch. This is supported by Baharaloo *et al.* (1998), who found that 31 per cent of those studying before the age of 7 had absolute pitch but only 5 per cent of those who started after age 7. Other smaller scale studies have supported this early learning hypothesis (Costa-Giomi *et al.*, 2001; Miyazaki, 1988; Hirata *et al.*, 1999).

One possible explanation for the early acquisition of absolute pitch relates to the fact that younger children have not yet undergone the critical transition in their cognitive development from pre-operational to concrete operations (Chin, 2003). Children aged from 3.5 to 4.5 years only understand pitch in an absolute sense and do not understand pitch direction, whereas most 5-year-olds do (White *et al.*, 1990). Adding support to this hypothesis, 3 to 4-year-olds are more likely than 5 to 6-year-olds to sing a song at the same pitch as they have been taught it (Sergeant and Roche, 1973). Further evidence comes from individuals with Williams syndrome. They have severely impaired spatial and other cognitive abilities, with unimpaired language skills and high levels of sociability, and often demonstrate an interest in music and a strong sense of rhythm (Levitin and Bellugi, 1998). They do not appear to have a critical period for the development of absolute pitch ending between 5 and 7 years, suggesting that it is mental rather than chronological age that may be important.

The particular types of musical training that lead to absolute pitch are not well established. Most possessors of absolute pitch acquire it naturally as they engage with formal music tuition. They have absolute pitch memory and learn to label those pitches (Levitin, 1994). While there have been reports of the successful teaching of absolute pitch in pre-school-aged children (Takeuchi and Hulse, 1993), this has not been easily replicated (Cohen and Baird, 1990). Highly motivated adults have trained imprecise absolute pitch in themselves, but the process has been lengthy and arduous (Brady, 1970; Meyer, M., 1899; Rush, 1989).

Most early research was based on an assumption that individuals either possessed absolute pitch or did not. Recently there has been an acknowledgement that this is an oversimplification (Bachem, 1937; Baharaloo *et al.*, 1998). There is diversity in the labelling, accuracy, consistency, and speed of labelling responses between individuals described as having absolute pitch. Absolute pitch varies when the attributes of the aural stimuli are manipulated (Miyazaki, 1990,

1992, 1993, 1995; Takeuchi and Hulse, 1993; Ward, 1999). Some possessors of absolute pitch can identify piano notes better than pure tones and some can identify white-key pitches better than black key tones (Miyazaki, 1989, 1990; Takeuchi and Hulse, 1993; Bahr *et al.*, 2005). Not only is absolute pitch multi-dimensional, but those who possess it have unique capabilities, their performance reflecting the diversity of their personal musical experiences (Bahr *et al.*, 2005). Responses are consistently more accurate for tones which are familiar, suggesting that knowledge of pitch is acquired incrementally over time as the result of on-going experience (Bahr *et al.*, 2005). Some musical experiences may be more conducive to developing absolute pitch than others. Using multiple coding strategies may be important, including fingering positions, musical notation and letter names (Zatorre and Beckett, 1989). Playing the piano may most easily facilitate its learning (Pantev *et al.*, 1998). Another factor may be differences in cognitive style (Chin, 2003). Costa-Giomi *et al.* (2001) showed that performance on tests of field independence (where individuals have to find hidden figures in pictures) was stronger in those possessing absolute pitch.

Perception of musical emotion in infants and young children

Infants respond to emotional expressiveness. They have been shown to be able to distinguish between lullabies sung by mothers to their infants, and lullabies sung without the infant present. They also preferred the former (Trainor, 1996). At 4 months they prefer consonant rather than dissonant intervals, even when the latter are placed in a naturalistic musical context (a Mozart minuet) (Trainor and Heinmiller, 1998). Six-month-old babies not only prefer listening to a consonant over a dissonant version of a melody, but demonstrate other behavioural changes – such as more vocalising and less fretting during the playing of consonant melodies (Zentner and Kagan, 1998). Whether infants can recognise emotions expressed through recorded musical excerpts is less certain (Nawrot, 2003).

The recognition of emotion in music develops in young children, although studies vary in identifying the ages when this occurs. Gentile (1998) found that adults and children as young as 3 agreed on the emotional content of 28 musical excerpts categorised as representing happiness, sadness and anger; while Kastner and Crowder (1990) found that 3-year-olds matched positive (happy/interested) and negative (sad/angry) faces to melodies played in either major or minor keys consistently in the same way as adults do. Pre-school children seem to develop understanding of the emotional meaning of music composed in major and minor keys (Kastner and Crowder, 1990), their performance improving with age (Gerardi and Gerken, 1995). Some research has found that 4-year-old children perform above chance in assigning affective labels to musical excerpts in agreement with adult performance, accuracy improving with age (Cunningham and Sterling, 1988; Dolgin and Adelson, 1990), but not all the evidence supports such early development (Nawrot, 2003; Gregory *et al.*, 1996; Robazza *et al.*, 1994; Terwogt and Van Grinsven, 1991). What is clear is that children in their early years begin to recognise musical depictions of emotion and to respond to them. The specific age at which this occurs is likely to depend on the extent of the child's exposure to music within and across genres and their general cognitive and emotional development.

Implications for music education

Human infants have the capacity to respond to music from birth. They are particularly receptive to the maternal singing of lullabies. Later, play songs fulfil a role in maintaining their attention. These musical activities have an important role in the development of communication skills. There are indications in the developed world, where our lives are increasingly dominated by the media, that the musical interactions between caregivers and children, for which there seem to be species-determined predispositions, are not always enacted. For some infants, exposure to music occurs through the media rather than face-to-face interaction with a caregiver. There is a need for the music community as a whole to encourage real-life musical interactions between infants, young children and their caregivers. These may be supported by recordings but should not be replaced by them.

The singing of play songs or nursery rhymes supports the development of language and, where actions are included in the songs, physical co-ordination. Very young children can participate in these activities and caregivers should be encouraged to provide appropriate opportunities for this to occur. Those engaged in formal childcare – for instance nursery nurses and child minders – need to be made aware of the value of participating in musical activities and encouraged to develop musical skills from the earliest ages. They may need support for this, including opportunities for training and the development of suitable recorded support materials. Musicians working within the community, and those offering services in compulsory education, should also consider how they can improve the provision of live musical experiences for pre-school children. Children's own musical performances of what they have learnt should be encouraged as this increases the involvement of parents and other caregivers in children's education, strengthening home– nursery links.

From infancy children acquire implicit knowledge about the music that they hear, and about its structures, rhythms and tonality. The greater the exposure to music, the more fully and speedily this knowledge will be acquired. It is not necessary for children to focus on listening to music for this knowledge to be acquired. It is acquired without conscious awareness. This means that in early years educational environments children can enhance their implicit knowledge of music while undertaking other activities. The most obvious ways in which this might be achieved are through movement or dancing, but calming music could be played while children undertake other activities – for example, painting and drawing. As we shall see in Chapter 12, calming music can optimise arousal levels, facilitating learning.

Children are likely to be exposed to music in the home through the radio, recordings and the television. The nature of that music will influence their musical enculteration. Globalisation has meant that worldwide most children are exposed to Western popular music. This may be in addition to other genres or world musics. Those engaged in early years education may find it useful to explore with the children the kinds of music that they hear at home. This information can then be used to ensure that links are made between home and school through music. Opportunities can also be made to complement what is learnt at home by introducing music from different genres and world musics. This may be through music for dance or movement and that played to accompany other activities, or through active engagement in music making. While the latter may be limited by the particular musical knowledge and expertise of the carer, the availability of recorded music means that children can easily experience a wide variety of musics and genres.

Developing awareness of emotions, one's own and those of others, has been shown to be important for success in life (Goleman, 1996). In early years education music can be used to develop initial awareness of different emotions, particularly happiness and sadness, and to provide a starting point for children to explore what makes them feel happy or sad in a non- threatening environment. This may supplement emotional literacy work.

If it is considered desirable for children to develop absolute pitch, the evidence suggests that they should receive formal music tuition at an early age and that this tuition should include learning the piano, or possibly another keyboard instrument. Labelling of pitches that have been internalised is crucial to the process. This usually occurs through familiarisation with note names through learning to read music. It is not possible to say with any confidence whether this will ensure that absolute pitch is developed. Teaching practices which encourage relative pitch with a tonic that changes but retains the same name – for example, Solfa – are likely to discourage the acquisition of perfect pitch. Whether it is desirable to promote the acquisition of absolute pitch is debatable. For the transcription of heard music into notation it can be very useful, but where instrumentalists have to transpose written notation into different keys it can interfere.

From birth, infants have well-developed capabilities for processing pitch, melody and rhythm, and enjoy musical stimulation – particularly interacting with caregivers. Singing promotes language development, and where it is coupled with movement can enhance physical co-ordination. Music can be used as a vehicle to explore simple emotions. These are benefits that should not be ignored. Music should play an important part in early years education, not least because engagement with music is of itself rewarding for both children and adults.

Further reading

Chin, C.S. (2003) 'The development of absolute pitch: a theory concerning the roles of music training at an early developmental age and individual cognitive style'. *Psychology of Music*, 31(2) (pp. 155–171).

Dowling, W.J. (1999) 'The development of music perception and cognition'. In D. Deutsch (ed.) *The Psychology of Music*. (2nd edition) London: Academic Press (pp. 603–625).

Trehub, S.E. (2003) 'Musical predispositions in infancy: an update'. In I. Peretz and R.J.A. Zatorre (eds) *The Cognitive Neuroscience of Music*. Oxford: Oxford University Press (pp. 3–20).

4 Musical ability

Conceptualising musical ability

When someone is described as being musical or having 'musical ability', this is usually because they are involved in making music in some way. Individuals are rarely referred to as musical if they listen to music, even if this constitutes an important part of their lives. In the music psychology literature 'musical ability' is often used interchangeably with a range of other terms, including 'musicality', 'musical aptitude', 'musical potential' and 'musical talent'. Overall, there are no universally agreed definitions of these terms. The meanings are socially constructed and reflect the cultural, political, economic and social factors pertaining in the time and place where they are adopted (Blacking, 1971). In this chapter the terminology adopted will reflect that of the research to which it refers.

The development of musical ability testing

The development of tests to assess 'musical ability' paralleled that of intelligence testing. In the early and mid-twentieth century, there was an assumption that individuals were endowed with different levels of 'intelligence' that were genetically based, relatively immutable and unchanging. Such measures of intelligence have continued to be used to identify individuals with learning difficulties, and sometimes in situations where it is necessary to select individuals for limited educational or employment opportunities. In parallel with intelligence tests, musical ability tests were first developed to assist music teachers in the selection of those pupils most likely to benefit from music tuition. Testing began in 1883, when Carl Stumpf suggested a number of simple aural tests which music teachers might undertake to select pupils. Subsequently, a range of tests have been developed which can be administered to groups of children of different ages. The content of the tests varies, although they all focus on aural skills (for reviews see Shuter-Dyson, 1999; Hallam, in press, b). The most comprehensive set of measures is that of Gordon (1965, 1979, 1982, 1989a, 1989b), who has devised tests to be used with pre-school children through to adults, taking account of prevailing cultural norms based on tonal imagery, rhythm imagery and musical sensitivity. Recent testing procedures reflect technological advances. Individualised computer-based systems can assess the recognition of change in synthesiser-produced melodies and allow for individual speed of responding, increasing validity and reliability (Vispoel, 1993; Vispoel and Coffman, 1992) through minimising the reliance on the general cognitive processing skills needed to perform well on earlier tests (Doxey and Wright, 1990). What these various tests have in common is that they assess the ability to discriminate sounds that vary in subtle ways.

Teachers often use other ways of selecting pupils, commonly singing, but the relationship between tonal aptitude and use of the singing voice may be very small (Rutkowski, 1996). Singing in tune seems to be more related to motor response schema and can be improved by training where knowledge of results is given (Welch *et al.*, 1989). Other active measures include tests of musical performance (Watkins and Farnum, 1954), although these assess attainment rather than potential.

Perceptions of the nature of musical ability

The devisers of the various musical ability measures held different beliefs about the nature of musical ability. Revesz (1953) adopted the term 'musicality' to denote the 'ability to enjoy music aesthetically' which was assessed by establishing the depth to which a person could listen to and comprehend the artistic structure of a composition. Seashore *et al.* (1960) believed that musical ability was a set of loosely related basic sensory discrimination skills, which had a genetic basis and would not change over time except for variation due to lapses of concentration or other environmental changes. Seashore did not believe that subtest scores should be combined to obtain a single score, but rather that a profile should be obtained that could be divided into a number of clearly defined characteristics which were unrelated to each other (pitch, loudness, rhythm, time, timbre, tonal memory). In contrast, Wing (1981) believed in a general ability to perceive and appreciate music rather than a profile. He held that the elements in his battery of tests should be related to each other and an overall score should be reported.

Gordon (1979) viewed musical ability as consisting of three parts: tonal imagery (melody and harmony), rhythm imagery (tempo and metre) and musical sensitivity (phrasing, balance and style). His tests contrasted with earlier work in that musical ability was viewed in part as sensitivity to the prevailing musical cultural norms. For instance, the phrasing and style tests were designed to assess interpretative ability, while the balance tests were designed to assess melodic and rhythmic creative ability. He used the term 'audiation' to describe the ability to give meaning to what is heard, identifying five stages. The first two, perceiving and giving meaning to the sound through tonal and rhythmic patterns, for him constituted musical aptitude. In stages 3 to 5, the listener asks what they have just heard, where they have heard it, and what they will hear next. These stages assess achievement.

Increasingly it has been recognised that aural skill is only one of many skills necessary for the development of musical expertise. Gilbert devised tests of motor skills, performance on which was highly correlated with musical attainment (Gilbert, 1981). Ways of assessing creativity have been developed (Vaughan, 1977; Webster, 1988), the evidence suggesting that, generally, musical creativity factors seem to be discrete from those assessed by musical ability tests (Swanner, 1985), while Hallam (1998a) has identified a range of skills required for becoming a successful professional musician.

Challenges to the concept of musical ability

The concept of musical ability has been severely criticised in recent years. Focusing on the importance of effort, some have proposed that it is time spent practising which underpins the development of expert performance, not inherited ability. This issue will be considered fully in Chapter 8. The evidence regarding teachers' perceptions of the role of genetic factors in musical ability is mixed. Substantial proportions of education professionals and music teachers believe that playing an instrument, singing and composing requires natural talent (Davis, M., 1994), although most also stress the importance of learning and effort. Where talent is mentioned, speed of learning and musical communication are seen as key (Hallam and Woods, 2003). There seem to be two simultaneously held views: one suggesting that musicality is biologically inherited, and a more relativistic one that assumes equal musical possibilities for everyone (Brandstrom, 1999).

A number of researchers have explored how different groups in society conceptualise musical ability. Haroutounian (2000) analysed the level of importance attached to particular criteria in identifying musically able children. General behaviours of 'sustained interest' and 'self-discipline' received higher mean responses than music-specific characteristics indicative of music aptitude. Hallam and colleagues (Hallam and Prince, 2003; Hallam and Shaw, 2003; Hallam and Woods, 2003) explored the conceptions of musical ability held by a cross-section of the population including adults and children, musicians and non-musicians, using both qualitative and quantitative research methods. Six categories emerged from the initial qualitative study: aural skills, receptive responses to music, generative activities, the integration of a range of skills, personal qualities, and the extent to which musical ability was perceived as being learnt or inherited. By far the largest response in any category was that musical ability was being able to play a musical instrument or sing (cited by 71 per cent of the sample). Personal qualities including motivation, personal expression, immersion in music, total commitment and metacognition (being able to learn to learn) were cited most by musicians. The findings did not indicate a general conception of musical ability as genetically determined. Overall, the musicians gave more complex responses, including many more elements in their statements. A follow-up study, based on responses to rating scales derived from the qualitative research, indicated that musical ability was most strongly conceptualised in relation to rhythmic ability, organisation of sound, communication, motivation, personal characteristics, integration of a range of complex skills and performing in a group. Having a musical ear came lower in the list than might have been expected, given its prominent position with regard to musical ability historically. The conception of rhythm as being most important may reflect its central role in much popular music. Musicians expressed the strongest agreement that musical ability was related to communication, being able to play in a group, emotional sensitivity and the organisation of sound, indicating that these skills are crucial at the highest levels of expertise. Overall, the conceptions of musical ability generated by this research were complex and multi-faceted, and reflected the wide range of expert endstates that occur in the music profession.

Skills needed for musical success

There has recently been a greater recognition of the diverse and complex skills involved in musical endstates and the relationships between them. McPherson (1995/6), for instance, exploring the relationships between different types of musical performance, identified five distinct skills: sight reading, performing rehearsed music, playing from memory, playing by ear, and improvising. Scores obtained on improvisation and performing rehearsed music were very different, while those obtained for playing by ear and improvising were very similar. Children learning their instruments for longer showed closer agreement between scores, suggesting that while there may have been initial preferences for one approach to learning and performance, over time the children were able to develop other skills.

Hallam (1998a) set out a range of skills that may be developed in the course of becoming a successful professional musician: aural, cognitive, technical, musicianship, performance, learning, and life skills (see Table 4.1). Different combinations are required for any particular musical task or branch of the music profession. Gardner (1999), in his theory of multiple intelligences, identifies music as a separate intelligence along with eight others: linguistic, logico-mathematical, spatial, bodily kinaesthetic, interpersonal, intra-personal, naturalist, and spiritual/existential. He suggests that we each have a unique blend of intelligences that leads to variation in our performance. For instance, while musical intelligence might be central for pursuing a career in music, each of the other proposed intelligences may contribute to the development of particular skills. Table 4.1 sets out the skills which may be important in relation to success across the music professions (Hallam, 1998a), with an indication of which of Gardner's multiple intelligences may contribute towards that success.

A weakness of Gardner's theory in relation to music is that it fails to address the issue of motivation and commitment, and the relationship between these, the various intelligences and their endstates. To learn to play an instrument, sing or compose requires practice and dedication. For commitment to be sustained, this motivation needs to be generated from within the individual, not derived from external pressures (Hallam, 1998a). Gardner argues that an individual may be motivated in a domain unrelated to their abilities in that domain. While this may be possible, the evidence relating to drop-outs from musical tuition suggests that there is often a strong relationship between perceived success and motiva-tion (see Chapters 7, 8 and 9). Gardner also has little to say about the processes involved in the acquisition of musical skills and the way in which the various intelligences operate together. His original

Table 4.1 *Multiple intelligences implicated in musical skill development*

Skills contributing towards musical success	Gardner's intelligences which may be involved in the development of the skills
Aural skills are required for developing: • rhythmic accuracy and a sense of pulse; • good intonation; • the facility to know how music will sound without having to play it; • improvisational skills.	Musical Spatial Bodily–kinaesthetic
Cognitive skills are required in the processes of: • reading music; • transposition; • understanding keys; • understanding harmony; • understanding the structure of music; • the memorisation of music; • composing; • understanding different musical styles and their cultural and historic contexts.	Logical–mathematical Spatial Linguistic Musical
Technical skills are required for developing: • instrument-specific skills; • technical agility; • articulation; • expressive tone quality.	Bodily–kinaesthetic Intra-personal Spatial
Musicianship skills are concerned with: • being able to play expressively; • being able to project sound; • developing control; • conveying meaning.	Musical Bodily–kinaesthetic Intra-personal Spatial Inter-personal Spiritualist/existential
Performance skills include: • being able to communicate with an audience; • communicating with other performers; • being able to co-ordinate a group; • presenting to an audience.	Interpersonal Linguistic Bodily–kinaesthetic

Table 4.1 (Continued)

Skills contributing towards musical success	Gardner's intelligences which may be involved in the development of the skills
Learning skills are related to being able to learn, monitor and evaluate progress independently.	Intra-personal
Life skills include:	
• social skills (being able to work with other musicians, promoters, the public);	Interpersonal
• planning and organisational skills (planning practice schedules, programmes, travel arrangements);	Intra-personal
• time management (being punctual, meeting deadlines).	Logical–mathematical

theory proposed no 'executive' processing system that would co-ordinate, monitor and evaluate the functioning of the other intelligences – although, in response to criticism, Gardner has argued that the intra-personal intelligence takes on this role. There are also limitations of the theory in relation to the development of the skills necessary for particular musical endstates as most of the 'intelligences' are implicated in even the simplest of musical activities. A further problem is that some individuals are able to perform extremely complex musical skills while having severely limited intellectual, personal and social capabilities.

Is musical ability genetically determined?

There is on-going controversy about the heritability of musical ability. There are two debates: one relating to whether human beings as a species have a capacity for music, the other concerned with whether there are inherited individual differences in the capacity to develop musical skills. These two issues are often confused. As we saw in Chapters 1 and 2, there is an increasing body of evidence indicating that all humans have the potential to make music and that musicality is as universal as linguistic ability (Blacking, 1971; Messenger, 1958; Wallin *et al.*, 2000). However, whether everyone inherits the same level of potential continues to be hotly debated.

In exploring this issue, one strand of research has focused on comparisons of measured musical ability between identical and fraternal twins and other family relationships. The evidence from this research is mixed (Shuter-Dyson and Gabriel, 1981; Shuter-Dyson, 1999; Hodges, 1996a; Gardner, 1999). A second strand has considered the impact of learning to play an instrument, receiving training in singing, or practising aural skills on musical ability scores. Findings indicate that engagement in active music making improves performance, suggesting that 'ability' is learnt (for a review see Shuter-Dyson and Gabriel, 1981). Advances in research on genetics to date have had little impact on the debate. Few human behaviours or traits have been traced to specific gene pairs, and it is likely that those who exhibit musical skills are drawing on a range of different gene combinations, which exert an influence on our physical make-up in addition to our cognitive and emotional development. Interactive rather than additive models of the relationship between the environment and genetic inheritance are now generally accepted (Ceci, 1990), supported by evidence from studies of expertise which demonstrate that the acquisition of knowledge, in itself, affects the efficiency and effectiveness of the processes by which more knowledge is acquired. This is supported by evidence that the cerebral cortex has an amazing ability to self-organise in response to outside stimuli – including music, as we saw in Chapter 2. While we cannot completely rule out the possibility that there may be some innate functional and structural brain differences which may predispose some individuals to become musicians, there is ever increasing evidence that musical training itself leads to changes in brain function and structure (Schlaug, 2003). This suggests that whatever genetic inheritance an individual may have is greatly enhanced by a musically enriched environment.

While interactive models provide the most plausible explanations for the differences in a range of learning outcomes, including those relating to music, there are instances where high levels of musical skill emerge very early in life, suggesting a strong genetic disposition in the individuals concerned. Idiot savants are individuals whose general cognitive functioning is below normal levels but who nevertheless are able to undertake some activities – for instance, drawing, calculating calendar dates, playing music – with apparent ease and outstanding skill. The evidence from these individuals suggests that some cognitive functions operate independently (Young and Nettelbeck, 1995; Sloboda *et al.*, 1985). Howe (1989), for instance, describes a man who was an excellent sight reader, could play by ear, had perfect pitch and extensive knowledge of music and musicians, played the piano sufficiently well to play at rehearsals of a leading American chamber orchestra and whose technique had been commented on favourably by a number of prominent musicians. When he listened to music played by others, his approach was critical and informed. He had become interested in music very early in life and would hum tunes he had heard before he could speak. However, his other cognitive functions and social and personal behaviour were equivalent to those of a 10-year-old. He learnt to read but did not understand the content, could not think abstractly and had no reasoning ability. He had to rely on other people to provide care and protection in his daily life. The discrepancy between his musical ability and his overall competence in everyday life was striking.

There are remarkable similarities between many of the character- istics of the savants and child prodigies. Ruthsatz and Detterman (2003) reported the case of a musical prodigy who had no formal tuition on an instrument, did no formal practice and had gained his skills by listening to other performers and improvising his own musical pieces. His family had no particular musical background, although his mother played the piano. He could sing in two languages and had taught himself to play numerous instruments.

His musical behaviours seemed self-motivated. He engaged in them spontaneously and with pleasure, and particularly enjoyed entertaining people. He spent a great deal of time in playful imitation of other musicians, but the improvement in his performance was a by-product of this practice, not the product of it. He had extremely high scores on tests of musical ability and intelligence, the latter revealing an extraordinary memory as measured within his cognitive profile.

It is difficult to explain the highly developed skills of savants and prodigies without resorting to genetic explanations, although many of the savants have limited sight and language disorders, which may have led to increased development of auditory-processing skills and the use of music as a means of communication. They also spend a great deal of time practising their skills, in part because they receive considerable positive reinforcement for their musical expertise. This they have in common with prodigies. Both seem to find their musical activities intrinsically rewarding and spend much time engaged with them. This indicates that even where there may be genetically determined predispositions towards developing musical skills, time spent rehearsing them is crucial to their development.

Issues of ability testing in music education

Our current knowledge does not enable us to state beyond doubt whether observed differences in musical ability are the sole result of genetic inheritance, learning or an interaction between the two. As we have seen in earlier chapters, there is abundant evidence that humans as a species are 'musical', that we share similar brain structures that respond to music, and that exposure to music and engagement with it improve measured musicality. It may be that we shall never be able to establish, beyond doubt, to what extent individual musical ability is learnt or inherited. If that is the case, we should provide all children with opportunities from the earliest age to develop their musical skills.

The first tests of musical ability were developed to select children to play an instrument in formal educational settings. The reasons for selection were essentially pragmatic. They were based on assumptions that musical ability was innate or at least determined at an early age. Resources were limited and the best way to ensure that resources were well used was to select children on the basis of ability. The tests focused on aural abilities, usually pitch and rhythm – although some later tests attempted to assess musicality. We now know that these tests assess what has already been learnt and may therefore discriminate against those who have experienced an impoverished musical environment prior to testing. The assessment of musical ability, particularly when assumptions are made about its genetic basis, has an impact on expectations of what can be achieved. It places limits on what is perceived as possible in the eyes of the individual concerned, their parents, and teachers. Labelling students as of high or low ability leads teachers to have expectations that are then fulfilled (Rosenthal and Jacobsen, 1968). Students recognise the level of expectation that teachers have of them from the way that they are treated and over time conform to them. This phenomenon (the self-fulfilling prophecy) can be avoided by ensuring that there are high expectations for all students, with appropriate challenges set for them. These should be communicated through goal setting, followed by praise when goals are attained.

There are ways in which tests of musical ability can be used positively. Adopted as part of formative assessment procedures, they can provide feedback to the learner and the teacher about strengths and weaknesses in aural skills and indicate which areas need further attention. However, using psychometric musical tests to assess progress or even diagnose problems in individual children may be time consuming. Instead, progress can be checked and monitored in the course of lessons and linked with other ongoing musical activities.

If resources are limited and selection procedures are needed to allocate those resources, interest in music and motivation to engage with it may prove to be better determinants of success than traditional tests of musical ability. If an individual attains high scores on a test but has no interest in music, they will not devote the amount of time to practice essential for the development of high levels of musical skill. Further, the use of motivation to determine the provision of opportunity ensures that the skills which are acquired are likely to be well utilised in the long term. In a society where it is not possible, or desirable, for everyone to become professionally engaged in music, the long-term aims of music education must surely be ensuring a love of music and engagement with it throughout the lifespan. This may be through listening to music or active involvement in music making at an amateur level. If motivation rather than prior musical knowledge is used to select pupils to take advantage of limited learning resources, these long-term educational outcomes are more likely to be achieved.

Further reading

Gardner, H., Kornhaber, M.L. and Wake, W.K. (1996) *Intelligence: Multiple perspectives,* New York: Harcourt Brace College Publishers.

Hallam, S. (in press, b) 'Musicality'. In G.E. McPherson (ed.) *The Child as Musician: A handbook of musical development.* Oxford: Oxford University Press.

Shuter-Dyson, R. (1999) 'Musical ability'. In D. Deutsch (ed.) *The Psychology of Music.* (2nd edition) London: Academic Press (pp. 627–651).

5 Listening, appraising and responding to music

Whenever we engage with music – whether as performers, composers or audience – we are listening, appraising and responding to it. As we saw in Chapter 3, we are born equipped with the necessary structures and mechanisms to perceive and respond to music. As we become encultured into the music of our immediate environment, we learn to appraise it.

Listening to music

A number of writers have distinguished between listening and hearing. Hearing is seen as essentially passive, a form of reception; while listening involves concentration, focus or activity on the part of the listener. Hearing occurs without conscious attention and is part of the constant process of monitoring our environment. Listening requires conscious cognitive activity and involves focusing on particular elements in the music. Both hearing and listening provide valuable means through which different kinds of learning can occur. Repetitively hearing particular music enables aural representations to be developed, a crucial element of enculturation. Music educators sometimes underestimate the importance of the incidental learning that can occur from just hearing music, believing that only active listening to music, consciously undertaken, where some form of cognitive evaluation is undertaken, is of value.

Historically a number of educators have stressed the importance of learning music by ear, through sound, rather than notation – notable among them John Curwen (Rainbow, 1980), Kodaly (Szabo, 1969) and Jacques-Dalcroze (Bachman, 1991), the last named also emphasising the importance of bodily movement in understanding music. Some instrumental teaching methods have been devised which have as their basis learning through listening – for instance, the Suzuki method (Lipman, 1987). Until recently, much formalised music tuition has tended to neglect the importance of playing by ear, which in some cases has been actively discouraged. However, many musicians working in the popular music field cannot read music and rely totally on their aural skills to enable them to perform, some having developed their aural skills to an incredible extent (Macek, 1987). Savants, discussed in the previous chapter, can also memorise lengthy pieces of music by ear more efficiently and effectively than professional musicians (Sloboda *et al.*, 1985). This suggests that human beings have structures in the brain which are not only pre-programmed to remember music, but can make links with motor programmes to turn what has been remembered into sound.

Listening frequently to music enables it to become internalised so that we know and remember it. This facilitates the development of audiation (Gordon, 1993), the ability to hear internally and comprehend music for which the sound is no longer or may never have been physically present. This includes the ability to hear internally and understand notated music without actually playing it. This is a highly advanced skill, and some professional musicians only partially acquire it. Audiation is important in both improvisation and composition.

The process of listening to music

Although listening to music is crucial for the development of all musical skills, we know relatively little about the way in which we process music in real musical situations. Much research has concentrated on the study of how we listen to short fragments, exploring the perception of melodic contour, harmonic structure and aspects of timing. Such artificial studies provide few insights into the ways in which individuals listen to music in normal circumstances and their actual experience of listening. As we saw in Chapter 3, the structures and processes required for musical perception are well developed by school age. When we listen to music, we process an enormous amount of information rapidly, often without conscious awareness. The ease with which we do this depends on our prior musical experiences and the culturally determined tonal scheme to which we have become accustomed (Dowling, 1992, 1993). This knowledge is implicit (not always available to conscious thought) and is then applied automatically whenever we listen to music. Studies of listening in realistic situations have suggested that repeated listening to a piece of music changes a listener's perceptions, leading to a greater understanding of the structure of the music and the relationship of themes within it (Pollard-Gott, 1983). There is also evidence that listeners tend to encode the music that they hear in absolute, not relative, terms. The memory represents very precisely what is heard (DeWitt and Crowder, 1986), to such an extent that, when asked to sing a familiar pop song, most people sing it at the correct absolute pitch. Tempos also tend to be accurately remembered (Levitin, 1994; Levitin and Cook, 1996). Memory for music typically operates in terms of precise representations.

Although musical experience leads to greater sophistication in the store of implicit knowledge, non-musicians typically acquire the fundamentals from their experience of listening to music. They are sensitive to shifts in tonality and to the multi-level structure of rhythmic organisation. Untrained adults do not usually find melodic contour recognition more difficult than trained subjects (Dowling, 1978), but they do find interval recognition (Cuddy and Cohen, 1976) and the hearing of partials in a complex tone more difficult (Fine and Moore, 1993). Both perform worse at memory tasks with atonal than tonal melodies (Dowling, 1991), and are error prone when dealing with non-standard quarter steps (Dowling, 1992). There are only small differences between musicians and non-musicians in identifying musical structures. Musicians demonstrate the same sorts of difficulty as non-musicians in resolving musical puzzles, both experiencing great difficulty in integrating local harmonic structures within a global structure (Tillman *et al.*, 1998a, 1998b). Musicians do not seem to have better comprehension of large musical structures than non-musicians (Poulin *et al.*, 2001), nor do they perform better in recognising similarity in canons of 12-note sounds written in the style of Webern (Bigand, 2003). The perceptions of the two groups barely differ in exploring different kinds of cadence and chord progression (Tillman *et al.*, 2000), in relation to melody (Bigand, 2003), or on a neurophysiological level (Koelsch *et al.*, 2000; Maess *et al.*, 2001). This suggests that listeners without musical training are musical experts, in spite of their inability to describe explicitly what they hear. However, those with musical training perceive the importance of the thematic material quicker than the musically naïve, categorising themes which are similar and different into groups (Aiello *et al.*, 1990). There are differences among professional musicians in the way in which they listen to music (Aiello *et al.*, 1990). Some adopt a Gestalt, holistic mode of perception; while others adopt a more analytic, segmented approach, focusing on the details of the work. These differences do not appear to depend on the instrumental specialism of the musician or their level of training, although they may depend on the type of training.

Responses to music

Human beings respond to music in a variety of different ways. Responses can be physiological, motor, intellectual, aesthetic, emotional or in relation to mood or arousal. In education the focus has been on the intellect and aesthetics. However, the other responses may be the most powerful.

The effects of music on heart rate, skin conductivity, respiration rates, blood pressure, muscular tension, movement, posture, finger and peripheral skin temperature, blood volume, and stomach contractions have all been investigated (Bartlett, 1996). No clear patterns emerge relating the music and the physiological measures. Most studies indicate that stimulating music leads to an increased response in most physiological measures, but not all do. Similarly, calming music does not always lead to a reduction in physiological response. Broadly, however, the evidence suggests that music influences physiological arousal in the expected direction – that is, exciting music leads to increased arousal; calming music to the reverse. Individual cognitive responses to music may mediate physiological responses and explain some of the variability in findings (Ogata, 1995; Vanderark and Ely, 1993). Differences may also depend on how often the individual listens to music, whether they are musically trained, whether they like the kind of music played, how they interpret the music, their personality and their typical level of physiological arousal. The model outlined in Figure 5.1 (LeBlanc, 1980) suggests that music has direct effects on mood and arousal through primitive brain mechanisms which operate without conscious cognitive control. Certainly there is evidence of decreased alpha electroencephalography (EEG), indicating increased arousal in children aged 8 to 9 years when music is played (Furman, 1978). Zimny and Weidenfeller (1962) also reported that stimulative music increased excitement (galvanic skin response) in children.

Music affects our behaviour. Most of us will have found ourselves tapping our feet to music or having the urge to get up and dance to music that we find particularly stimulating. Scientific observations of the behaviour of young children when lively music is playing indicate that they become more active, suggesting that this is a 'natural' response (Ferguson *et al.*, 1994). Some athletes report using music to help them in training (Ferguson *et al.*, 1994; Pujol and Langefield, 1999), although this seems more to distract them from any discomfort they are feeling than directly to affect their performance (Anshel and Marisi, 1978). There is also evidence that muscular tension can be reduced by listening to quiet, sedative music (Bartlett, 1996). An extreme example of the effect of music on behaviour is the part it plays in creating trance-like states (Neher, 1962). The impact of music on behaviour will be discussed further in Chapter 12.

Music affects our moods, arousal levels and emotions. Generally, music that is slow and quiet tends to encourage relaxation and reduce

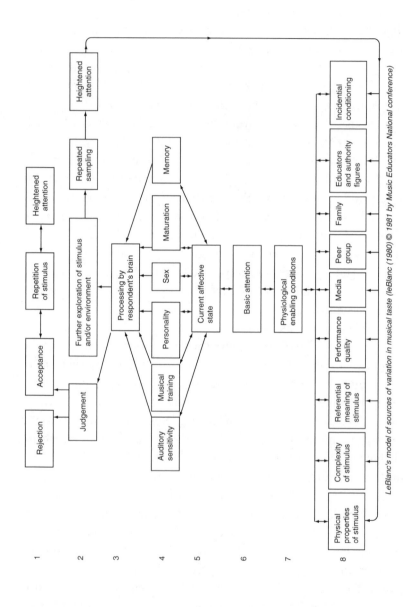

Figure 5.1 *A model of sources of variation in musical taste*

LeBlanc's model of sources of variation in musical taste (leBlanc (1980) © 1981 by Music Educators National conference)

anxiety, while stimulating music tends to increase our arousal levels (Abeles and Chung, 1996). The characteristics of music that induce different moods seem to relate to three main dimensions: pleasure–displeasure, arousal–non-arousal and dominance–submissiveness (Crozier, 1997), although it has proved very difficult to specify with any degree of accuracy which musical structures evoke particular moods. There is some evidence that minor and major modes tend to be associated with happiness and sadness; firm rhythm tends to evoke feelings of dignified and vigorous character; and flowing rhythm, happy feelings (Hevner, 1936). Specific reactions to music – for example, shivers down the spine, laughter, tears and a lump in the throat – may be related to particular musical structures (Sloboda, 1991). Beyond these rather general trends, the evidence with regard to the effects of particular types of music on the mood and emotions of particular groups of people is mixed. Exploration of gender, age and social class differences have revealed no clear patterns. Some studies have shown the effects of formal training (Abeles and Chung, 1996), but quite different types of music can change mood in the same direction (Field *et al.*, 1998). This may be because the individual characteristics of the listener and their prior experiences with music are important mediators (Robazza *et al.*, 1994). There is some evidence that music can affect our moods, emotions and physiological responses whether we like the music or not (Iwanaga and Moroki, 1999). In one study, favourite music of whatever type lowered feelings of tension, while physiological responses were greater during exciting music regardless of whether the listeners liked it. Similar effects have been found with young children undertaking a writing task. While they enjoyed writing with exciting background music playing, their task performance was better when the music was quiet and classical (Hallam and Godwin, 2000).

Individuals can have very strong emotional experiences to music (Sloboda, 1992) (see Gabrielsson, 2001, for a review), although music can also play an important role in helping overcome powerful emotions. For instance, adolescents who report a high frequency of personal problems listen to music more frequently than their peers (Behne, 1997). Increasingly, music is used to mediate moods and emotional reactions, fulfil spiritual or 'transcendent' functions, and provide cues to reminiscence (Sloboda *et al.*, 2001; Sloboda and O'Neill, 2002).

There are three main explanations for our physical and emotional responses to music. First, there may be 'pre-wired' connections between musical stimuli and emotional responses, particularly in relation to the 'primitive' components of music – for example, loudness, timbre, pitch and tempo (Gabrielsson, 1993). Second, cognitions may play a mediating role – for instance, a particular piece of music might be connected with an emotional event in our lives. Third, emotion may be aroused when musical expectations are disconfirmed or delayed (Meyer, I.B., 1956, 2000, 2001). It is likely that all three explanations are valid, in relation to different kinds of emotional response, on different occasions, for different individuals, or working in combination.

Aesthetic responses to music are subjective, personal responses to beauty. Such responses are highly individualistic and will depend on the taste and judgement of each listener. Aesthetic experience requires involvement with the music, the perception of interacting events within the music, cognition of the interplay among the events within the music and an emotional reaction of some kind to the music (Knieter, 1971; Reimer, 1970); the essential difference between aesthetic and affective experience being that the former requires the involvement of both perception and cognition. There is little agreement as to what makes some interactions aesthetic and others not. Some have argued that the term 'aesthetic experience' can be applied to more or less any reaction that any person might have to any work of art, defined in the broadest possible sense. So the reaction of a teenager to the latest pop release is equivalent to the response of a music critic to a new musical composition (Hargreaves, 1986).

In addition to the effects of music on our physiology, movement, mood and behaviour, music is a source of intellectual stimulation. Listening to music, identifying its structures and forms, analysing it, learning about its history and nature across different cultures, learning to play an instrument or sing, composing, improvising and performing, all offer intellectual stimulation and challenge (Hallam, 1998a). While these are the main focus of education, motivation might be increased if there were a greater acknowledgement by teachers of the mood changing and emotional power of music.

Appraisal and evaluation

Appraisal and evaluation are central activities for musicians. The musician constantly appraises their work and that of colleagues. This guides future planning and activity. The process of appraising involves listening and making comparisons (implicit or explicit) with internal representations of music already acquired. These may be specific – that is, of the same piece of music; generalised but still pertaining to particular types of music; or generalised relating to particular features of performance – for example, intonation, tone quality. The principle of comparison, either implicit or explicit, is central. Without comparison with some conception already held, appraisal cannot occur. The process of appraisal may take place on a number of different levels: description, comparison and evaluation within the broader musical context. Even quite young children are able to articulate ideas about their listening processes, and as they get older they more frequently predict, compare, evaluate, express preferences, reflect, recognise and make judgements about music (Bundra, 1993). Musically trained children demonstrate similar skills to adults, including classifying, elaborating, comparing, predicting and evaluating (Richardson 1996, 1998), suggesting that the ability to think critically while listening to music is related to experience with music rather than age.

Musical preferences

Appraising involves learners making judgements about their liking of particular pieces of music. These judgements can be made independently of whether the individual has any understanding of the music, although being able to justify preferences has educational value (Swanwick, 1994). There is evidence that the more familiar we are with a piece of music, the more we like and value it (Zajonc, 1968; Smith, K.C. and Cuddy, 1986). However, not all the evidence supports this view. Overfamiliarity may lead to boredom (Berlyne, 1971) or dislike (North and Hargreaves, 1997). A critical aspect of music that determines whether it is liked is its complexity. Complexity refers to the degree of variability or uncertainty in the music. The relationship between complexity and liking can be described by an inverted U-shaped curve. A moderate level of complexity elicits the maximum liking for the music. The effect of exposure to music, repetition, training or practice is to lower the perceived complexity of the music. These changes seem to develop cyclically, occurring in a spiral as music is listened to more than once (Bamberger, 1991). This suggests that musical preferences can be changed through prolonged exposure, although the evidence indicates that this does not guarantee liking. Education may alter and expand musical preference, but the results are not always predictable (Radocy and Boyle, 1988). Why might this be the case? Musical taste is not acquired in a vacuum. It is an integral part of the lifestyle of the individual concerned and reflects cultural, historical, societal, familial and peer-group background. Whether someone will like a piece of music depends on a hierarchical set of factors (LeBlanc, 1980). These are set out in Figure 5.1.

At the bottom level of the hierarchy is the nature of the music itself and the listening situation. This includes the physical properties of the music, its level of complexity, its meaning for the individual, and the quality of the performance. The listening situation includes the media through which it is presented and who is present: members of the listener's peer group, members of their family, authority figures – for example, the teacher. Beyond this initial level a range of factors act as filters. First, there are physiological and psychological factors, such as ease of hearing, the level of attention being paid to the listening process, and the current mood of the listener. Any of these may preclude careful listening. Continuing the filtering process are things which the individual brings to the listening process themselves – their level of auditory sensitivity in relation to music; their level of musical training; their personality (in particular whether they are generally receptive to new experiences); and their gender, ethnic group, socio-economic status and maturity. For instance, we know that young children respond positively to a wide range of music, whereas adolescents tend to prefer popular music. These all affect the way the process to listening is undertaken, what is attended to, and how the listener processes the music. Having passed through these filters, the music is processed. This may occur at a holistic level or the listener may take note of the detail, paying attention to instrumentation, structure, the style and so on. A judgement is then made about whether they have sufficient information to make a decision about whether they like the music. It may be that more information is required, in which case the music may be listened to again or listening may continue more carefully. The individual will then be in a position to make a preference judgement. The factors that affect developing preferences for particular kinds of music are therefore complex.

Promoting the development of listening and understanding

The acquisition of listening skills is important for musical development in its broadest sense. Most children have well-developed listening skills from exposure to music in their everyday lives. Those who are not receiving specialist musical training have listening skills that are in most ways as well developed as the skills of those who are. These skills can be utilised to good effect in music lessons. Setting different kinds of listening tasks can encourage detailed or holistic listening. Concentrating on similarities and differences can be used as a guiding principle for identifying musical structures. Repeated listening to the same piece of music increases understanding, although care needs to be taken to judge when it is becoming too well known and boredom is setting in. To develop appraisal skills, attendance at live performances can provide stimulation and opportunities for critique of both performance and composition. Introducing into the classroom music that will be perceived as 'shocking' can stimulate discussion. Facilitating peer review of performance and composition can assist in developing critical skills and increased understanding of creative processes.

Listening to music while undertaking other related activities also has benefits. For instance, getting young children to move to music encourages learning which is multi-sensory. Encouraging students to listen to music while following a part or score will also begin to develop the process of audiation (being able to hear music from the written page), and will enable the development of internal aural representations of phrasing in different musical styles as musicians do not play written notation literally (Gabrielsson, 1988). We need to encourage students to engage with a wide variety of different types of music. Exposure to different genres, for instance, through formal instrumental tuition leads to appreciation of a wider range of music (Kotsopoulou, 2001). Savan (1999), in her work with children with emotional and behavioural difficulties (see Chapter 12), found that some of those exposed regularly over long periods of time to the music of Mozart while they were studying science came to enjoy the music and continued to listen to it at home after the research was over. Opportunities for playing music while children are engaged in other activities frequently present themselves, particularly in the early years, and may be preferable to formal 'listening' opportunities for developing wider musical preferences. Music can be used as a stimulus for art, writing and a range of other creative activities, in addition to being played in assemblies, during lunch times and at other social occasions.

Educators need to acknowledge the power of music to change mood and to influence emotions. Too often music is seen as an intellectual pursuit with little reference to what it may mean to young people. At the earliest stages of secondary education children begin to use music to express feelings and change moods in their home environment (Tolfree, 2005). These emotional responses to music can be used as a way of encouraging exploration of structure, instrumentation, timbre and so on. Engaging rather than ignoring the emotional power of music will make lessons more enjoyable and interesting for everyone.

Further reading

Aiello, R. and Sloboda, J.A. (eds) (1994) *Musical Perceptions.* Oxford and New York: Oxford University Press.
Hodges, D.A. (ed.) (1996a) *Handbook of Music Psychology.* (2nd edition) San Antonio, TX: IMR Press.
Juslin, P.N. and Sloboda, J.A. (eds) *Music and Emotion: Theory and research.* Oxford: Oxford University Press.

6 Composing and improvising

Creativity and music

Music is both a creative and a performing art. Composition, improvisation and the interpretation of music all require creativity. Research on creativity has adopted several perspectives which variously consider the processes involved in it, the individuals who contribute to it, the environments which may be conducive to it, and its products (Sternberg, 1988). In this chapter these will be considered in relation to composition and improvisation. Compared with research on musical processing and learning to play an instrument, there has been relatively little research on creative processes in music, although promoting creativity is acknowledged to be important. There is also some debate as to whether there are different levels of creativity in music dependent on the permanence of the end-product and the scale of the endeavour, composing being at the highest level and interpretation and at the lowest.

The products of the creative process in music

A creative product is one that is both novel (to its creator) and is appropriate or valuable in the context of a domain (Mayer, 1999). What is considered appropriate or valuable varies, depending on subjective appraisals. In music, composition, improvisation and, to a lesser extent, performance lead to creative products. While in the professional music world the distinction between composition and improvisation is relatively clear, in education – because compositions are not always notated – the boundaries are blurred.

Changing conceptions of composition
Historically, the Western musical tradition conceived of the composer as a highly talented individual who created a unique

work of art. Composition was taught from models derived from the accepted masters, with students learning the rules, writing in a variety of genres, and gradually developing their own distinctive styles. In other cultures, particularly where music is not notated, music making is a social activity where the role of the individual is less important. During the twentieth century composers explored a much wider range of sounds in their compositions, and technology has made composition at a very high level possible for those who do not have highly developed technical skills on an instrument. This has opened up the possibility of composition for all and made possible a revolution in the music classroom. Educationally, there have been enormous benefits. Active composing increases pupils' interest in music, giving them an opportunity to control what they are doing and a greater understanding of sound, structure and emotional expression.

What do we mean by improvisation?

The term 'improvisation' covers a wide range of musical phenomena and incorporates a multiplicity of musical meanings. It may involve slight deviation of rhythm or articulation from what had been rehearsed, the relatively planned realisation of notated or rule-governed music, free unplanned music, or variation in the interpretation of graphic scores. In the same way that what is creative is determined by societies, what is purported to be improvisation is also constructed. Some see improvisation as a subset of composition (Paynter, 1992), but it can be viewed in many ways, from an exploratory means of composing to a highly skilled performance skill which leads to the creation of an exactly specified product. Overall, there is no single concept of improvisation: it includes a range of activities that involve improvisational elements. As we saw in Chapter 2, young children improvise songs, and free improvisation can be used as a means of communication in music therapy or to develop self-esteem and a range of skills in those with special educational needs or mental health problems. With the exception of free improvisation, it is typically based around some predetermined structure, form, chord sequence or melody, where some aspect is left undetermined or unrealised. The quality of the improvisation lies in relation to its stylistic conventions, and in order to appreciate it the listener has to understand the genre. The common element is that creative decisions take place within the real time of the performance. To improvise, musicians must have a knowledge base, acquired over time through practice, which is idiomatic to a particular genre, from which they generate novel routines in performance.

Creative processes

While there is disagreement about the exact nature of the creative process among researchers, they agree that it is time consuming, both in the extensive period of training required to develop appropriate skills and in the time taken in each creative act. The actual processes involved depend on the particular domain within which the individual is working, although there seem to be some overarching principles which apply across all domains (Sternberg, 1988). One influential theory has been that of Wallas (1926). He proposed four stages in the creative process: preparation (gathering of relevant information, assessment of the initial problem), incubation (time to mull over the problem, playful activities associated with it), illumination (flash of insight, derivation of a solution), and verification (formalisation and adaptation of the solution which may lead back to the preparation or incubation stages). Ross, M. (1980) proposed a similar model which includes initiating (tactile explorations, doodling, playing, chance and accidents), acquainting (becoming conversant with sound, practice, invention), controlling (mastery of basic skills and techniques, manipulation, dealing with constraints and limitations) and structuring (gathering the creation into a comprehensible whole, relatedness, rescanning, reviewing). There is considerable agreement between these two conceptualisations of creative processes, although the stages into which each activity fits and the exact terminology adopted vary.

Gestalt theorists reject the idea of stages. For them creative problem solving is a process where individual sub-elements are gathered into a whole structure. Restructuring, or the flash of illumination, occurs when the problem solver or creator sees an unexpected solution to the problem (Duncker, 1945). Emerging systems theory (Gruber, 1980) suggests that there are many moments of insight during the course of creative effort (Gruber and Davis, 1988; Gilhooly, 1996). Generative ideas evolve over significant periods of time, often with many goals and subgoals, false starts and dead-ends. For information processing theorists, creativity is seen as a form of problem solving characterised by the ill-defined nature of the problem and the notion of novelty or newness (Johnson-Laird, 1988, 1993). Trial-and-error searches take place through a variety of possibilities in a problem-space. The problem-solver moves from the initial stage of the problem to its goal state, working within the structures imposed by a particular rule system. In music the composer needs to have knowledge of particular musical rules and grammars (Newell and Simon, 1972).

Compositional processes

Research has focused on the compositional practices of experts and novices. Reitman (1965) studied a professional composer working on a fugue and postulated several transformational characteristics: constraint proliferation (more constraints emerge as the process proceeds); attribute discontinuity (the composer ignores or suspends attention to particular attributes); and connected alternatives (the composer defers plans or actions until suitable conditions arise for their implementation). The recursive nature of creative thinking was a strong feature of the process. Collins (2005), studying a single composer, demonstrated strategies operating at micro- and macro-levels. At the outset, a clear mental picture of the composition was in place which acted as a loose framework throughout the process. Problem proliferation and successive solution implementation occurred not only in a linear manner, but also recursively. Moments of Gestalt creative insight were observed which related to problem restructuring; some were seen to overlap in real time with others, indicating an element of parallelism in thinking. There were no clear boundaries between the various stages. For each problem arising, solutions themselves were conjectured, implemented or deferred. Overall, it was a complex process.

Similar processes have been identified in the creative activities of children. Studies of children's spontaneous creativity in developing playground songs suggest a deliberate process of innovation, reorganisation of formulae, elaboration and condensation across all ages (Marsh, 1995). The stage theory of Wallas, outlined above, has provided an explanatory framework in several studies (Bennett, 1976; Burnard and Younker, 2002), indicating linearity, recursivity and moments of illumination. Seddon and O'Neill (2003), using computer technology, identified exploratory, rehearsal and construction phases in musical composition, with students moving in linear and recursive fashion between these phases; while Bamberger (1977) identified strategies of searching for continuity, setting goals, structuring parts into wholes, and grappling with crucial questions involving the interaction between local and global structure and between detail and larger design.

Identification of the factors contributing to successful composition supports the importance of conceptualisation of an intended product, the process itself depending on 'enabling skills' (music aptitudes, conceptual understanding, craftsmanship, aesthetic sensitivity) influenced by enabling conditions (motivation, subconscious imagery, personality and environment). Divergent and convergent thinking, enabling skills and conditions ultimately interact in the creation of the final product (Webster, 1988, 1991). Children more successful in composition seem to adopt different strategies from those who are less successful. Highly creative groups tend to generate more musical ideas, and experiment and repeat them more than other children. Ideas for the final composition also emerge early on (Hickey, 1995). Daignault (1997) found that highly creative groups tended to generate product-oriented music rather than process-oriented improvisations. Some children rated high for craftsmanship generated the musical material in their finished compositions by manipulating the notation rather than by improvising. Taken together, these studies identify clear differences in composition processes between groups perceived as high and low in creativity.

The development of compositional skills

Some researchers have considered the development of compositional skills over time. Kratus (1989) examined ten-minute segments of children's compositions, categorising activities into exploration, development, repetition and silence. Older children used more strategies of development, and repetition in relation to exploration and silence. Younger children were unable to conceptualise complete musical ideas and centred their time around process-oriented versus product-oriented thinking, reflecting Daignault's (1997) findings. As children progress through elementary education, the processes adopted become more similar to those of adults (Kratus, 1994). The developmental process is clearly delineated by Swanwick and Tillman (1986), who devised a descriptive spiral which builds on the ideas of mastery, imitation, imaginative play and metacognition, with data derived from children given opportunities to compose in various ways. Eight areas of development were identified: sensory, manipulative, personal expressiveness, vernacular, speculative, idiomatic, symbolic, and systematic. These describe the development of compositional processes from pre-school through to adolescence.

Comparisons between expert and novice performance

Comparisons of experts and novices suggest that experts take a more holistic view of the whole composition and maintain this conceptually while working on problems arising. Davidson, L. and Welsh (1988) found that in writing a modulating melody novices tended to work on a note-by-note basis, while the experts were able to chunk information into larger units, holding the focus of attention on the task in hand and looking forwards and backwards through the music at the same time. Similarly, Younker and Smith (1996) found that novices considered only local features or isolated individual sound events, while those working at a higher level reflected a Gestalt-like approach in which they demonstrated the ability to consider the detail of the task within the structured whole. Colley *et al.* (1992) asked an expert and three novices, within a specified time scale, to harmonise part of a Bach chorale. While the experts approached the task considering general strategic factors, novices took less of an overview and approached the task on a bar-by-bar basis.

Despite these differences, novices and experts approach some aspects of composition in similar ways. Folkestad (2004), undertaking a meta-analysis of qualitative data derived from several studies, showed that the basic qualities and elements in composition were very similar for all participants, from early childhood through adolescence up to adulthood. The data used included that derived from Sundin's (1998) investigation of 3–6-year-old children's spontaneous songs created in a day-care centre; Nilsson's (2002) study of 8-year-old children using synthesiser and computer to compose music; Folkestad's (1996) study of 15–16-year-olds creating music using computers and synthesisers; Vesterlund's (2001) project investigating the creative music making of 18–20-year-old students using music technology and computers; the in-depth study of a professional composer by Collins reported above; and preliminary results of an interview study of adult students in composition (Folkestad and Hultqvist, in press). The findings showed that the process was one of interaction between the participant's musical experiences and competences, their cultural environment, the available tools and instruments, and the instructions. This relates closely to the analysis undertaken by Webster described earlier. The findings also suggested that the process was supported by the constraints imposed externally – the professional composer's commission and the instructions given to the students by the teacher. These provided the framework for the process. Composing without such a framework was reported to be the most difficult task. Crucial was the way the conditions were formulated; they needed to be able to be incorporated into the act of creation. Participants referred repeatedly to the relationship between 'whole–parts', 'figure–ground' and 'framework/texture' details. The evidence suggested that instructions defining the parts or details were limiting, while instructions providing an overarching framework were not only helpful but necessary.

Notating compositions

Notations are 'cultural tools for leaving an intentional trace of communicative and cognitive acts'; central to these notations are 'the features of intention, communication, cognition and representation of something internal to the mind' (Karmiloff-Smith, 1992:139). Children's notations of their compositions have been described as windows into musical cognition (Davidson, L. and Scripp, 1988; 1992). Their immediate verbal accounts of their notations indicate meaningful intention (Barrett, 2001). A common feature of their invented notations is the borrowing of symbols and strategies from a range of symbol systems, including drawing, music, number and writing. With increasing experience, they build a repertoire of notational strategies with symbol choices moving from enactive and representational to more abstract depictions, although the acquisition of strategies is accumulative rather than rigidly hierarchical (Barrett, 1997) and choice is influenced by the nature of the task and those features perceived to be dominant (Barrett, 1999). When notating song material, representation of lyric content dominates (Barrett, 2000). For retrieving musical meaning over time, abstract symbolic notational strategies are more effective than representational/pictorial notational strategies (Barrett, 2003).

Bamberger (1982, 1991, 1994) distinguished between figural (conveying the shape and musical expressiveness of the rhyme) and metric drawings (accurately conveying the number of claps but not the musical sense) of children's notation of the clapped rhythm of part of a nursery rhyme. Children varied the size, shape and placing of the units they used to represent the taps on the page, inventing their own notations – including pictures, words and symbols. Bamberger suggested that these might represent different hearings of the piece. Children familiar with and competent users of conventional music notation attend to and construct rhythmic patterns in different ways from those for whom such notation is an unknown. Mastery of the denotive system shapes and reflects musical perception and conception (Bamberger, 1991).

The process of improvisation

The process of improvisation at a professional level requires the utilisation of complex cognitive abilities. Much improvisation is rule governed, providing constraints within which the musician must operate; for instance, in jazz, a particular song, the harmonic structure, characteristic rhythmic patterns (Pressing, 1998). These limit the musician's creative choices. Most improvisations operate within a framework of rules, leaving the musician to choose between several alternatives available. The process of improvisation relies to a great extent on long-term memory and the simultaneous interaction of unconscious automatic processes with conscious cognitive processes (Pressing, 1988). Johnson-Laird (1988) argues that to improvise effectively in a particular genre, the subconscious knowledge-base processes need to be automated and submerged so that the performer cannot access their own subconscious processes at the moment of creation. If the knowledge base is sufficiently internalised in long-term memory and automated through practice and performance experience, the resources used to generate surface melody are free to focus on developing coherence and structural unity. The performing musician must be able to generate and execute motor programmes 'online' through having access to a large stock of style-specific knowledge in the form of common patterns and sequences. Improvisers programme what Schramowski calls 'movement images' (1973:239). Entire movement sequences are anticipated that hinge on particular notes constrained by the physical characteristics of the instrument.

Johnson-Laird (1991, 2002) suggests that at the deepest level improvisers commit basic structures to memory, at a middle level they make feedback decisions that concern the structure of the referent, and at the surface level improvised melody is generated. As the player becomes more experienced, ever more complex actions become automated, but in the early stages of learning to improvise very simple processes using short-term memory can generate acceptable improvisations, although they may be somewhat mechanical (Johnson-Laird, 1988). Part of the process of developing improvisation knowledge includes feedback where ongoing monitoring of performance enables new ideas, perhaps initially unintended wrong notes, to be incorporated into future performances (Kenny, B.J. and Gellrich, 2002). The creative impetus for improvisation is interaction with fellow performers, the audience and the environment. These make each performance distinctive (Johnson-Laird, 1991).

Development of improvising skills

Several authors have noted the differences between expert and novice improvisers (Kratus, 1991; Hargreaves *et al.*, 1991). For the expert improviser, knowing how a melody will sound before it is played seems central. Gordon (1993) calls this ability to create a mental image of the sound 'audiation'. An expert improviser will have:

(i) the skill to hear musical patterns internally as they are about to be played;
(ii) knowledge of the relevant musical structures;

(iii) the skill to manipulate an instrument or the voice to achieve musical intentions fluently;
(iv) knowledge of strategies for structuring an improvisation and the flexibility to change strategies if necessary;
 (v) knowledge of stylistic conventions for improvising in a given style;
(vi) the skill to transcend stylistic conventions to develop personal style (Kratus, 1991).

In reaching this expert level, the learner appears to develop through a series of stages (Kratus, 1996). Stage 1 consists of exploration through play; Stage 2 is process oriented, for example musical doodling without any overall coherence; Stage 3 is product-oriented improvisation where some musical techniques are adopted into the playing; at Stage 4 improvisation becomes more fluid and there is more control over the technical aspects of performance; at Stage 5 improvisation is increasingly structured; and at Stage 6 the learner demonstrates a developed style. The improvisation becomes fluent and the appropriate musical style is adopted for the improvisation. So how are these skills acquired?

Sudnow (1978) documented how tedious, effortful and frustrating was the experience of acquiring jazz improvisation skills as an adult professional classical musician. He experienced difficulties in relation to acquiring knowledge bases from aural sources, and frustration with the technical constraints imposed by particular instruments that impacted on the improvised response, and with the relationship between spontaneously created material and improvised fillers. As his skills developed, he reported that conscious application of his internalised knowledge produced what he described as 'frantic' playing. To overcome this, he had to give up cognitive control and allow each hand to find the notes intuitively. This risk taking led to more 'right' notes falling under his fingers, and his improvisation became more relaxed and sounded more like that of experienced players. Performance that incorporates flow states and risk taking may hold the key to achieving optimal levels of musical communication. Berliner refers to the attainment of this level of performance as being 'within the groove' (1994:389). In some performances improvisers experience peak experiences or flow states (Csikszentmihalyi and Rich, 1997) which assist them in moving beyond their own cognitive limits. This quasi-narcotic flow state may also be a powerful motivator.

A number of factors seem to be important in facilitating the development of improvising skills, including appropriate early musical environments, using the jazz community as an educational system, developing a jazz repertoire, developing a jazz vocabulary, musical interactions, musical conversations, making jazz a way of life, thinking about jazz, making music in the moment (Berliner, 1994) and commitment (Sudnow, 1978).

Improvisation in the classroom environment

Improvisation in educational settings differs from that in professional settings in that it is not normally rule governed and can be accessed by all students. Very young children spontaneously improvise music, usually songs (Dowling, 1988), and can engage productively with free improvisation (see Azzara, 2002, for a review). Typically, pre-school children improvise exploring tone, timbre and rhythmic patterns with a steady beat and asymmetrical patterns, trying to make sensory-motor connections between the structure of their activities and sound qualities (Mialaret, 1994). Older children use a greater variety of rhythm patterns (Reinhardt, 1990). As children mature, they are able to improvise patterns relating to musical stimuli and from verbal stimuli; as they do so, their tonal orientation and the cohesion of their improvisations improves (Moorhead and Pond, 1978; Flohr, 1985). Working with older children, aged 6–12, Brophy (1999) demonstrated developmental trends for rhythmic and structural dimensions of improvisation performances but not for the melodic dimension. With increasing age, improvisations included more formally organised content, the creation of more rhythm patterns and increased motivic development. Changes were particularly evident from ages 6 to 9, but seemed to reach a plateau at 9–11, resuming again at age 12. Not surprisingly, the improvisations made by children reflect the musical culture within which they have been brought up and the musical experience of the teacher (Kalmar and Balasko, 1987). Children can learn to improvise within specific genres. Freundlich (1978) showed that by fifth grade, children could produce authentic musical ideas without notation within the framework of a 12-bar blues. Formal instruction also makes a positive contribution to improvisation skills, particularly those within a harmonic context (Ott, 1996; Laczo, 1981).

The benefits of learning to improvise

While learning to improvise is valuable in its own right, the skills acquired provide students with clearer comprehension of music performed with notation (Azzara, 1992; McPherson, 1993). Montano (1983) found that improvisation of particular rhythms improved rhythmic accuracy in sight-reading achievement in college elementary-group students compared to a control group. Similarly, Azzara (1992) found that elementary students who received instrumental music tuition that included improvisation performed significantly better than controls on etudes, while Wilson (1971) found that students with improvisation experience made greater improvements than controls in aural recognition of melodic and rhythmic elements, idioms and sight reading.

There also seem to be personal and social benefits to group improvisation. Students who reported anxiety regarding solo performances found that playing in group improvisations and making rhythmic embellishments of familiar tunes helped alleviate their concerns. They felt that they had more freedom of expression in a jazz band than in a concert band setting. The keen improvisers also forged friendships with each other (Leavell, 1997). Group improvisation is effective in reducing performance stress and helps musicians become more aware of issues relating to performance anxiety through experience in a safe environment, the transformation of stress through creativity, and bonding in the spirit of the community (Montello, 1990).

Developing creative individuals

In music there is a tradition of considering creativity in terms of the characteristics of creative individuals. However, these are very different from each other and do not fit easily into simple categories, although expert composers and improvisers do share some common experiences (Simonton, 1997) including the opportunity to engage with music, the length of time they have devoted to musical activity, extensive knowledge of music, and dedication and commitment to their work. Studies predicting the development of jazz improvisation skills in students have shown strong correlations between vocal jazz improvisation, jazz theory knowledge, imitative ability, prior ensemble experience, jazz experience and length of time of having instrumental lessons – all indicating the importance of time engaged with jazz-related activities as predicting levels of attainment (Coy, 1990; Greennagel, 1995). The way in which the individual's identity is related to music is also important for motivation, as we shall see in Chapter 9. Simonton (1997) points out that the very greatest composers began composing when they were very young, made their first contributions to the repertoire at a very young age, and continued to be prolific in their writing throughout their lives. Commitment and time spent in musical activities are key to developing high levels of expertise.

Attempts have been made to identify the particular character traits which creative individuals possess. Across domains no single personality characteristic has emerged as common to creative individuals, although some patterns have emerged. Commonly cited characteristics include willingness to confront hostility, willingness to take intellectual risks, perseverance, curiosity, openness to new experiences and growth, driving absorption, discipline and commitment to work, high intrinsic motivation, being task focused, and a high degree of self-organisation (see Sternberg, 1988, for reviews). These are related more to motivation, commitment and ways of working than to general personality traits. Some have argued that factors in the creative individual's upbringing contribute to the development of this pattern of motivation, independence and drive – for instance, a number of renowned composers are first-born children (Simonton, 1997). Other experiences which may contribute towards the development of the creative individual are the loss of one or both parents in childhood; unusual living situations; and being reared in a diversified, enriching and stimulating home environment (see Sternberg, 1988). An underlying theme that has been suggested is one of the creative individual as being in conflict. There is evidence, for instance, of conflict between self-criticism and self-confidence, social withdrawal and social integration (see Sternberg, 1988).

In studies specifically relating to the personality of musicians, Kemp (1996) has shown that musicians in general share certain personality traits in common: introversion, independence, sensitivity and imagination, and radicalism. Composers tend to exhibit these characteristics in more extreme forms than other musicians. Studies of composers' lives support these findings, suggesting that they are individualistic, have a capacity for solitude, and are attracted to complex and ambiguous symbolic enterprises. They are also highly motivated. Although there are some commonalities, the range of characteristics and experiences attributed to creative individuals is broad and varied, and there is insufficient clarity to enable the identification of creative individuals in childhood. It is the interaction between the individual and the environment that ultimately shapes creativity.

Creative environments

No individual can be considered in total isolation from their environment. Our behaviour is determined not only by our own characteristics but by the environment within which we find ourselves. To become a musician, an individual needs opportunities to engage in stimulating musical activities. In the early stages of development a relatively uncritical environment may be important, but once motivation is well established constructive criticism is necessary for development. Educators need to provide opportunities, resources, stimulation and the time for children to acquire the musical skills that are essential for any professional creative act. Expertise is a prerequisite of high-level creativity.

Setting creative tasks

While open-ended tasks are optimal for creativity (Amabile, 1996; Sternberg, 1988), having some constraints seems to support the creative process. The task for the teacher is to provide a framework that is appropriate for the intended outcome and for particular groups of students. Students may vary in their preferences. Burnard (1995) found that prescriptive directions were preferred by adolescent students with advanced practical and theoretical backgrounds, but a free task in which directions indicated merely that they were to write for the voice was preferred by students who had strong interpersonal interest, desire for individuality in expression, and independent working styles. However, Brinkman (1999) found a preference for open-style problems in high-school participants, but no interaction between problem solving (open or closed) and creative style.

Intrinsic motivation (valuing the task for its own sake and enjoying doing it) is central to creative work. Where extrinsic rewards are offered, musical creativity tends to decline (Bangs, 1992). If pupils see that their compositions are valued and that the process is important, this can immunise them against the negative effects of extrinsic rewards (Gerrard *et al.*, 1996). Closely related to intrinsic motivation is the concept of flow – an exhilarating feeling that can develop when a task is rewarding and enjoyable (Csikszentmihalyi, 1975, 1988). For 'flow' to occur, participants must not be anxious about failure, clear goals must be provided, instant feedback must be given as the task proceeds, and there must be a balance between challenge and current skill level so that the individual feels in control (Csikszentmihalyi, 1996). MacDonald *et al.* (in press) have shown that as group flow increases, university students working on a compositional task become more creative. Group working supports the provision of spontaneous feedback and provides opportunities for reflective discussion in relation to goals.

Feedback and self-assessment

Monitoring of progress and critical evaluation of the developing product are crucial to creative processes. These can be through self, peer or teacher evaluation. Constructive feedback from others provides pointers for enhancing future compositions and can act as inspiration. Providing informational feedback sensitively does not discourage creativity. School-aged children are able to assess the compositions of their peers (Hickey, 2001); however, their assessments do not match those of their teachers (Hickey, 2001; Seddon and O'Neill, 2001, in press). Clearly they are adopting different criteria. Some children's judgements may be coloured by their lack of confidence in their compositional skills, relating to their lack of formal instrumental tuition (Seddon and O'Neill, 2001, in press; Vispoel and Austin, 1993, 1998). Teacher and peer evaluation may support the development of self-criticism that is central to creativity. The most creative student composers set personal goals, negotiate the relationship between global and specific parameters, experiment and constructively criticise their work; and while demonstrating an optimistic outlook and internal locus of control, they are more critical of their work than their peers (Priest, in press).

The benefits of working in groups

When learners are developing improvisation skills, they benefit from becoming members of communities of practice. Observations of amateur bluegrass banjo players revealed a progressive sequence of intentional stages through which they progressed as auditors, competent listeners, inceptors, beginners and competent banjoists within the group. The players proceeded through a series of important encounters with the music, model players and the instrument (Adler, 1980). Professional jazz musicians report the importance of developing keen listening skills through interacting musically with others to develop the skills to anticipate and respond to one another's musical ideas (Monson, 1992). Interactions based on a set of cues; the role of instruments in the ensemble; and the personality, experience, age, and status of the ensemble members are also central to learning to perform the Solonese pathetan repertoire (Brinner, 1986). Encouraging students to engage with musical groups, in and out of school, in the area of expertise that they wish to develop is of huge benefit to the learner.

There are many advantages in group composition: collective involvement and decision making, support for the less confident, opportunities for playing and practising together, exchange of ideas, opportunities for the less skilled to learn from the more experienced, increased opportunities for experimentation, more choice of instrumentation, and shared opportunities for the rejecting and selecting of ideas. Other benefits can include increased confidence, the development of negotiation skills, the ability to defer to other people, respect for the work of others, the ability to give constructive criticism, and the ability to work freely within a disciplined environment. Allocation of pupils to groups can be made on the basis of the nature of the task (Hallam *et al.*, 2002a), although children working on a collaborative composition with someone nominated as their best friend produced compositions rated as superior to those of children working with someone who was only an acquaintance. The communication, both verbal and musical, between best friends was characterised as being of a type more conducive to good-quality collaboration (MacDonald *et al.*, 2002a; Miell and MacDonald, 2000).

Facilitating composition and improvisation practices

The starting point for the teacher in facilitating improvisation or composition must be to consider the specific purpose. Free improvisation or composition to enable self-expression requires little structure. However, constraints at the global level are necessary to develop musical understanding and creative skills, although if they become too detailed they can impede creativity. As students become more expert, the teacher can negotiate with them the level of guidance that they need. Providing constructive feedback is important for the development of the critical thinking so significant in relation to creative work. Teachers need to encourage students, while offering informative feedback that can guide future planning. Group work also promotes these skills.

Very young children can participate effectively in creative musical activities and should be encouraged to do so. The benefits extend beyond music to a range of other group-working skills. As children mature and wish to emulate the music they hear in their everyday lives, lack of musical skill may impede their progress. Use of technology can overcome this – computers enable the creation of sounds without the need for technical expertise. Intrinsic motivation is central to creativity, so tasks must be enjoyable, students must feel that they have ownership and control of them, and they must be set at a level which is challenging but not too difficult. Whether children work alone, in pairs or groups may impact on motivation and can be negotiated with them, as can the extent to which compositions are notated.

Creativity takes time, both at the level of the individual task and in developing the knowledge required to attain high levels of expertise. Differences between children described as exhibiting high or low levels of creativity are similar to those between experts and novices, suggesting that experience rather than ability is the cause. The only characteristics which highly creative individuals seem to share relate to their motivation, commitment and expertise in the field, developed over long periods of time. Attempting to identify creative individuals at an early age within a formal educational environment is not realistic.

If students are to work creatively within particular musical genres, they need to acquire considerable knowledge of them. This knowledge can be acquired through listening, imitation, analysis and participating in making music with others more expert than themselves. For instance, in jazz students can analyse selected performances of jazz musicians – particularly the melody, rhythm and harmony (Moorman, 1985). They can develop skills by ear – either through developing musical responses to particular patterns (Bash, 1984) or through memorising melodies, harmony, repertoire, counterpoint and other elements – and develop them, taking musical risks (Azzara, 1999). They can use jazz texts or interactive computer programs (e.g. Fern, 1996) and join jazz groups. Whatever specific strategies are adopted, developing high levels of expertise takes time and effort. Similar processes are required whatever the genre: extensive aural immersion, semi-structured experimentation and, particularly important, active participation in the improvising genre (Berliner, 1994). Over time this will enable audiation of the material to become possible (Gordon, 1997).

Music educators sometimes have concerns about teaching composing and improvising effectively (Byrne and Sheridan, 1998; MacDonald and Miell, 2000). Perhaps because of this, creative tasks tend to be underused in music education (Miell *et al.*, in press). However, there is clear value in encouraging creativity from the earliest years. The development of creative skills reinforces other musical skills, including listening and understanding and – particularly where children work in groups – can enhance children's personal and social development.

Further reading

Hickey, M. (2002) 'Creativity research in music, visual art, theatre and dance'. In R. Colwell and C. Richardson (eds) *The New Handbook of Research of Music Teaching and Learning*. Oxford: Oxford University Press (pp. 398–415).

Hickey, M. (2003) *Why and How to Teach Music Composition: A new horizon for music education*. Reston, VA: MENC, The National Association for Music Education.

Kenny, B.J. and Gellrich, M. (2002) 'Improvisation'. In R. Parncutt and G.E. McPherson (eds) *The Science and Psychology of Music Performance: Creative strategies for teaching and learning*. Oxford: Oxford University Press (pp. 117–134).

7 Learning to play an instrument and develop vocal skills

Opportunity and choice

Not all children have the opportunity to learn to play an instrument or have specialised vocal tuition. Where resources are scarce, selection procedures operate. While these are often based on ability to pay for lessons, they can include assessment of musical ability (see Chapter 4). Some teachers believe that physical characteristics should be taken into account in instrument selection, although research investigating the relationships between progress and the appropriateness of physical characteristics has found no clear relationships (Lamp and Keys, 1935), but some have suggested motivation may be enhanced if playing is a physically rewarding experience (Ben-Tovim and Boyd, 1990).

Factors affecting the choice of instrument are complex and include convenience, availability, gender, parents' views, influence of the school or music service, friends' influence, interests, and enthusiasms. Commitment to a specific instrument is important to continuing motivation (Ben-Tovim and Boyd, 1990). There are gender differences in instrument preference – girls preferring small high-pitched orchestral instruments; boys choosing large low-pitched ones (Delzell and Leppla, 1992). Parents also tend to have stereotypical views of which instruments are appropriate for each gender. One study showed that clarinets, flutes and violins were preferred for girls; drums, trombones and trumpets, for boys; with cello and the saxophone seen as having no significant gender association (Abeles and Porter, 1978). Another study indicated that harp, piccolo, glockenspiel, cello, piano, french horn and oboe were preferred for girls; while guitar, cymbals, saxophone, double bass and tuba were preferred for boys (Griswold and Chroback, 1981).

Predictors of success in playing and singing

A range of factors are important in determining the level of expertise attained in music, including practice (Ericsson *et al.*, 1990; Sosniak, 1990; Sloboda *et al.*, 1996; Hallam, 1998c; 2004b), parental support (Davidson, J.W. *et al.*, 1996), motivation (O'Neill, 1996, 1997; Hallam, 2002), personality (Kemp, 1996), prior knowledge (Hallam, 1997a), ability to understand instructions (Hallam, 1998c), and approaches to learning (Hallam, 1997a, 2001b, 2001a). These issues are dealt with in Chapter 8. Longer-term aims in relation to becoming a professional musician or being involved in music in an amateur capacity are best predicted by self-esteem, self-efficacy and enjoyment of performing. Professional aspirations are further predicted by membership of high-quality performing groups and effective practising strategies, while amateur aspirations are predicted by parental support (Hallam, 2004b). Where the quality of performance has been considered rather than the level of expertise attained, the amount of practice undertaken is not a good predictor (Hallam, 1998c; Williamon and Valentine, 2000). Other factors – in particular, teachers' ratings of musical ability, self-esteem and involvement in extra-curricular music activities – are important (Hallam, 2004b).

Research on drop-out has enhanced our understanding of those factors which contribute to success. Socio-economic status, self-concept in music, reading achievement, scholastic ability, measured musical ability, mathematical achievement and motivation are all predictors of continuing to play a musical instrument (Young, 1971; Mawbey, 1973; McCarthy, 1980; Klinedinst, 1991; Hallam, 1998c), as is the amount of practice undertaken (Sloboda *et al.*, 1996; Hallam, 1998c; 2004b). Frakes (1984) found significant differences between musical achievement, academic achievement and attitudes towards musical participation between drop-outs, non-participants and participants in musical activity. Drop-outs perceived themselves as less musically able, received less family encouragement, tended to feel musically inadequate, and turned to sport and other leisure activities instead of music. He concluded that positive self-perceptions of musical skills were linked to the desire to continue music education voluntarily. Supporting this, Hurley (1995) found that students who dropped out viewed continuing to play as demanding too great a time cost for the relatively small rewards it offered.

Skill acquisition

Learning to play an instrument or develop vocal skill requires the development of a wide range of skills. There are generally considered to be three stages in skill learning (Fitts and Posner, 1967). In the cognitive – verbal–motor – stage, learning is largely under cognitive, conscious control. The learner has to understand what is required to undertake the task and carries it out while consciously providing self-instruction. Teachers can support this by ensuring that students understand what is required of them and providing learners with opportunities to develop a mental template of what they are aiming to achieve. This may be aural (knowing the sound), visual (knowing what a movement looks like) or kinaesthetic (knowing what a movement feels like). The teacher can act as a verbal prompter, providing a simultaneous scaffold for the learner and gradually phasing out the prompts as the learner becomes proficient. In the associative stage, the learner begins to put together a sequence of responses that become more fluent over time. Errors are detected and eliminated. Feedback from the sounds produced and the teacher play an important role in this process. In the autonomous stage, the skill becomes automated, is carried out without conscious effort, and continues to develop each time it is used, becoming more fluent and quicker.

In learning to play a musical instrument many skills are acquired simultaneously, new skills constantly being added to the repertoire. As mastery of more advanced skills is acquired, skills learnt earlier are continuously practised so they achieve greater automaticity. As one set of skills is becoming increasingly automated, others will be at the associative and cognitive stages. The teacher needs to guard against expecting pupils to acquire too many skills at the same time as the load on processing will become too great. In developing skills, learners need to have goals that provide a focus for attention and facilitate motivation. They can be set in the short, medium or long term. To sustain motivation, the mastery of each small goal and subgoal needs to be acknowledged and praise given (Hallam, 1998a).

Informal learning

In recent years there has been interest in informal learning in music – for instance in rock, pop and hip-hop (Fornas *et al.*, 1995; Berkaak and Ruud, 1994; Green 2001; Soderman and Folkestad, 2004; Mito, 2004) and folk music (Cope, 2002). Informal learning is based on combinations of trial and error, repetition, watching and taking advice from other players, reading, listening, and emulating – processes already considered in relation to the development of improvisation skills. Informal learning experiences often go beyond musical skills, encompassing organisational and practical skills, linguistic training and the formation of personal identity.

Musical memory

While we generally think of musical memory in relation to memorising music for performance, memory plays a part in all aspects of learning. In the development of musical skills there is an interplay between declarative (knowing something) and procedural (knowing how) knowledge. Declarative memory can be thought of as a network of cognitive units in which knowledge is linked. In contrast, production memory consists of a set of rules for carrying out tasks. This knowledge, once learnt, is stored in long-term memory. Memories in long-term memory can be retained over many years, motor skills being particularly resistant to forgetting. Working memory operates in the short term and allows us to rehearse information and maintain it in consciousness, encoding incoming information so that it can be stored in long-term memory. It also allows information from long-term stores to be retrieved and utilised to deal with the particular task in hand. Working memory is limited in its capacity and can deal with only a small amount of information at any one time. Materials need to be rehearsed for transfer to long-term memory. Rehearsal falls into two main types: maintenance rehearsal (repetition) and elaborative rehearsal (relating new material to existing information). It is easier to learn new information and concepts if they are related to knowledge structures that are already established. Some learning takes place incidentally, without our making a conscious effort to learn. The repetition that is an integral part of musical practice lends itself to incidental learning and much musical learning takes place in this way.

We learn more effectively when we are aware of the various learning strategies available to us. This awareness is known as metacognition. Adults and older children have sophisticated meta-memories, and are very conscious of their strengths and weaknesses in relation to remembering things, the strategies that they can utilise to memorise information, and which strategies are likely to be effective for which tasks. They are also able to monitor successfully their progress towards the goal of memorisation and, if the strategies they have adopted are not being effective, can make changes. Recognising the need to work at remembering information is something that develops only gradually. Children below the age of 7 years may not realise what they have to do to memorise (Hallam and Stainthorp, 1995).

Memorising music for performance

Playing or singing from memory enhances musical communication and musicality in performance (Williamon, 1999), enabling the audience to see the communicative movements and gestures of the performer better (Davidson, J.W. 1993, 1994). However, it can be extremely anxiety provoking for musicians. To feel more secure, musicians need to develop strategies that assist them in memorising efficiently and retrieving securely. Early studies exploring the ways in which memory performance might be improved found that there was superior retention of musical fragments when they were learnt away from the keyboard (Kovacs, 1916). Rubin-Rabson (1937, 1939, 1940a, 1940b, 1941a, 1941b, 1941c, 1941d) developed this work, adopting experimental procedures to consider the most effective ways of memorising music. Her research suggests that memorisation is improved when analytic pre-study is undertaken prior to physical practice; when practice is distributed over time; when hands are learnt separately; when some mental rehearsal takes place part way through the rehearsal schedule; and when the work is learnt in small sections. Adoption of these strategies has a greater effect on learning outcomes for those who find the memorisation of music difficult. The findings from these early studies have been supported by more recent work. There is evidence that analysis of the music to be memorised supports learning (Ross, E., 1964; Williamson, 1964; Nuki, 1984; Kopiez, 1991; Hallam, 1997b), as do taking account of structural musical boundaries (Williamon and Valentine, 2002; Chaffin *et al.*, 2002; Ginsborg, 2002), starting memorisation early and monitoring progress (Ginsborg, 2002), and adopting multiple coding procedures (Nuki, 1984; Lim and Lippman, 1991; Hallam, 1997b). Playing the music is more effective than reading the score alone, even if the reading is accompanied by listening to the music (Lim and Lipmann, 1991), and for singers learning the words and music together rather than separately is more effective (Ginsborg, 2000, 2002). Overall, the most secure method of preparing for performance from memory is to use a wide range of strategies that result in multiple coding. Visual, aural and kinaesthetic strategies provide the basis for the development of schema which operate with little conscious awareness and which are fitted into a structural framework provided by conscious cognitive analysis of the music. Together these provide multiple retrieval structures. Studies observing instrumentalists memorising under naturally occurring conditions suggest that memorisation tends to take place towards the end of the learning process, when the performance of the music is already secure (Chaffin and Imreh, 1994, 1997; Chaffin *et al.*, 2002; Miklaszewski, 1995).

Changes in memorisation strategies occur as expertise develops (Hallam, 1997b; McPherson, 1995/6). Hallam (1997b) found that strategy use in professionals depended on the nature of the material to be memorised, individual preference and perceived levels of performance anxiety. Learning was based on combinations of aural, kinaesthetic, visual and analytic strategies. While novices adopted similar automated processing strategies, they made little use of conscious cognitive analysis. In a controlled study, where young instrumentalists were allowed a combination of playing and non-playing time to memorise short phrases, McPherson (1994) established a similar increase in the use of aural strategies and mental rehearsal as expertise developed. It seems that novice musicians tend to rely initially on automated processing, the use of conscious cognitive strategies developing as expertise increases.

Reading music

Many cultures have devised systems to encode and notate their music. The two main types of notation are phonetic notations (those using words or numbers) and diastematic notation (all forms of pictorial or graphic representation, such as staff notation). These notations do not provide all the information necessary for the music to be reproduced; aural, manipulative and translative abilities are required to decode them appropriately. When reading music, skilled readers do not fixate on each note; their fixations are directed across line and phrase boundaries. Their eye movements go further ahead in the score and return to the current point of performance. They seem to know what to look for (Goolsby, 1994). They scan the page more efficiently and require shorter and fewer fixations to compare or encode material for execution because they are able to grasp more information in one fixation (Waters *et al.*, 1997). They can continue to play about six or seven notes after removal of the printed page (eye–hand span), while poor readers manage only about three or four (Sloboda, 1984; Goolsby, 1994). Eye–hand span coincides with phrase boundaries, increasing or reducing as boundaries change, suggesting that musical content is organised into meaningful chunks (Sloboda, 1984). Readers of contrapuntal music tend to follow individual melodic lines more horizontally, while in homophonic music chords are scanned vertically, chord by chord (Weaver, 1943). Exact visual patterns vary between individuals. As readers become increasing familiar with the music, fixations become shorter and eye movements longer, presumably because part of the information is already known.

No methods have been demonstrated to assist children consistently in learning to read music. Hodges (1992), in a review of the literature, indicated that is was impossible to draw conclusions as the teaching strategies adopted were not underpinned by theory, findings were mixed, and there were few replications. Strategies adopted included the use of mnemonic devices, tonal pattern instruction, use of tape-recorded aural models, use of a computer, changes to notation systems, use of body movements, singing, practising with accompaniments and emphasising the vertical aspects of the score with pianists. Three successful strategies which have some theoretical basis include engaging students in creative activities such as composing, performing and listening (Bradley, 1974; Hutton, 1953), experiencing music reading activities before formal explanations (Hewson, 1966), and placing song texts higher or lower in conjunction with higher and lower melodic pitches (Franklin, 1977).

Sight reading

Sight reading is the unrehearsed performance of music. It places high demands on the performer's capacity to process complex visual input under real-time constraints, with no opportunity for error correction. Success in sight reading depends on aural imagery, sight-reading experience, cognitive and thinking styles, external locus of control (Kornicke, 1995), acquired expertise, speed of information processing, and psychomotor speed (Kopiez *et al.*, in press), and for pianists accumulated time spent in accompanying related activities and size of accompanying repertoire (Lehmann and Ericsson, 1996). There also seems to be a strong association between rhythmic ability and sight-reading performance (Boyle, 1970; Elliott, C.A., 1982). Expert sight readers rely on the context more in planning ahead (Waters *et al.*, 1997), are relatively more distracted by unexpected information (Waters *et al.*, 1997), and perform better on tasks where they are required to fill in blank spaces in a score with an appropriate note (Lehmann and Ericsson, 1996). Sight readers can be misled into making 'proof readers errors' (playing notes that are not really there) because they identify familiar patterns rather than reading each individual note (Sloboda, 1976). McPherson (1994) suggests that better sight readers are able to assimilate more information about the score before beginning to play than those who are less skilled. The most effective way to improve sight reading seems to be to practise it, preferably in conditions where momentum has to be maintained – for example, accompanying someone, or playing in a group (Banton, 1995; Kornicke, 1992; Lehmann and Ericsson, 1996).

Stages of becoming a musician

Musicians pass through different stages as expertise develops. Bloom (1985) and Sosniak (1985, 1990) suggest three phases: introduction to activity in the domain, the start of instruction and deliberate practice, and commitment to pursue activities on a full-time basis. Some musicians may not make the transfer between technical expertise and what is required for professional performance in 'musical' terms (Bamberger, 1986). Manturzewska (1990) suggests six stages in the life-span development of musicians, each having different developmental tasks and serving a different function. During stage 1 there is development of sensory-emotional sensitivity and spontaneous musical expression and activity. Stage 2 is a period of intentional, guided musical development where basic technical and performance capacities and musical knowledge are gained. Stage 3 concerns the formation and development of artistic personality. During stage 4 musicians establish themselves in the music profession and enter the period of greatest performing activity. Stage 5 is described as the teaching phase, with stage 6 the retreat from professional activity. Harnischmacher (1995) provides a more detailed account of development in school-aged students. In the activity stage (8–10 years), musical activity was play related. During the adoption stage (11–12 years), the work ethic developed and the young musicians thought about the causality and goal orientation of their practice. During the stage of integration (13–14 years), practice became part of the daily routine, while the playful element served for relaxation. At the stage of identification (15–18 years), there was reflection on the implicit self-relation of practice, as well as improving effectiveness and an awareness of standards. Changes in the structure of practice appeared to be accompanied by increased metacognitive awareness, a phenomenon also noted in relation to the development of composition skills (Swanwick and Tillman, 1986). These studies all focus on development within a Western classical music culture and may merely reflect the education systems of those cultures. We know little about musical learning within other cultures.

Performance

Performance is socially defined and its nature changes over time. Currently, most Western professional musicians tend to view performance in terms of public concerts given to an audience. However, with the increasing use of technology, many performances are no longer 'live' and performance is often in a studio where there is no immediate audience. Performance can be viewed in terms of a hierarchy of formal to less formal situations which create different levels of stress in the performer, the least stressful being private performance where one plays to oneself.

The key element of public performance is communication, with the audience and fellow musicians. This is acknowledged by professionals, music students and school-age pupils (Prince, 1994; Founta, 2002; Hallam and Prince, 2003). Communication depends on shared meanings, understandings and intentions on the part of performers and audience (Mead, 1934). These meanings may be embodied or referential (Meyer, 1956). An important element in the level of communication established between a performer and an audience is the way the music is interpreted. Human performance varies because it goes beyond the information in the printed score. When musicians play, each performance differs in subtle ways from any other performance. In fact, even within a single bar, there can be subtle variations of timing, loudness, tone quality and intonation. It is these variations which contribute towards an expressive performance (Shaffer, 1992). Musicians, in developing interpretation, tend initially to look or play through the music in its entirety to gain an overview of the whole work. One of two main approaches is then adopted: intuitive (interpretation develops during the course of learning to play the piece and is based on intuitive feelings and instincts, with no element of conscious planning) or holist (interpretation is planned in advance, based on extensive listening to music, comparison of alternative interpretations and the analysis of the structure of the music). Some musicians adopt both approaches, although most exhibit a preference for one approach (Hallam, 1995a). The musician's interpretation of the music to be performed constitutes the core message that they communicate to the audience. This has the greatest impact, more than a technically accurate but 'dead' performance. It is important that the performer does not lose sight of this in the preparation stage.

The communication of expression is more effective when listeners can detect variations in performance and interpret them. The most effective communicators seem to be more consistent in their use of expression and to exaggerate it more (Sloboda, 1983). They also tend to be the most experienced. The least effective are inconsistent and violate 'rules' which the majority of performers obey. The use in the music of expressive variation that is exaggerated helps listeners to understand the structure of a piece of music. This process is assisted through the visual aspects of performance. Davidson, J.W. (1993, 1995, 2001, 2002b) has shown that body movements made by performers while playing contribute to the expressivity of the performance as judged by observers. The movements seem to draw the observers' attention to particular aspects of the music. Playing from memory can also assist in the communicative process, partly because it enhances visual presentation (Williamon, 1999).

Performance anxiety

Performance anxiety relates to a configuration of symptoms, including excessive physiological arousal (increased heart rate, dry mouth, sweating, shortness of breath, upset stomach, nausea, diarrhoea, trembling, dizziness, flushing); psychological and emotional symptoms such as exaggerated feelings of apprehension, fear of failure, irritability and generalised panic; cognitive factors such as loss of confidence, lack of concentration due to negative thoughts including worry and fear of making mistakes, memory lapses and an inability to play sensitively; and behavioural changes including stiffness and muscular tension (Ely, 1991; Salmon, 1991; Wesner *et al.*, 1990). The physiological changes that occur before performance indicate that the sympathetic branch of the autonomic nervous system has been activated. This is not necessarily connected with anxiety. Similar autonomic changes are manifest when individuals undertake challenging tasks, are in situations involving anger, and anticipate pleasurable experiences. Studies that have used multi-methods to assess performance anxiety have shown that the relationships between physiological measures of anxiety, reported anxiety and performance are often not consistent (Kendrick *et al.*, 1982; Craske and Craig, 1984; Deffenbacher and Hazaleus, 1985; Fredrikson *et al.*, 1986; Abel and Larkin, 1990; Ryan, 2004). Worry concerning performance and the social implications of failure can be dissociated from perceived somatic arousal (Deffenbacher, 1980). Comparisons of anxious and non-anxious musicians show that both groups exhibit increased physiological activity when performing (Craske and Craig, 1984), while research on the effects of beta blockers has shown that, although physiological arousal may be reduced and there is an improvement in the quality of performance, these effects may not be translated into reductions in the subjective experience of anxiety (Neftel *et al.*, 1982; James and Savage, 1984; Fredrikson *et al.*, 1986). Other factors, apart from those related to physiology, would appear to be important.

Anxiety about performance is common among musicians (Goode and Knight, 1991; Steptoe and Fidler, 1987; Fishbein and Middlestadt, 1988; Van Kemanade *et al.*, 1995; Bartel and Thompson, 1997), but some degree of tension appears to be an integral part of good performance (Caldwell, 1990). It is only when stress becomes excessive that it can become debilitating, disrupt musical skills (Brotons, 1994), and discourage performers from further study of music (James, 1988; Wolfe, 1989). Many artists argue that they need to be aroused psychologically in order to perform well and that stress is an integral component of good performance. Hamann (1982) and Hamann and Sobaje (1983) found that increased anxiety tended to facilitate performance skills, especially for musicians with high mastery who had been learning for a greater length of time.

There are several theories of performance anxiety. The Yerkes-Dodson law proposes an inverted U-shaped relationship between emotional arousal and performance, stating that the arousal level of the individual increases performance up to an optimal point beyond which overarousal leads to deterioration. The law also states that the deterioration occurs more quickly when the task to be performed is complex or underlearnt. Catastrophe theory suggests that when a performance deteriorates in a stressful situation, it is unlikely to be restored even to a mediocre level (Hardy and Parfitt, 1991). Psychoanalytic theory views performance anxiety as a cluster of attitudes, traits and unconscious conflicts that are developed during childhood and that are re-enacted in particular circumstances – such as anticipating or giving a concert (Plaut, 1990). Brandfonbrener (1990) suggests that performance anxiety is simply a manifestation of psychological problems and cannot be considered in isolation. Anxiety symptoms have to be evaluated in relation to the individual's psychological make-up. Cognitive behavioural theories attribute performance anxiety to negative thoughts and irrational beliefs about the need for audience approval to maintain positive self-esteem, and the need for perfection for a performance to be acceptable. These persistent thoughts lead to lack of confidence and negate hours of preparation (Nagel, 1990).

Lehrer (1987) identified five elements of stage fright: worry about memory or distraction, worry about tension, fear of social disapproval, concern about performing abilities, and engaging in performance-oriented coping thoughts. Only worry about tension was associated with performance anxiety. In contrast, Tobacyk and Downs (1986) found that students with the greatest increase in anxiety prior to performance were more threatened by the possibility of failure and endorsed more irrational beliefs. They believed that they must be perfectly competent at musical performance in order to be a worthwhile person. This may be compounded by a tendency for musicians to feel that they are constantly evaluated and compared against a perfect standard (Gabbard, 1980). Steptoe and Fidler (1987) found that musicians reporting severe anxiety about performance sustained maladaptive cognitions which could be classed as catastrophising. They exaggerated the consequences arising from a minor error, believing that it would ruin the whole performance, or felt that they would not be able to perform without breaking down. Worry about anxiety, or catastrophising, can have severe negative consequences (Powell and Enright, 1990).

Multi-dimensional models

Recently, LeBlanc (1994) and Hallam (1998a, 2003) have proposed models of performance which are multi-dimensional and take account of the ways in which the various factors which affect performance anxiety develop in the period leading up to a performance. Factors include the characteristics of the performer, the characteristics of the planned performing environment, the nature of the music to be performed, the process of preparation, the performer's state immediately prior to the performance, the actual performance, and post-performance feedback. At any point in the preparation period circumstances may change, which can then have an impact on the performer and their actual performance. The model is set out in Figure 7.1. There is evidence which supports aspects of the model (for a detailed explanation see Hallam, 2003).

Approaches to dealing with performance anxiety

There has been a tendency in recent years for performance anxiety to be seen as a medical or psychological condition. Treatment has tended to be within a medical framework and has included the use of drugs, hypnotherapy, a focus on general health issues, and use of the Alexander Technique (for reviews see Hallam, 2003; Williamon, 2004). Most psychological approaches to reducing performance anxiety have focused on changing behaviour or cognition. Some behavioural techniques such as systematic desensitisation, cognitive attentional interventions and biofeedback have proved to be successful in reducing physiological and cognitive symptoms of performance anxiety, while improving performance (Appel, 1976;

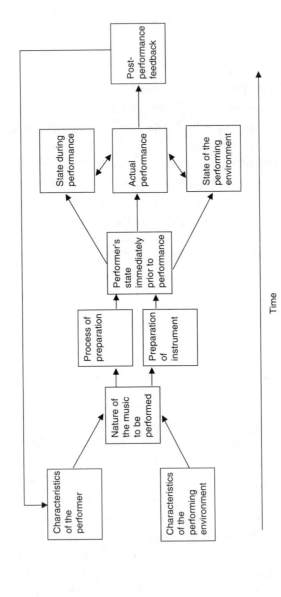

Figure 7.1 *Model of performance*

Fogle, 1982; Mansberger, 1988). Cognitive behavioural therapy involves changing the performer's thinking and has proved successful – sometimes in conjunction with other treatments – in reducing anxiety and improving performance (Clark and Agras, 1991; Sweeney and Horan, 1982). For instance, Kendrick *et al.* (1982) worked with a group of 53 pianists, identifying negative and task-irrelevant thoughts during playing and substituting optimistic task-oriented self-talk. The treatment also included verbal persuasion, modelling, stress on performance accomplishments, the use of group influences and homework assignments. Another technique, know as stress inoculation, is based on the assumption that it is important to implant realistic expectations about what will be experienced during performance as well as promoting optimistic self-comments. Performers are taught to accept the symptoms of anxiety that are bound to occur and to utilise them to provide energy for the performance (Meichenbaum, 1985; Salmon, 1991). These strategies are frequently adopted by musicians who have not felt the need to seek professional advice about reducing anxiety (Roland, 1994; Hallam, 1992).

Preparing for performance
Those who perform well are able to mobilise arousal specifically for performance (Bochkaryov, 1975; Hamann, 1982). Hamann and Sobaje (1983) have suggested that the critical anxiety management factor is mastery of the task. Steptoe (1989) found that most coping strategies cited by musicians did not relate to practice itself. They included distraction, deep breathing, muscle relaxation, sedatives and the use of alcohol. Bartel and Thompson (1994) reported a similar range of life-style coping strategies, but identified one group of strategies relating specifically to being technically and musically well prepared. This included doing warm-ups, rehearsal to mastery, slow practice, listening to recordings, practising more difficult materials than those required, sight reading new works, and ensuring that instruments were in excellent condition. Some

musicians practised performance by playing for peers. Imagining how the audience will perceive the performance in a range of different acoustical environments may also be useful (Edlund, 2000). Strategies for coping when performance is under way include concentrating on hearing the music before playing, the physical movement of playing, calming the mind, blocking out the audience, and ignoring the conductor. Thorough musical preparation is one of the most effective strategies for coping with stage fright, although it is often adopted in conjunction with other strategies. Hallam (1992) found considerable individual diversity in perceived levels of stress. Only a small minority of musicians experienced sufficient stress to consider adopting life-style coping strategies; some felt that they needed an audience to perform well. Others, while experiencing distressing physical symptoms from stage fright, enjoyed performing and experienced no impairment of performance. Biographical evidence from famous actors includes similar reports. It would seem that nervousness in itself does not mar performance, nor necessarily deter musicians from undertaking it. A novice sample exhibited a similar range of attitudes towards performance, but their coping strategies were less well developed. Their focus was on reducing feelings of fear rather than on alleviating detrimental effects on performance. The latter had clearly not developed the same significance as for the professional group.

In supporting students in utilising their arousal levels to improve rather than impair performance, teachers need to provide guidance at every stage of the process, ensuring that the music to be played is appropriate, that sufficient time has been allowed for preparation, that 'mock' performances have been undertaken to identify potential difficulties and strategies developed to overcome them, that students do not have an exaggerated notion of the importance of the performance, and that time is allowed for acclimatisation to the performing environment and to prepare calmly immediately before the performance. After performance, opportunities need to be available to reflect, evaluate and make future plans.

The importance of the family

Sustained parental support is an important factor in the attainment of high levels of musical expertise. As we saw in Chapter 3, the mother's interest in music, particularly her singing activities, may influence the development of early musical expertise, even before birth. A comparison of young musicians at different levels of expertise revealed that the highest achieving group sang a recognisable tune on average six months earlier, around 16 months of age, than the children in the four comparison groups. Rhythmically moving to music, showing high attentiveness to musical sounds and asking to join in musical activities did not differ between groups (Sloboda and Davidson, 1996). The age at which children first sang was related to the number of musical behaviours initiated by the parents (Howe *et al.*, 1995). Parental enrichment of the musical environment from birth seemed to stimulate the onset of early singing, which in turn contributed towards later success. Having musical parents or a musical home environment influences participation in music (LeBlanc Corporation, 1961) and musical development (Shelton, 1966; Wermouth, 1971; Jenkins, 1976). The success of Suzuki-type approaches (Sperti, 1970; Doan, 1973; Blaine, 1976) has been related to the level of parental involvement (Breamer, 1985). The parents of high achievers tend to be more involved in initial practice, attend lessons with their children, and receive feedback from the teacher (Davidson, J.W. *et al.*, 1996). Practical help in taking pupils to concerts and providing financial support is critical (Zdzinski, 1991). Sometimes family members are actively involved in music making themselves (Rexroad, 1985; Sosniak, 1985; Sloboda and Howe, 1991), although Davidson, J.W. *et al.* (1995/6) demonstrated that parental commitment to assisting, encouraging and supporting the child in the early stages of learning was a more important predictor of successful musical outcomes than any specialist knowledge on the part of the parent. Families can play a role in the identification of talent (Rexroad, 1985) and parents of high achievers tend to have very high expectations and are demanding in those expectations (Bastian, 1989; Lassiter, 1981). The child seems to internalise these, and achievement becomes a need in itself. However, this may not be a panacea for raising achievement as we do not know what happens to those children whose parents have high expectations which are unmet. Those children may develop low self-esteem and ultimately give up playing.

Creech (2001), studying the parents of violinists, suggested that parents who possess a strong sense of self-efficacy construct a role for themselves whereby they assist in selecting the choice of instrument, facilitate the child in receiving tuition, and engage in behaviour and activities which are linked to musical achievement (providing external motivation for the child, supervising practice, instilling focus and discipline in practice, attending lessons, communicating with the teacher, and responding to the child's wish for parental help and support). However, many parents felt less efficacious as the child progressed and matured past the age of 11, a phenomenon common in relation to school homework (Hallam, 2004a). Family dynamics, including the role of siblings, are important in relation to motivation (Davidson, J.W. and Borthwick, 2002) (see Chapter 9). Outstanding individuals in a range of fields have often been first-born or only children – although older siblings can act as inspiration for younger siblings, leading to imitation, with older siblings offering encouragement and support (Davidson, J.W. *et al.*, 1997).

One of the most dramatic accounts of the role of the family comes from a description of the arts in China in the 1980s (Lowry and Wolf, 1988). At that time, the role of the musician was determined by the state, and a very limited number of professional musicians were trained and assigned to fill existing places as players or teachers. Families identified talent in their children and provided initial opportunities either because they were musicians or worked in closely related careers. In learning an instrument, the focus was on technique and skill building, with considerable rote learning. Training involved discipline, fixed amounts of practice at set times, set tasks and punishments, although encouragement and rewards were also in evidence. Children tended to start between 4 and 6 years of age. Practice was highly structured, lasted for one to two hours each day, and was enforced by parents. The family provided all the necessary support and opportunities to enable their offspring to go on to train as a professional musician.

Not all studies have found parental support to be important in musical attainment, performance (Mitchell, 1985; Dregalla, 1983; Zdzinski, 1991) or musical perception (Brand, 1982, 1985, 1986). Age may be a factor here, with older students requiring less support, although parents of accomplished teenagers across all talent areas typically devote great amounts of time and energy to meeting the needs of their children, set high standards, encourage productive use of time, provide challenging opportunities, make sure lessons and materials are available, and set aside areas of the home where children can work privately (Csikszentmihalyi *et al.*, 1993). Despite this, there are famous instances where children have achieved professional status with little practical support from the family – for instance, Louis Armstrong (Collier, 1983) and the orphans at La Pieta in the time of Vivaldi (Howe, 1990) – but such cases are rare. In these examples other aspects of the wider environment compensated for the lack of family support. Some highly effective individuals in a range of domains have histories marked by severe frustration, deprivation and traumatic experiences. Personal determination enabled them to overcome these difficulties (MacKinnon, 1965).

Monitoring and supervision of practice

Few children appear to be totally self-motivated to practise. The parents of those achieving at a high level tend to support practice, by encouragement, monitoring the length of time spent practising, or supervision – although this sometimes leads to family friction (Sosniak, 1985; Bastian, 1989; Sloboda and Howe, 1991; Heaney, 1994; Davidson, J.W. *et al.*, 1996). Brokaw (1983) and Sperti (1970) concluded that the amount of parental supervision of home practice was a major contributor to student achievement. Brokaw found correlations with achievement of 0.44 to 0.54 for time spent practising but 0.58 and 0.57 with parental supervision. In a study of child prodigies using historical data, Lehmann (1997b) showed that all had been supervised in their practice during childhood. Vacher (1992), finding that much of pupils' practice time was spent ineffectively, concluded that practising skills should be taught and practice should be supervised, particularly in the early stages of learning. Marcoux and Toussaint (1995) have reported some success in developing ways of improving the skills of parents in supporting and encouraging their children in musical activities. In adolescence, parental supervision of practice, or even reminders to practise, are usually unwelcome. The child's motivation needs to be internalised before the teenage years if they are to become committed to music. If the parent continues to supervise practice in the teenage years, this it is likely to lead to resentment and ultimately may be counterproductive in that the child may give up playing (Sloboda and Davidson, 1996). Close supervision of practice may also have detrimental effects on intrinsic motivation (Lepper and Greene, 1975), and the benefits can be short term (Freeman, 1991).

Parent–teacher–pupil communication and responsiveness

The quality of interactions between parent, teacher and pupil may significantly influence personal and professional satisfaction, enjoyment of music, and musical achievement for all three participants. Duke (1999/2000) found close agreement amongst parents, pupils and teachers with respect to objectives and outcomes of piano study in research on effective piano teachers, while Jorgensen, H. (1998) – in her examination of features of instrumental teacher and student decision making – found that the level of agreement, with respect to expectations and preferences, was related to the intensity of conflict or co-operation. Creech and Hallam (2003) propose a model based on the work of Tubbs (1984), which synthesises earlier models and identifies three categories of variables, which affect interactions and are also modified as a result of them. The categories are background factors (personality, attitudes and values), internal influences (style of leadership, language behaviour, interaction roles, decision style), and consequences (solutions to problems, information sharing, interpersonal relations/growth amongst group members). Figure 7.2 sets out how these may interact within a musical context.

The aims of engaging with extra-curricular musical activities

While in the short term there may be many possible aims for participating in extra-curricular musical activities, in the long term the main distinction is between those who may wish to pursue a career in music and those who may want to be engaged as amateur musicians or active listeners. For most students, the last two categories are pertinent. Perhaps because of this, an increasingly important aim for extra-curricular tuition is that it should be fun and enjoyable (Schenck, 1989; Hallam and Prince, 2000). Teachers also perceive a wider range of benefits, including enhanced social skills; love of music; team working; a sense of achievement; increased confidence and self-discipline; opportunities for relaxation; enhanced concentration, physical co-ordination, cognitive, listening, creative and organisational skills; and giving enjoyment to others (Hallam and Prince, 2000). To enable lifelong engagement with music, pupils need to develop independent learning skills (Hallam, 1998a), have available a range of learning strategies, understand their own strengths and weaknesses, be able to assess what is required in undertaking a musical task, be persistent, be able to monitor progress, and be critical of learning outcomes. The implications of this for teaching are profound.

Implications for teaching

Most children learning to play an instrument or having vocal tuition will not go on to become professional musicians or work in careers related to music. Extra-curricular musical activities prepare most

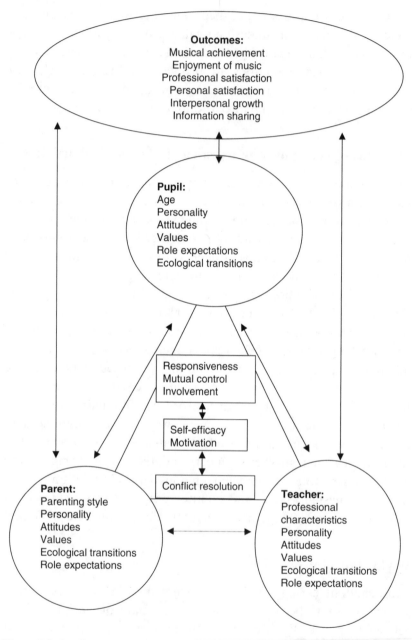

Figure 7.2 *Pupil–parent–teacher interactions (Creech and Hallam, 2003)*

young people with the basis for lifelong engagement with music in an amateur or listening capacity, and promote the development of generic skills that are useful in a range of occupations. The aims of instrumental/vocal teaching should therefore be to make music fun while still providing challenge and intellectual stimulation. Even where pupils wish to pursue a career in music, teachers should provide a broad, rounded curriculum which prepares students for professional music making in a changing and uncertain future. All students need to be facilitated to become independent learners so that they can adapt easily and rapidly to new musical environments and draw on the skills they have learnt to satisfy current needs.

Learning to play an instrument requires considerable time and effort, and motivation is crucial (see Chapter 9). Playing an instrument of choice may therefore be more important than perceived physical appropriateness. Playing a seemingly unpopular instrument can offer more opportunities for high-level group participation; and for some students this may be an attractive option, providing the rationale is explained to them.

The family is an important support for young children learning to play an instrument, and teachers should attempt to engage carers in the learning process in whatever ways are possible – including supportive, not critical, help with practice. Young children, in the earlier stages of learning to play an instrument, thrive on praise and encouragement. Teachers, family and friends are valuable sources of these and the provision of non-threatening performance opportunities can be valuable for enhancing motivation. For older students, family involvement, beyond providing resources and encouragement, may be counter-productive. As students' expertise develops, they appreciate constructive criticism as a way of improving their skills and their relationship with teachers is more task focused. As we shall see in Chapter 9, peer influence and a developing identity as a musician are crucial to motivation in adolescence.

The acquisition of the complex skills required to play an instrument takes time and practice (see Chapter 8). In the early stages of skill learning, clear explanations and feedback on progress are required. Aural templates of the desired end-product guide learning and enable errors to be identified more easily. Providing recordings of what is to be learnt can facilitate the development of appropriate aural schemata. As skill learning proceeds into the later stages, increasing automaticity is gained through use. This does not have to be through solitary practice. Skills can be developed in group activities which provide additional motivation through their social nature. Where groups play from notation, the development of reading and sight-reading skills is rehearsed and enhanced.

Taking part in public performance can be an exhilarating and rewarding experience, increasing motivation. However, for some students it provokes extreme anxiety and can act as a demotivator. Playing or singing in a group with others, particularly where there is no requirement to take a solo part, can reduce anxiety while still providing the positive outcomes related to public performance. However, is not essential that those learning to play an instrument or having vocal tuition perform in public. Playing for or singing to oneself can be rewarding, providing enjoyment and emotional release. Similarly, while playing or singing from memory may enhance communication with the audience, it is not essential. Where it is considered desirable, learning the piece thoroughly, using multiple coding strategies with extensive opportunities for 'mock' performance, should provide security. Total mastery of the music, a focus on communicating with the audience, accepting nervousness as necessary to give a 'spark' to performance and utilising it to provide that energy, can all assist in ensuring that nervousness does not mar performance but serves to enhance it.

Most instrumental and vocal teaching practices continue to be based on those developed in the latter part of the nineteenth century, when formal tuition was one-to-one and available only for the privileged few. More children now have the opportunity to learn to play an instrument and most will not go on to be engaged with music professionally. There is a need for educators to redefine what they consider to be successful learning outcomes. These are likely to vary depending on the particular instrument learnt, the genre, the aspirations of the students and the opportunities available for them to engage with music in the longer term.

Further reading

Creech, A. and Hallam, S. (2003) 'Parent–teacher–pupil interactions in instrumental music tuition: a literature review'. *British Journal of Music Education*, 20(1) (pp. 29–44).

Hallam, S. (1998a) *Instrumental Teaching: A practical guide to better teaching and learning*. Oxford: Heinemann.

Parncutt, R. and McPherson, G.E. (2002) *The Science and Psychology of Music Performance: Creative strategies for teaching and learning*. Oxford: Oxford University Press.

Snyder, B. (2000) *Music and Memory: An introduction*. Cambridge, MA: The MIT Press.

Thurman, L. and Welch, G.F. (2000) *Bodymind and Voice: Foundations of voice education*. (2nd edition) Iowa City: National Center for Voice and Speech.

Williamon, A. (ed.) (2004) *Musical Excellence: Strategies and techniques to enhance performance*. Oxford: Oxford University Press.

8 Learning through practice

Practice is central to the development of all aspects of musical expertise. Musical practice is multi-faceted. The musician not only needs to consider the development of technical skills but also must develop musical interpretation. They may have to play or sing from memory, rehearse and perform in co-operation with other musicians, improvise, and contend with stage fright. These elements require aural, technical, cognitive, communication, performance and learning skills. Such complex skills cannot be acquired, improved and maintained by simple repetitious practice.

Ericsson *et al.* (1993) introduced the concept of 'deliberate practice' (goal oriented, structured and effortful), and outlined several constraints (motivation, resources, attention) which may determine the amount and quality of practice. Sloboda *et al.* (1996) distinguished between formal and informal practice, the former closely related to 'deliberate practice', the latter playing previously learnt material or improvising. An alternative perspective stresses the importance of conscious strategy use in learning (Jorgensen, H., 1995; Ribke, 1987). Jorgensen, H. (1995) views practice as 'self-teaching', and suggests that during practice musicians need to take account of their aims, the content, available learning media, allocation of time, and methods. Four strategy types are proposed: planning; the conduct of practice; the evaluation of practice; and meta-strategies, the last named taking an executive role. A similar conception is that of practice as self-regulated learning (McPherson and Zimmerman, 2002).

Effective practice has been defined by Hallam (1997c) as 'that which achieves the desired end-product, in as short a time as possible, without interfering negatively with longer-term goals'. In other words, effective practice is 'what works' in the short term without interfering with progression in the long term – for instance, by creating undue muscular tension. This definition assumes that effective practice might take many forms and implies that the musician requires considerable metacognitive skills to facilitate the completion of task requirements or, in the case of the novice, appropriate support. Models have been developed to provide a framework which encompasses the multi-faceted nature of practice in musical creativity and performance (see Hallam, 1997c; Chaffin and Lemieux, 2004).

The impact of practice on attainment

Time spent practising has been proposed as underpinning the development of expert performance. Typically, 16 years of practice are required to achieve levels that will lead to international standing in playing an instrument. The individual usually begins to play at a very early age, with 25 hours of practice being undertaken weekly, increasing by adolescence to as much as 50 hours (Sosniak, 1985). Ericsson *et al.* (1993) suggest a monotonic relationship between 'deliberate practice' and an individual's acquired performance. Evidence from higher education music students and school-aged musicians supports this, showing that those with the highest levels of expertise accumulated considerably more hours of practice than their less successful peers, although there are substantial individual differences (Ericsson *et al.*, 1993; Jorgensen, H., 2002; Sloboda *et al.*, 1996). Other support comes from Donner (1987), Vacher (1992) and a study in Germany of 1,000 music students participating in a national music competition, which found that prize winners reported higher practice times prior to the competition and in normal practice (Deutscher Musikrat, 1993). Neiman (1989), teaching basic conducting techniques to adolescents, also found that success depended more on motivation and daily practice than on age, sex or handedness.

While there is general agreement that practice is important, several studies have questioned the simplicity of the monotonic

relationship. Sloboda and Howe (1991) found that students identified as having greater ability by their teachers had undertaken less
practice on their main instrument, their practice time having been
spread more equally across three instruments. Wagner, M.J.
(1975) found that increased practice did not lead to any greater
improvement in performance over an eight-week period, and
Zurcher (1972) found no relationship between total practice time
and performance achievement. Kafer (1982) failed to reveal any
significant differences between students having 30-minute practice
sessions before and after private lessons and those students with no
special sessions.

Reported correlations between achievement and time spent
practising vary considerably. Doan (1973) found a correlation of
0.25 between hours of practice per week and performance test scores
for violin students from public schools. Brokaw (1983) reported that
the amount of time spent by students in home practice was correlated with achievement, 0.44 for technical–physical factors and 0.54
for musical factors. Sloboda *et al.* (1996) reported correlations of
0.30 and 0.37 between teachers' ratings of performance level and
accumulated amounts of formal practice at ages 8 and 13 respec-
tively. Hallam (1998c) found a correlation of 0.67 between an
overall achievement score, taking account of grade level and mark,
and accumulated practice. However, when length of time learning
was correlated with achievement, as opposed to time spent practising, the correlation rose to 0.84. It seems that the overall length of
time over which learning has taken place may be as important as the
actual amount of practice in determining level of expertise (Hallam,
1998c, 2004b). Starting to play at an early age, when physically the
body is more flexible, may be important. Wagner, C. (1988) has
demonstrated that pianists' hands can change physically if they
begin playing when very young. Cumulative practice does not seem
to predict the quality of performance at any point in time
(Hallam, 1998c; Williamon and Valentine, 2000; Hallam, 2004b).
Other factors – in particular teachers' ratings of musical ability,

self-esteem and involvement in extra-curricular music activities – are better predictors of examination marks than time spent practising (Hallam, 2004b).

Evidence from students who have dropped out (see Chapter 7) suggests that there are complex relationships between prior knowledge, motivation, effort and perceived efficacy. When a child begins to learn an instrument, prior musical knowledge affects ease of learning and the time needed to achieve mastery of a task. While undertaking additional practice may compensate for lack of prior knowledge, this has a time cost and requires perseverance. If a task proves challenging, the effort required to complete it may be perceived as too great and the individual may give up. Difficulties may be attributed to a lack of musical ability, leading to a loss of self-esteem, loss of motivation, less practice and a downward spiral followed by the termination of lessons (Asmus, 1994; Chandler *et al.*, 1987).

Time spent practising

The amount of practice required for different instruments varies (Jorgensen, H., 1997). At conservatoire level, keyboard players have the highest rate, followed by string and wind players (Jorgensen, H., 1997). These differences are in part determined by the technical demands of the instrument and the extent of the repertoire for it. Time spent in practice increases as expertise develops (Doan, 1973; Hallam, 1992; Harnischmacher, 1993; Sloboda *et al.*, 1996), and this increase is greater for those who go on to become experts than for amateurs (Freyhof *et al.*, 1993; Krampe, 1994). However, after entrance to the profession, duration of regular practice time decreases (Harnischmacher, 1993; Krampe, 1994). Skill maintenance requires less practice time than skill acquisition. The amount of practice sustainable is limited. Three to four hours daily seems to be the maximum sustainable over long periods without burnout occurring (Ericsson *et al.*, 1993; Bastian, 1989; Hallam, 1995b; Jorgensen, H., 1996). Measures of time spent practising do not take account of the quality of the practice undertaken. There are differences in students' practising strategies and metacognitive skills, the former being inextricably intertwined with the acquisition of expertise (Hallam, 2001a, 2001b).

Expert strategy use

Research on the way in which experts practise (Wicinski, 1950; Miklaszewski, 1989, 1995; Chaffin and Imreh, 1994, 1997; Chaffin and Lemieux, 2004; Chaffin *et al.*, 2002; Hallam, 1992, 1995a, 1995b, 2001b; Nielsen, 1997a, 1997b, 1999; Williamon and Valentine, 2002; Williamon *et al.*, 2002), taken together, suggests the following:

(i) Most professional musicians acquire an overview of the music that they are to learn in the early stages of practice of a new work. The way that this is acquired depends on their ability to develop an internal aural representation of the music from examination of the score alone.

(ii) The structure of the music determines how it is divided into sections for practice.

(iii) Subsections may be identified within musical structure to attend to technical problems.

(iv) The more complex the music, the smaller the chunks which are dealt with.

(v) As practice progresses, the units become larger, although smaller sections may still be worked on.

(vi) As practice on a work nears completion, the length of the passages worked on tends to become more similar.

(vii) A hierarchical structure appears to develop, in which performance plans are gradually integrated into a coherent whole. This plan is guided by musical rather than technical considerations.

(viii) There is considerable individual diversity in the ways that musicians practise. Strategies include playing through the music without stopping, playing through and stopping en route to practise sections, or selecting sections for particular focus. Choice of these depends on the particular stage of practice reached.

(ix) Technical practice may depend on slow analytic work, repetition, deliberate attempts to speed up, and variation of material – for example, rhythm, bowing, tonguing.

(x) The detailed progression of practice on a particular piece differs in response to the actual music itself, but the learning outcome, the integrated performance plan, appears to be similar for all. The routes to achieve it seem to be different, depending on the preferred automated and conscious strategies adopted.

At expert level, multiple coding and a diverse range of strategies are used (Grondahl, 1987), related to the particular requirements of the instrument, the repertoire and performance demands. Problem solving, monitoring and reflection are crucial (Whitaker, 1996).

Many musicians use warm-up exercises to begin practice, although there is considerable individual variation in the extent to which these are perceived to be necessary (Hallam, 1995b). Technical exercises often follow with repertory work left until last (Duke *et al.*, 1997; Jorgensen, H., 1998). Exercises are sometimes used to address specific challenges within a given composition (Harvey *et al.*, 1987; Pacey, 1993; Pierce, M.A., 1992; Hallam, 1995b; Nielsen, 1999a), but the alternative and more common solution is to practise difficult sections within the music being learnt (Hallam, 1995b; Harvey *et al.*, 1987). When passages need to be played at speed, typically they are learnt slowly and speeded up, sometimes with the aid of a metronome. As performances at different speeds can activate different muscles (Winold *et al.*, 1994), combinations of slow and fast practice may be best (Donald, 1997). Musicians also adopt a range of strategies for memorising music for performance (see Chapter 7).

Approaches to practising and personality

There are differences in learning style, approaches to practice and the length of time taken by professional musicians to learn repertoire (Miklaszewski, 1995; Ghent, 1989; Hallam, 1995a; 1995b). Diverse strategy use has also been observed where woodwind specialists have to change instruments during performance (McLaughlin, 1985). In some cases, the adoption of particular strategies is seen to lead to particular learning outcomes (Miklaszewski, 1995; Ghent, 1989), while in others all of the musicians demonstrated high professional performing standards, regardless of the approach adopted (Hallam, 1995a; 1995b; McLaughlin, 1985). Similar diversity has been identified in school students (Cantwell and Millard, 1994). Students adopting a deep approach to studying defined the practice task in musical rather than technical terms, although they were aware of the need to achieve fluency in technical matters. Surface-approach students adopted rote-learning strategies and sought external support. A deep approach was consistently linked with high-level cognitive strategies and a high level of planning (Sullivan and Cantwell, 1999). To promote more effective practice, Cantwell and Millard (1994) suggest that pupils should be encouraged to attend to the musical aspects of their playing; while Barry (1992), in conclusions drawn from a study of cognitive style and gender, suggests that structured supervised practice is more effective than free practice, particularly for boys. Age differences in the students studied may account for the differences in recommendations, more structured work being appropriate for younger students, with greater emphasis on musical factors for older students who are already self-regulating.

In developing interpretation, three main approaches have been identified. Some musicians plan interpretation at the outset, based on ideas gleaned from listening to a wide range of music and different interpretations of the same piece. For others the interpretation develops intuitively as they work on the piece (Hallam, 1995a).

Nielsen (2001), studying music students rather than professionals, found that some musicians developed a performance plan after mastering most of the technical challenges. For some instruments, musical interpretation dictates fingerings, bowing or breathing, so interpretation and technical issues are irrevocably intertwined. This affects the approach adopted. Experienced performers report taking the audience perspective into account when developing expressive ideas (Oura and Hatano, 2001). A useful strategy is working deliberately on communication ideas in the final stages of practice (Williamon *et al.*, 2002).

Personality factors may also affect practising. Kemp (1981, 1994), in research examining the personality characteristics of performing musicians, suggested that the relatively high levels of introversion exhibited by musicians might assist them in undertaking repetitive practice. Support for this comes from Hallam (1998b), who observed that there appeared to be a relationship between concentration in practice and arousal levels in performance in professional musicians. Those who described themselves as effective, focused learners experienced higher arousal levels in performance that were often problematic. Strategies were developed by both groups to overcome their perceived needs.

Differences in practice between novices and experts

Gruson (1988) and Hallam (1997a, 1997b, 2001b, 2001d) have examined changes in practice as expertise develops. Their findings demonstrate the following in relation to novices:

(i) They often appear to be unaware that they are making errors. This may be because they do not have the appropriate internal aural schemata.

(ii) They have problems in identifying difficult sections. This may be because their technical schemata are insufficiently developed.

(iii) They tend to practise by playing through music rather than focusing on difficult sections.

(iv) When they begin to identify errors, they initially correct them by repetition of the single wrong note.

(v) As they become more expert, they repeat small sections (half bar or a bar) when errors are made.

(vi) They gradually change to focus error correction on 'difficult sections' which are then worked on as units.

(vii) When learning to read music, they tend to focus first on playing notes which are at the correct pitch. Attention is then directed to rhythm. This then extends to all of the technical aspects of playing. Finally, attention becomes focused on dynamics, interpretation and the expressive aspects of playing.

(viii) They report the use of strategies in practice before they are actually adopted. This reflects findings from research in the development of memory development, where it is known as a 'production deficiency' (Flavell *et al.*, 1966).

(ix) The use of more advanced strategies is more closely linked to developing expertise than to age.

(x) Strategy use does not seem to determine the quality of performance.

(xi) They reflect more on performance itself as expertise develops.

Once a certain level of expertise has been attained (around Grade 8 standard), it is possible to identify similarities with professionals in strategy use. There is greater concern with interpretation, and individual differences emerge in approaches and orientations to practice. Whether this individual diversity develops over time, or is present in novices but unrevealed because of their relatively unde-veloped metacognitive awareness, is debatable. It is likely that there is a complex interplay between preferences for automated proces-sing strategies, conscious selection of particular approaches and orientations, and metacognitive awareness. However, it is only as metacognition develops that these are revealed. This seems to occur at a late stage in the development of musical expertise (Swanwick and Tillman, 1986).

The quality of practising processes

Individuals may be more or less effective when they are practising. There are differences in organisation, planning, concentration, use of appropriate practising strategies, understanding of the nature of the task, monitoring and evaluation. Playing in groups allows repetition of required skills and some skills – for instance, sight reading, listening and improvising – may be better developed through playing with others than through individual practice.

Developing aural schemata

It is particularly important that appropriate schemata against which to evaluate practice are developed. Hallam (1997a, 2001b, 2001d) showed that novice violinists, when learning a new piece unaided, often did not correct mistakes. They were unaware of their errors. Only when they had developed considerable expertise were errors consistently corrected. Whitaker (1996) – studying performers, arrangers, conductors and composers – established the necessity of possessing a mental template that served as the focus for all learning and performance activities. In contrast to professionals, most students are unable to generate auditory schemata from written notation (Grondahl, 1987). These skills need to be developed. Recorded aural models may assist in this process (Folts, 1973; Rosenthal, 1984; Rosenthal *et al.*, 1988; Puopolo, 1971), although Hodges (1975) found that, for beginners, aural models alone had no positive effect on performance achievement.

Making effective use of feedback

Research on feedback has generally focused on practical applications – for instance, improving technique, relaxation, and aural perception – although some (delaying or removing feedback) has addressed theoretical issues. Practical applications of feedback have included work on improving violin posture (Salzberg and Salzberg, 1981), visually displayed computer feedback for pianists to aid improvement in technique (Tucker *et al.*, 1977) and computer feedback for trainee conductors (Schwaegler, 1984). All have had some measure of success. Precise feedback regarding pitch, jitter and formant can improve the quality of singing and has been found particularly valuable as a substitute for human feedback (Fourcin and Abberton, 1971; Murray *et al.*, 1979; Wilson, 1982). Brick (1984) found that trombonists who had received training on the TAP Pitch Master improved pitch accuracy more than a control group, while Salzberg (1980) found that verbal feedback produced more accurate intonation than recorded or model performance feedback in university-level string players. A number of studies (Johnstone, 1993; Yarborough *et al.*, 1979; Yarborough, 1987) have devised feedback techniques for use with conductors, with positive results.

The literature on children who have problems singing in tune has highlighted several successful feedback techniques. Cobes (1972) and Jones (1971, 1979) illuminated coloured lights when intonation improved; Joyner (1969) and Roberts (1972) relied on teachers' verbal ratings of pitch performance. Ekstrom (1974) reports the use of tape recordings in experimental singing clinics to give poor pitch singers the chance to listen to their attempts at singing in tune. These methods have all had at least some degree of success. Welch (1985a, 1985b) used visual feedback and knowledge of results to improve pitch accuracy. Both were necessary. The importance of knowledge of results in learning to sing in tune has consistently been demonstrated (Welch, 1985a; Welch and McCurtain, 1986; Howard and Welch, 1987; Cleveland, 1988; Welch *et al.*, 1989).

To be effective, feedback needs to be appropriate and relevant to the task. Conditions of restricted and unrestricted vision, for instance, had no differential effects on string players' intonation

(Salzberg, 1980); while Smith, A. (1973) found no significant effect of knowledge of results provided by a system of electric boxes in the training of young children who were required to monitor the musical form of unfamiliar classical minuets and movements in sonata form.

Biofeedback techniques have proved very useful in enabling musicians to learn to relax specific muscles as they are playing. Irvine and LeVine (1981) and LeVine and Irvine (1984) used biofeedback techniques to help violinists and violists to play their instruments without tensing their left thumbs. Morasky *et al.* (1981) used similar techniques to relax the forearm muscles in violinists. Basmajian and White (1973) studied biofeedback in relation to control in trumpet players' lips, while Basmajian and Newton (1974) used visual electromyographic feedback with wind players, who learnt within minutes to suppress or activate specific parts of the buccinator muscle in the cheek. Other studies report similar results with different technical problems (e.g. Morasky *et al.*, 1981, 1983; Evoskevich, 1979; Levee *et al.*, 1976; Basmajian and White, 1973). The effectiveness of biofeedback techniques in reducing muscle tension while performing on a musical instrument is now well accepted. Further, Cutietta (1986) demonstrated that biofeedback training sessions reduced muscle tension while students performed passages from the repertoire with which they were having difficulty. This indicates that biofeedback can be used in normal practice rather than exclusively in relation to specific exercises (for a review see Gruzelier and Egner, 2004).

Some research has been concerned with the nature of the feedback perceived by the musician, as distinct from another listener. Patterson (1974), studying the intensity ranges of professional bassoon players, found that the largest range they achieved was 17 decibels. As a range of 30 decibels is possible, it seems that the players' own feedback is different from audience perceptions, making external feedback necessary. Several studies have also demonstrated that trained musicians demonstrate a tendency towards sharpness of pitch in performance (Madsen *et al.*, 1969; Madsen, 1974; Small, 1937; Papich and Rainbow, 1974). This suggests that the feedback musicians experience directly is systematically different from that experienced by other listeners. The implications of this for performing and teaching are considerable.

Distributed and variable practice

Distributed practice is more beneficial than massed practice for the long-term development of skills (Rubin-Rabson, 1940a). Short amounts of regular practice are better than long, infrequent sessions. Schema theory suggests that motor programmes, including those required for playing a musical instrument, are strengthened by increased variability in practice (for instance, practising a passage with different articulations, at different tempos, or a technique using different examples), rather than repetition of the same actions. This facilitates transfer to other tasks (Schmidt, R.A., 1975, 1976). Variable practice is more likely under conditions of distributed practice (Shea and Morgan, 1979). Pacey (1993) studied the effects of variable practice in teaching stringed instruments, in particular the acquisition of skills relating to loudness, tempo and pitch. Variable practice was effective, particularly with children at lower levels of expertise. Owen (1988) also found advantages for variable practice over other formats, although the findings may have been confounded as the group adopting it, overall, received the most comprehensive levels of training. Not all the evidence supports the efficacy of variable practice (Harvey *et al.*, 1987). Training on a variety of intervals resulted in less transfer to the task of imitating a single interval than did training on a different single interval. Given the equivocal findings, it is difficult to draw any meaningful conclusions. The relative effectiveness of each approach is likely to depend on the nature of the task being undertaken and the desired learning outcome. For the long-term development of technical skill, variable practice may be more beneficial, whereas the learning of specific pieces for performance may benefit from repetition based on actual performance requirements. There may also be mediating factors relating to the effects of repetition on motivation.

Part vs whole practice

Particularly relevant to the acquisition of musical skill is the question of part–whole transfer of training. In learning to play some musical instruments, considerable part learning takes place and there has been controversy amongst teachers as to the extent to which skills should be broken down into simpler tasks. One of the earliest experimental studies of part–whole learning in music was undertaken by R.A. Brown (1928), who found that a whole strategy was the most effective. In contrast, Rubin-Rabson (1940b) found that in the memorisation of piano music, learning of hands separately was more effective than learning both hands together; while Neiman (1989) found that, where sufficient practice was undertaken for the behaviour to become relatively automatic, part learning was successful in assisting the development of successful conducting techniques. Adams (1987), in an overview of research on part- and whole-task training in areas apart from music, suggested that in general there is transfer from part-task training. Sometimes part-task training is as good as whole-task training, but usually whole-task training is better. In the musical context, it is likely that the most effective training will depend on the nature of the task, the characteristics of the learner, their level of prior knowledge, and the context of learning.

Transfer of learning

Closely related to the issue of part–whole training is the question of transfer of learning. In the long term, almost all musical skills, once learnt, transfer to new tasks. For the learning of specific repertoire the issues are different. Duke and Pierce (1990) found that performing a piece at a different tempo from that at which it had been learnt (slower or faster) negatively affected performance. Fast and slow speeds of movement seem to be controlled in different ways

(Winold *et al.*, 1994), although both are learnt in relation to the desire to express a musical idea. Systematic vocal training has transfer effects in relation to improving instrumental performance and accuracy of intonation (Davis, L.P., 1981; Schlacks, 1981; Brick, 1984), while effects for memorisation of songs (Williamson, 1964) and the facilitation of sight-reading skills (Peitersen, 1954; MacKnight, 1975) depend on the extent to which the conditions pertaining to the original and transfer tasks are similar. Transfer of learning in music needs to be considered in relation to particular tasks and different time scales. In the short term, practice seems to be most effective when it relates specifically to the task being undertaken, with the conditions for learning and performance being as similar as possible.

Comparisons of different types of practice

A number of studies have compared the effects of different practice techniques. Zurcher (1975) compared model-supportive practice, where pupils were supplied with tapes that included instructions, reminders and model play-along performances with a control group. The model supportive practice was found to improve some aspects of performance. Rosenthal *et al.* (1988) compared modelling (listening to a recording) with singing (singing the composition), silent analysis, free practice and a control group. Significant differences in the effects of the different practice techniques were found for different aspects of performance. For maximum effectiveness, practice techniques need to be tailored to suit specific task requirements.

Mental rehearsal

Mental practice, where the learner thinks through the procedures without actually playing, can be effective (Wapnik *et al.*, 1982). However, Kopiez (1990), comparing the performance of guitar students who either played short atonal phrases or adopted cognitive analytic techniques to study them, found that playing through was the most effective method of learning them. Ross, S.L. (1985) concluded that a combination of mental and physical practice was most effective because mental practice allowed concentration on the cognitive aspects of music performance without the distractions of exercising motor control.

Task requirements

The nature of particular learning tasks inevitably affects the way in which practice is undertaken. The particular ways in which this occurs have been little explored. Miklaszewski (1995) studied the differences in pianists' practice of a late romantic miniature and three contemporary variations. All three musicians worked for a shorter period of time on the romantic composition, perceived it as easier, and learnt it from memory. More time was spent analysing the contemporary piece, although overall the general pattern of practice was similar. Hallam (1992) reported that professional musicians expressed greater difficulty in learning contemporary music; indicated greater use of 'conscious cognitive' strategies, particularly in relation to rhythmic difficulties; and stated that it would be difficult to memorise, although there was considerable individual variation. The adoption of memorisation strategies depends on the nature of the task and the context within which the music is to be performed (Hallam, 1997b). Musicians are more likely to rely on automated aural memory without resort to conscious cognitive analysis if a piece is short, simple and to be performed in a relatively unthreatening environment – for example, a school concert. Lehmann and Ericsson (1995) suggest that the increasing technical demands of twentieth-century music have influenced the nature of practice. Where the repertoire of the instrument is limited, we might also expect relatively lower levels of practice. Some support for this comes from Jorgensen, H. (1996), who reports differences in average practice time between students playing different instruments, pianists and string players practising the most. These differences may relate to historically different traditions and the physical and cognitive demands made by the instruments themselves.

Executive strategies to support practice

Metacognitive strategies are concerned with the planning, monitoring and evaluation of learning. They are crucial to all aspects of practising, and can be considered at the level of a particular task or in relation to the more global concerns of the musician to maintain or improve the standard of their playing. In both cases, knowledge of personal strengths and weaknesses, the nature of the task to be completed, possible strategies and the nature of the learning outcome are important. There are considerable differences between beginners, novices and experts in their knowledge and deployment of different practising and self-regulating strategies (Hallam, 2001a, 2001b; Pitts *et al.*, 2000a, 2000b; Sloboda *et al.*, 1996), as well as individual differences among musicians and novices at the same level of competence (Nielsen, 1997, 1999a, 1999b, 2001; Austin and Berg, in press). Hallam (2001d) demonstrated that professional musicians had well-developed metacognitive skills – including self-awareness of strengths and weaknesses, extensive knowledge regarding the nature of different tasks and what would be required to complete them satisfactorily, and strategies which could be adopted in response to perceived needs. This not only encompassed technical matters, interpretation and performance, but also issues relating to learning itself: concentration, planning, monitoring and evaluation. Novices demonstrated less metacognitive awareness, the amount and structure of their practice tending to be determined by external commitments such as examinations.

The planning and organisation of practice may contribute to its effectiveness. Manturzewska (1969) found that high and low achievers among professional pianists differed significantly in the way they reported organising their work. Prize winners, while working more than four hours daily, did not work as intensely as the most diligent students, but their work was more regular and systematic and took priority over other activities. Jorgensen, H. (1998) found that some students had a regular routine, while others changed their strategies from session to session. Some students practise at the same time every day (Duke *et al.*, 1997), while others integrate practice into a daily or weekly plan (Jorgensen, H., 1997). The morning may be the best time for high levels of concentration. Ericsson *et al.* (1993) found that conservatoire students at the highest levels of expertise practised in the morning, took naps in the afternoon, and then put in more practice in the evening. While practice may be most effective when it is organised in sequential and logical manner (Santana, 1978; DeNicola, 1990; Price, 1990; Barry, 1992), conservatoire students often start practice without clear goals (Jorgensen, H., 1998). Self-reinforcement can help in the development of more effective habits (Smith and Singh, 1984). External factors have a major impact on planning and practice time. Time spent practising increases as expertise develops and repertoire becomes more demanding; more time is spent practising in the run-up to examinations (Hallam, 2001d) and before lessons (Lehmann and Ericsson, 1998), while school holidays usually result in a decrease in practice activity (Sloboda, 1996).

Motivation and self-regulation are important dimensions of music practice (Austin and Berg, in press; Gellrich, 1987; McPherson and Zimmerman, 2002; McPherson and Renwick, 2001; Nielsen, 2001). Some activities which students engage in during practice sessions are not related to learning – for instance, day-dreaming – or are avoidance behaviours (taking a long time to set up a music stand or maintain an instrument) (Hallam, 1992; Pitts *et al.*, 2000a; McPherson and Renwick, 2001). Practice motivation and regulation are associated with the quality of the home environment, personal interest, effort and emotional responses during practice (Austin and Berg, in press). McPherson and Renwick (2001) found that over a period of three years, as students became more self-regulating in their practice, a higher percentage of practice time was focused on improving performance, with less time spent responding to distractions, talking to others, day-dreaming or expressing frustration. High-achieving students tended to strike a balance between formal or required practice tasks and informal, creative or motivating activities such as playing a favourite piece or improvising (McPherson and McCormick, 1999; Sloboda and Davidson, 1996). Self-regulated learners managed their environment to optimise learning (Barry and McArthur, 1994; McPherson and Zimmerman, 2002).

Attempting to improve undergraduate students' concentration, Madsen and Geringer (1981) required them to keep a record of their practice, rate each practice session for productivity over an eight-week period, and complete a distraction index. This increased observed attentiveness and performance, but the index was time consuming to complete. Nielsen (2001) suggests that students can enhance self-guidance by covertly or overtly describing how to proceed, giving comments on progress, and noting concentration lapses and changes in motivation (Nielsen, 2001). Focus is crucial to avoid mindless repetition. The regulation of strategies requires deliberate effort, task selection, speed and intensity (see Nielsen, 1999b).

Motivation to practise

There are complex relationships between motivation, achievement and practice (Hallam, 1997a; 1998c; McPherson et al., 1997; O'Neill, 1997) (see Chapter 9). Many children view practising as boring and a chore (McPherson and Davidson, in press; Pitts et al., 2000a; 2000b). Motivation to practise seems to be based on extrinsic, intrinsic and combined motives in both professional and novice musicians (Hallam, 1995b; Gellrich et al., 1986; Howe and Sloboda, 1991). Howe and Sloboda (1991) found that most students in their sample required parental encouragement and support to practise, although family tensions relating to practice were also reported.

Harnischmacher (1995) identified short- and long-term goals which influenced motivation – including wanting to play with others, playing particular favourite pieces of music, pleasing teachers, and sometimes love of the instrument. Constraints on practising included the environment, the interference of close relatives, dislike of particular music, the distractions of leisure activities and the weather.

Studies of teachers' encouragement of practice have suggested that negotiating individual practising contracts (Wolfe, 1987) and asking students to keep written practice reports (Wagner, M.J., 1975) can be effective. The latter led to significantly more practice but no better performance than controls. Rubin-Rabson (1941a) found that extrinsic rewards and verbal encouragement were not necessarily effective ways to motivate students to practise, while Hallam (in press, a) found that the support of teachers and parents was important for encouraging practice in girls but that boys tended to be influenced more by their peers. Overall, the most important attitudinal predictor of practising was the individual's own self-determination. Motivation to practise is increased by allowing students more control in setting their own goals, selecting repertoire, and determining time spent practising (Greco, 1997). Engagement in self-evaluation also enhances perceived attainment and develops greater independence and planning ability (Brandstrom, 1995–6).

The influence of the environment on practising

Teaching about practice

Instrumental teachers are an important influence on practice. Their characteristics and the interactions that they have with students are considered in Chapter 11. Research on the way in which they teach about practising has had mixed results. Jorgensen, H. (1995, 2000), in research with beginning conservatoire students in Norway, reported that 40 per cent indicated that their previous teachers had invested 'little' or 'no' effort in teaching them how to practise.

However, in the United States, teachers have reported that they always or almost always include instructions about practice in their lessons (Barry and McArthur, 1994). Specific practice techniques are discussed with pupils, the use of different approaches is encouraged – particularly slow practice, marking of the music, analysis, setting goals, mental practice and appropriate distribution of practice. Students do seem to be able to learn how to use expert practising strategies (Barry, 1992), and having done so report more positive attitudes towards practising, are more likely to engage in practice planning and problem identification, are better able to select appropriate performance goals, and are able to formulate more cognitively complex goals (Kenny, W.E., 1992). This suggests that there can be benefits in teaching about practice (see Hallam 1998a for ways to approach this).

The learning environment

Parents and the home are important influences on engagement with music and practising, as we saw in Chapter 7. The impact of institutional learning environments has been less studied. Research at conservatoire level in Norway (Jorgensen, H., 1996, 1997, 1998) reported constraints on practising relating to institutional factors. Forty per cent of students wishing to undertake more practice reported pressure of work from other study activities as a barrier. Comparison of reported time spent practising with departmental expectations of weekly practice – as defined in the curriculum – revealed a close match for instrumentalists, a lower level of practice for vocalists, and a higher level for church musicians and educationalists. Jorgensen interpreted the additional practice of church and educational musicians in terms of the dual role conflict these students experienced, between the dominating value system of the institution related to high instrumental standards and their particular course curriculum. Undertaking higher levels of practice than required by their courses enabled them to maintain status within the institutional value system.

Rehearsing in groups

Research on rehearsals in small groups has shown that there is no single best strategy for rehearsing repertoire (Davidson, J.W. and King, 2004). Individual ensembles find their own best ways of working. Berg (2000) found that high-school student ensembles adopted four main activities: initiating, performing, orienting and assisted learning. They focused on intonation, dynamics, articulation and rhythmic accuracy in relation to individual parts and the ensemble. Professional groups usually have a draft plan of the material to be covered across a series of rehearsals, with room for extra sessions should they be needed (Goodman, 2000). As in individual practice, warm-up sessions can be useful, and sequential and non-sequential strategies are adopted, the former being particularly useful in generating new thoughts about subsections of the work (Goodman, 2000). Cox (1989) stresses the need for the pace and intensity of work to be varied throughout sessions to maintain concentration and interest. Group cohesiveness centres around the music (Davidson, J.W. and Good, 2002), but trust and respect are crucial for the functioning of groups working together continuously over long periods of time, for example, string quartets (Young and Colman, 1979). To be successful in the long term, rehearsals have to be underpinned by strong social frameworks. The smaller the group, the more important personal friendship seems to be (Blank and Davidson, 2003). In larger groups – for example, orchestras – the player's sense of self has to be sublimated to facilitate group affiliation (Atik, 1994). The interactions of small-group members tend to be characterised by conflict and compromise (Young and Colman, 1979; Murningham and Conlon, 1991), and are mainly concerned with musical content and its co-ordination, although some are of a more personal nature (e.g. approval). As performance approaches, non-verbal communication increases (Williamon and Davidson, 2002). Such communication often solves problems when discussion has failed (Goodman, 2002; Murninghan and Conlon, 1991).

Implications for educators

To be successful, practice must be thoughtfully approached and tailored to the needs of the particular task. It may be exploratory, deliberate, playful, mental, physical, expressive or performance oriented, depending on the task and the stage reached in bringing it to fruition. Musicians wishing to practise more effectively are advised to:

(i) develop metacognitive skills (identify the nature of the task and what will be most effective in tackling it, identify strengths and weaknesses, monitor and evaluate progress);

(ii) identify clear goals and work towards them;

(iii) listen to high-quality models of musical performance of all kinds and of repertoire to be learnt;

(iv) search out and act upon feedback from others;

(v) think about the task outside practice time – engage in mental rehearsal;

(vi) invest time in analytic work;

(vii) plan practice;

(viii) develop strategies for managing motivation;

(ix) ensure that the learning environment is conducive to practice;

(x) take advantage of opportunities to play with others (this develops a wide range of skills);

(xi) acknowledge the relationship between time engaged with music and achievement and set out to invest the time necessary.

Teachers and parents wishing to support students in their practice should encourage them to follow these suggestions. Time invested in practice and the quality of that practice impact on the level of musical expertise developed. Learning how to practise makes practice more productive, challenging and enjoyable.

Further Reading

Barry, N.H. and Hallam, S. (2002) 'Practising'. In R. Parncutt and G.E. McPherson (eds) *The Science and Psychology of Music Performance: Creative strategies for teaching and learning.* Oxford: Oxford University Press (pp. 151–166).

Davidson, J.W. and King, E.C. (2004) 'Strategies for ensemble practice'. In A. Williamon (ed.) *Musical Excellence: Strategies and techniques to enhance performance.* Oxford: Oxford University Press (pp. 105–122).

Hallam, S. (1997c) 'What do we know about practising? Towards a model synthesising the research literature'. In H. Jorgensen and A. Lehman (eds) *Does Practice Make Perfect? Current theory and research on instrumental music practice.* NMH-publikasjoner 1997:1, Oslo, Norway: Norges musikkhgskole (Norwegian Academy of Music).

Jorgensen, H. (2004) 'Strategies for individual practice'. In A. Williamon (ed.) *Musical Excellence: Strategies and techniques to enhance performance.* Oxford: Oxford University Press (pp. 85–104).

McPherson, G.E. and Zimmerman, B.J. (2002) 'Self-regulation of musical learning: a social cognitive perspective'. In R. Colwell and C. Richardson (eds) *The New Handbook of Research on Music Teaching and Learning.* Oxford: Oxford University Press (pp. 327–347).

9 Motivation and musical identity

The study of human motivation has a long history. Theorists have attempted to explain it from a wide range of different perspectives. These fall into three main groupings: those which emphasise motivation as deriving from within the individual, those where the individual is perceived to be motivated by environmental factors, and those where motivation is seen as a complex interaction between the individual and the environment mediated by cognition (for reviews see Asmus, 1994; Hurley, 1995; O'Neill and McPherson; 2002; Hallam, 2002). Most modern theories of motivation have evolved from the major meta-theoretical positions (behaviourist, psychoanalytic, humanist), taking much greater account of cognition, the way our perceptions of events are determined by our construction of them, and the ways in which our interpretations of them subsequently influence the constantly changing perceptions we hold of ourselves. They acknowledge the capacity of the individual to determine their own behaviour, whilst also recognising the role of the environment in rewarding or punishing particular behaviours, which then influences thinking and subsequent actions.

A further key issue for understanding motivation which modern theories have begun to address is the way in which motivation operates at different levels and in different time scales. At the highest levels, motivation to behave in particular ways may be determined by needs deriving from the individual's personality and goals which are specified over the life span. In the medium term, behaviour may be determined by the need to achieve intermediate goals, while maintaining self-esteem. Actual behaviour at any single time, while it may be influenced by longer-term goals, will also depend on decisions made between competing motivations and needs, and 'coping' with the demands of the environment. The study of motivation is extremely complex and needs to take account of many different and inter-related factors.

A model of motivation

Figure 9.1 provides a framework illustrating some of the complex interactions that may apply within a musical context. Our personality, self-concept and self-esteem are, in part, determined by feedback from the environment. We are motivated because we desire social approval,

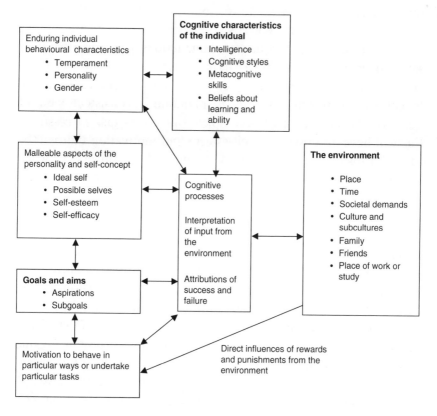

Figure 9.1 *Interactions between individual and environmental factors in determining motivation*

particularly from those we admire and respect. Such praise is internalised, raises self-esteem and enhances confidence. Individuals set themselves goals, which determine their behaviour. These goals are influenced by personality, ideal and possible selves as well as by environmental factors. Behaviour is the end link in the chain, but at the time of enactment it too can be influenced and changed by environmental factors. There is interaction between the environment and the individual at every level, and in the long and short term. Individuals can act upon the environment to change it, or seek out new environments more conducive to their needs. The model recognises the importance of cognitive factors and self-determination in behaviour. While we have needs and desires, we are aware that we need to consider the consequences of our actions before we attempt to satisfy them. Cognition plays a role in the ways in which we attempt to enhance our self-esteem, leading us to attribute our success or failure to causes which will allow us to maintain a consistent view of ourselves. When a learner has completed a learning task successfully, this will have an impact on self-esteem and motivation that will be carried forward to subsequent learning tasks. Conversely, when learning outcomes are negative, motivation is often impaired.

Expectancy value models

Much of the research on motivation in music has not been embedded within motivational research paradigms or theoretical positions. Psychological research exploring musical motivation has been almost exclusively concerned with motivation to learn and continue to play an instrument. There has been little interest in motivation to listen to music or compose. In education more generally, expectancy-value models have provided a theoretical framework for recent research. While the models have focused on motivation at the level of particular tasks (e.g. Eccles, 1983; Feather, 1982), the framework can be utilised for considering motivation to engage with music in a more general way. Expectancy–value models have three main components:

value components – students' beliefs about the importance and value of the task(s); expectancy components – students' beliefs about their ability or skill to perform the task; and affective components – students' feelings about themselves or their emotional reactions to the task. These components are not independent of each other. There are complex interactions between them.

Value components and musical identity

Value components incorporate three elements: the individual's perception of the importance of the task; the intrinsic value of, or interest in, the task; and the utility of the task for future goals (Eccles, 1983). In music, each of these is linked to the individual's sense of identity as a musician, their intrinsic motivation to engage with music, and their musical aspirations for the future. An individual's identity or self-concept represents the way they think about themselves and their relationships with others (Sullivan, H.S., 1964; Rogers, C.R., 1961; Mead, 1934). Behaviour is influenced by the individual's interpretation of situations and events, their expectations, and the goals that they have that mediate and regulate behaviour (Mischel, 1973). Some theorists have also stressed the needs of the individual (Murray, H.A., 1938). In education, need for achievement (to be more successful and better than others) (McClelland *et al.*, 1953; Atkinson, 1964) and need for competence are of particular importance (Koestner and McClelland, 1990). Need for achievement is based on two complementary elements: the motive to achieve success, which enhances the ego; and the motive to avoid failure, which involves the fear of losing face. Gellrich *et al.* (1986) identified three levels of achievement-related motives in music: a general achievement motivation; a specifically music-oriented achievement orientation; and a sensual–aesthetic motive, the pleasure and joy of playing certain pieces of music.

In developing and consolidating identity, individuals set them-selves goals. These take account of both context and cognition. One example is 'possible selves'. If an individual perceives themselves as successful and attributes this success to high ability, they may come to include in their self-concept a 'positive possible future self' in that domain (Markus and Ruvolo, 1989). Possible selves can be powerful motivators, providing long-term goals and encouraging the setting up of interim goals which need to be achieved en route. If an individual does not have a positive possible self as a musician (professional, amateur or listener) in the long, medium, or short term, they are unlikely to maintain their interest in music. Some theorists have developed conceptualisations of how individuals move towards their desired selves – for example, 'personal strivings' (Emmons, 1989); 'personal projects' (Little, 1989); 'life tasks' (Cantor and Kihlstrom, 1985, 1987); and 'current concerns' (Klinger, 1975, 1977, 1987). These all emphasise the individual's capacity to choose life activities and preoccupations and to express their intentions in action.

The importance of musical identity emerged in Kemp's (1996) studies of the personalities of young musicians. He found that those who emerged as the most highly accomplished appeared to be self-motivated almost to the point of obsession, as if they were unable to separate their developing self-perception from that of being a musician. This level of commitment is demonstrated by evidence that some children playing musical instruments experience bullying or loss of popularity as a result of their involvement (Howe and Sloboda, 1992), but nevertheless continue to play. Sloboda (1991) suggests that this commitment may depend on the experience of intense, aesthetic, emotional reactions to music, initially occurring in early childhood. Autobiographical accounts of the memories of professional musicians' emotional responses to music in childhood support this (Manturzewska, 1990; Sloboda, 1990). Some, with no commitment to music, reported negative emotions associated with strong criticism by teachers, which created anxiety and reduced motivation.

The development of a high level of commitment to music is influenced by societal and family factors (also see Chapter 7 for consideration of family influences). Music is not valued equally in all cultures. In some it is viewed as decadent and is forbidden; in others it is highly valued and those involved in its composition or execution are highly revered members of society. In some places and at some times, the environment is very conducive to musical activity and there are considerable rewards for being musical. Institutions can also be supportive of musical engagement. Instrumental teachers have reported that the support of the head teacher and class music teacher in school are crucial in the extent to which their instrumental teaching is effective (Hallam and Prince, 2000). The music teacher is central to motivation (Wragg, 1974). An enthusiastic teacher can modify pupils' attitudes towards music and counteract negative social influences. Their interest and musical competence contribute to pupils' attitudes towards music and subsequent attainment (Szubertowska, 2005). Where teachers motivate pupils to engage with music, identities as musicians develop, leading to more positive attitudes towards school music and teachers (Lamont, 2002). In adolescence the peer group is very powerful and can bring negative pressure to bear in relation to engagement with some types of music (Finnas, 1987, 1989). To withstand this, musical identities need to be well developed. The influence of early teachers who are viewed as warm and sympathetic seems to be particularly important in this respect (Sosniak, 1985; Sloboda and Howe, 1991). Relatively uncritical encouragement in the early stages of engagement with music encourages the development of a positive musical identity. Once this is established, later teachers provide high-status role models with whom the young musician can identify and whom they emulate (Manturzewska, 1990).

The role of the family, as we saw in Chapter 7, is crucial in the development of interest in music. In providing early opportunities for pleasing interactions with music, parents are likely to develop motivation for further involvement. Later, parents may play a role in identifying potential in their child and selecting an instrument to be played. Borthwick and Davidson (2002) studied families where at least one child was labelled as a 'musician'. They found that the musical beliefs and experiences of the parents were of central importance in shaping the way in which the subsequent generation experienced and valued music for themselves within the family. A united musical group identity bound all family members together in routines that were music related. The musical influence was not uni-directional but bi-directional. The child's behaviour was shaped, but also shaped the musical identity of parents and siblings. Parent–child coalitions were often formed where one parent and one child had a strong musical link that often led to negative relationships with others in the family. External factors sometimes led to the 'parenting script' being amended rather than replicated. Birth order was important, the eldest usually having been identified as musical, and other children finding their own niches to avoid being 'second best', particularly where there were two children. Overall, family expectations, some based on transgenerational influences, were highly powerful forces with regard to the study of a musical instrument. The combinations of the parents' family histories, emergent expectations, role allocations and current dynamic interactions within the family played a central role in defining musical identity. For those who went on to become performing professional musicians, music was an important determinant of self-concept. Music making was viewed as having positive physical and psychological benefits, and performance became a critical means of self-expression (Burland and Davidson, 2002).

Musicians may also identify themselves as part of musical subgroups – for example, singers, violinists, conductors. For singers the issue of musical identity is central as the voice, for all of us, in part defines who we are and how we are perceived by other people. It conveys our feelings and inner states to ourselves and to others (Thurman and Welch, 2000; Welch, 2000). Jazz players develop a specific 'jazz' identity although they play across a range of other musical genres, usually for financial reasons (MacDonald and Wilson, in press). The relative lack of financial reward in playing jazz is offset by musical satisfaction, indicating high levels of intrinsic motivation. Fatigue, hectic schedules and financial demands tend to be seen as obstacles preventing a focus on practising and playing the music of their choice.

Intrinsic motivation is a crucial aspect of developing self-identity as a musician. However, not all musical activities may be intrinsically motivating. Novice and professional musicians exhibit diversity in motivation to practise. Many students require parental encouragement to practice (Howe and Sloboda, 1991) or other rewards, including playing favourite pieces of music or pleasing teachers. Practising for love of the instrument is rare (Harnischmacher, 1995). The interplay of intrinsic and extrinsic motivation is also demonstrated in relation to drop-outs. Those ceasing to play tend to do less practice and have attained less (Sloboda *et al.*, 1996; Hallam, 1998c). They perceive themselves as less musically able, musically inadequate, and receiving less family encouragement, and feel that they have greater strengths in other recreational activities (Frakes, 1984). They do not develop a musical identity and prefer to engage in other extra-curricular activities (Hurley, 1995).

Expectancy components

Expectancy components relate to students' beliefs about their ability to perform a task, their judgements of self-efficacy and control and their expectancy for success (Rotter, 1966; Mischel, 1973; Bandura, 1977). When people approach a task, they form expectations about how well they think they will be able to carry out that particular task. Such expectations will be based on their previous performance. This is known as self-efficacy (Bandura, 1977). Motivation for an activity will be at its peak when strong self-efficacy beliefs are combined with some moderate uncertainty about the outcome, for instance when a person feels competent but challenged (Bandura, 1989). Confidence in ability does not necessarily facilitate motivation when individuals are faced with failure. Students with records of success and high levels of confidence are often the most vulnerable when they meet failure (Henderson and Dweck, 1990; Dweck, 1999). In music, McCormick and McPherson (2003), McPherson and McCormick (in press) have shown that self-efficacy is extremely important in predicting examination performance.

In education, particular goal orientations have been explored: performance and learning (Diener and Dweck, 1978, 1980; Dweck and Elliott, 1983; Elliott, R.S. and Dweck, 1988). Performance goals are concerned with gaining positive judgements of competence and avoiding negative ones. In contrast, learning goals are concerned with increasing mastery, reflecting the desire to learn new skills, master new tasks or understand new things.

Where students' goals and beliefs about their likelihood of success have been manipulated, those adopting performance goals were more vulnerable to developing helpless responses (Elliott, R.S. and Dweck, 1988) – particularly when they were focused on the possibility of failure (Elliot and Church, 1997). Dweck (1975) described how some students believed that once failure had occurred, the situation was out of their control and nothing could be done. In contrast, those students who adopted a learning goal orientation tended to use deeper, more effective learning strategies and apply what they had learnt more effectively (Ames and Archer, 1988; Pintrich and Garcia, 1994). There is also a relationship between students' theories of intelligence and their goal choices. Where students hold an entity theory of intelligence (fixed and immutable), they are more likely to adopt performance goals; while those holding an incremental view of intelligence are more likely to choose a learning goal (Dweck and Leggett, 1988). Henderson and Dweck (1990) and Sorich and Dweck (2000) found that students who had a fixed view of intelligence performed less well than those with an incremental view, even when the latter had low confidence in their ability. Those with entity theories also tended to minimise the amount of time they put into their school work (Maehr and Midgely, 1996), and believed that if they did not have sufficient ability, hard work would not compensate (Stipek and Gralinski, 1996). They believed that being good at something meant that it was not necessary to work at it (Mueller and Dweck, 1998). Some students self-handicap – deliberately make no effort on difficult tasks to protect their beliefs about their ability (Berglas and Jones, 1978).

Research in music has found no significant effects of goal structure. Self-esteem appears to be related to motivation, but not necessarily to achievement. Austin (1991) showed that students with low music self-esteem were less interested in music and gave significantly less endorsement to effort and affect as explanations for success in music than students with moderate or high levels of music self-esteem. Successful music students who reported that they intended to continue playing attributed their success to ability, not luck, although they also regarded personal effort as important (Chandler *et al.*, 1987). They were more satisfied with their current level of performance, enjoyed playing more, believed that technical knowledge was an important influence on performance, practised more, expected to play the instrument longer, aspired to promotion within their musical group, valued help from their teacher, and believed that it was valuable and important to play an instrument. Chandler *et al.* (1987) suggest that practice operates as cause and effect. If satisfaction is derived from playing an instrument and the individual expects to continue to play, it is likely that more practice will be undertaken. As a result of increased practice the individual will become more competent and confident, which will lead to increased success, promotion within the group and more enjoyment. Effort attribution will then contribute to further increased practice.

Affective components

Affective components relate to anxiety regarding performance (discussed in Chapter 7) and the need for individuals to maintain self-esteem and self-worth. Covington (1984) suggests that, because individuals are motivated to establish, maintain and promote a positive self-image, they develop a variety of coping strategies to maintain self-worth, some of which may be self-defeating – for instance, reducing effort. Important in this respect is how we attribute our successes and failures (Weiner, 1986). The causes of success or failure can be seen as stable or unstable, controllable or uncontrollable, and internal or external. If we attribute failure to something which is unstable – for example, bad luck – which may not occur in the future, expectations about future performance are likely to be unaffected. However, if failure is attributed to a stable factor – for example, lack of ability – then there will be an expectation of continued failure (Weiner, 1986). Some causes are perceived to be within our control (e.g. the effort we make), while others (e.g. the difficulty of the test) are not. Some are internal (e.g. intellectual capabilities), others are not (e.g. the quality of the teaching we receive). In explaining success and failure, these three elements interact with each other. More recently, an alternative approach to attribution has been identified: strategy attribution (Clifford, 1986). Here failure is explained by a lack of specific strategies or skills rather than of effort or general ability.

Considering the effect of attributing success or failure to the use of particular learning strategies in music, Vispoel and Austin (1993) found that students who explained their failure in relation to using poor learning strategies or to making insufficient effort anticipated improving their performance, effort and strategy use in the future. Where failure was explained by lack of effort, students were likely to try harder in the future but not necessarily to improve their learning strategies. Where explanations were in terms of inadequate learning strategies, individuals indicated that they would improve their learning strategies and try harder. Explaining failure in terms of the adoption of less than optimal learning strategies seemed to be effective in improving these and increasing effort. Emotional reactions to success and failure in music students were also explored. While anger, upset and guilt at failure or feedback about failure were likely to lead to positive responses for future work, this applied less when the responses were characterised by shame or embarrassment. For those engaged in individual instrumental tuition rather than class music, responses to failure were stronger. This was particularly the case where pupils explained the failure in terms of their lack of ability. Children learning to play instruments seemed to have a more personal investment in music. They may have also been more accustomed to success, therefore being told that they lacked ability may have been more ego threatening. While emotions like anger, upset or guilt might motivate a general music student, for students involved in instrumental music no such benefit was apparent. Emotional reactions to failure seemed to have a debilitating effect. Taken together, these studies indicate the motivational importance of being successful and, where one is not, making appropriate attributions that serve to maintain high musical self-esteem.

Implications for education

Identifying oneself as a musician requires a commitment to music which in turn demands that engagement with music is enjoyable and active (in most cultures listening to music seems to be insufficient to constitute this self-labelling). Family, in the first instance, and later teachers, are key in determining the extent to which musical activities are enjoyable and set at an appropriate level to be both challenging and successful. Praise is crucial to the development of self-confidence, particularly early on. If failure occurs, it should be attributed to specific circumstances rather than to lack of ability. As students progress, their intrinsic motivation will be enhanced if they have control over the repertoire that they learn and the musical groups that they participate in. Where activities have a rewarding social dimension, motivation is likely to be further enhanced. While it might be tempting to offer external rewards for practising or other musical activities, in the longer term if motivation is not generated from within the individual, the activities are unlikely to be sustained.

Further Reading

Hallam, S. (2002) 'Musical motivation: towards a model synthesising the research'. *Music Education Research*, 4(2) (pp. 225–244).

MacDonald, R.A.R., Hargreaves, D.J. and Miell, D.E. (2002b) *Musical Identities*. Oxford: Oxford University Press.

O'Neill, S.A. and McPherson, G.E. (2002) 'Motivation'. In R. Parncutt and G.E. McPherson (eds) *The Science and Psychology of Musical Performance: Creative strategies for teaching and learning*. Oxford: Oxford University Press (pp. 31–46).

10 Assessment

The effects of assessment on learning are powerful. 'The assessment tail wags the educational dog; tests drive instruction to concentrate only on what these tests seem to measure' (Snow, 1990). This effect is so powerful that Elton and Laurillard (1979) have suggested that if educators want to change the way that students learn, they should change the assessment system. The effect that assessment has on learning and teaching is called 'backwash'. Backwash can be cognitive or affective. Cognitive backwash refers to the strategies used in preparing for assessment, while affective backwash refers to the effects of different kinds of assessment on affective outcomes – for example, emotions, attitudes and motivation. Biggs (1996) suggests that the aims of learning, the processes adopted and assessment should be aligned so that backwash effects are positive. In music the most appropriate way of achieving this is to ensure that assessment procedures are authentic.

Backwash effects apply to summative assessment. This assesses the degree of learning at the end of a course. Formative assessment is part of the learning process and enables the teacher and learner to assess progress and from this adjust old goals or set new ones. Formative assessment is sometimes known as feedback, and has been considered in earlier chapters. Assessment can be norm or criterion referenced. The results of norm-referenced tests are interpreted according to the performance of an individual in relation to others. Only a certain percentage of candidates are able to achieve each level. Many educational tests fall into this category, in part because their purpose is selection. Criterion-referenced tests assess whether a particular performance meets task demands. A good example of this is the driving test. Candidates are considered sufficiently expert to drive or not. The quantitative–qualitative distinction in assessment is concerned with the distinction between the amount that has been learnt and the quality of that learning.

It is surprising, given the power of assessment to affect teaching and learning, there has been relatively little research relating to assessment in music. Authentic assessment in music is normally based on performance (this subsumes composition and improvisation), although assessment of critical listening and thinking skills is also important. The nature of performance can vary: it may be public, in front of examiners, part of a competition, recorded, solo, or part of a group. Critical listening and thinking skills are usually assessed by written work that might be in the form of examinations, coursework, or portfolios, although interactive computer assessment is becoming more common.

Assessing composition

In educational contexts, composition is normally assessed through its performance, in part because it is not always notated – although computer-generated compositions are an exception to this. Differentiating between the performance and the composition can be problematic for assessors. There is debate about whether evaluations of composition should be through objective analyses of their specific content; or global, holistic, subjective, qualitative judgements. Amabile (1996) developed a consensual assessment technique to assess the creativity of artistic products. Inter-judge reliabilities for the measure are consistently high (see Hickey, 2002), and the technique has been modified and used for assessing musical compositions and improvisations (Bangs, 1992; Hickey, 1995; Daignault, 1997; Brinkman, 1999; Amchin, 1996; Priest, 1997). Webster and Hickey (1995) compared the reliability of open-ended consensual-assessment type scales to more closed, criterion-defined scales for rating compositions and creativity, and found that the rating scales using consensual assessment were more or at least as reliable as scales with more specific criteria.

In establishing reliability in assessing composition, the level of expertise of the individual undertaking the assessment is an important factor. Hickey (2000) sought to find the best group of judges using a consensual-assessment technique to rate the creativity of children's music compositions. Reliability of creativity ratings of 10-year-old children's original musical compositions was compared among different groups of judges. The inter-judge reliabilities were 0.04 for composers, 0.64 for music teachers, 0.65 for instrumental music teachers, 0.81 for general/choral teachers, 0.7 for music theorists, 0.61 for seventh-grade children, and 0.5 for second-grade children. Hickey suggested that the best experts for judging children's compositions were not experts in the field, but teachers. Professional composers were the least reliable judges of children's compositions when compared to peer and music-teacher judgements. They approached the assessment of music in a more detailed, technical way than the non-experts, who took a more holistic approach (Gromko, 1993; Mellor, 1999). Seddon and O'Neill (2001) found similar differences between primary music-specialist teachers and non-specialist teachers, comparing the evaluations of compositions written by 11-year-olds. Specific and overall ratings were highly correlated, and both specialist and non-specialists were able to give reliable global evaluations of the compositions. However, the specialist teachers were more aware of the specific structural characteristics that affected the overall composition, while non-specialists did not distinguish between global qualities and specific musical attributes.

Assessment of improvisation

Assessment of improvisation needs to take account of the particular genre within which the improvisation is being developed. Within that framework, issues relating to the appropriateness of the style; the development of ideas; the use of different sound textures; melodic, rhythmic, harmonic, dynamic, and expressive qualities;

the extent to which the improvisation is structured; and originality, imagination, and effectiveness need to be considered. A number of checklists have been developed to assess improvisation skills. Gorder (1980) developed materials which enabled scores to be given for the number of improvised phrases produced (fluency), shifts of musical content (flexibility), varied use of musical content (elaboration), rarely used content (originality) and what Gorder called 'music quality'. Based on this work, a model was developed for use in schools (Hassler and Feil, 1986) which included five categories: first impression, originality, imaginativeness, general impression, and final appraisal. McPherson (1993) devised the Test of Ability to Improvise for use with high-school instrumentalists. It rates performance on instrumental fluency, musical syntax, creativity, and musical quality, using five-point scales. Results show high inter-judge reliability. There are also rating scales for the assessment of jazz (Pfenninger, 1991; Horowitz, 1995). All of these tests show high levels of reliability. If improvisation is undertaken within a group, then a decision has to be taken as to whether it is group performance, individual performance or a combination which will be assessed.

Computers and music assessment

Increasingly, interactive-computer assessment systems are being developed. For instance, Venn (1990) has developed such a system to measure common objectives in elementary general music: melody, rhythm, texture and tonality. Tasks were devised to assess the child's ability to detect change in an element, identify compositional devices related to an element, and identify a place in a musical selection where a change in an element occurred. Test– retest reliability was 0.79 for the total measure. Such interactive tests can provide a reliable means of assessment, releasing teacher time for more creative work.

Assessment of performance

The benefits of performance

Performance increases motivation to practise and, if successful, has a positive impact on self-esteem and confidence. There is variability in the extent to which students enjoy performance. Some dislike it intensely (Prince, 1994), while for others it can bring experiences of real joy (Howe and Sloboda, 1991) – although there are differences in what elicits these responses: the attention of the audience, the winning of competitions, or actual enjoyment of the music making. Being 'judged' in competitions can be particularly harrowing. Singers report profound and emotional performing experiences (Davidson, J.W., 2002a; Beck *et al.*, 2000), while for rock bands performance can facilitate increased self-esteem and more extroverted social behaviours (Cohen, 1991).

Types of assessment

In the United Kingdom, systems of graded examinations have been developed for instrumentalists and vocalists. These are taken when the child is ready and provide an assessment of level of expertise and quality. Such examination systems promote motivation, give a clear guide of the level that the learner has attained which can be compared with other learners nationwide, provide a structure for learning, measure musical achievement, enable individuals to compete against their previous examination performance, and enable some assessment of the effectiveness of teachers. However, there have been criticisms of the nature of the examination syllabuses and their relative lack of change since the inception of the examinations in the late nineteenth century (Salaman, 1994). Although students are motivated to increase levels of practice prior to impending examinations, they find graded examinations the most anxiety-provoking performance context because there is a concrete outcome, a mark (Hallam, 1997a). Teachers sometimes find themselves under pressure from parents and pupils to follow examination syllabuses rigidly, inhibiting what they teach and how they teach it. In the United States there are performance scales for some instruments (e.g. Watkins-Farnum Performance Scale) which require sight reading and performance of exercises of increasing difficulty. A range of measures using bipolar adjectives (Repp, 1990) and rating scales (McPherson, 1993) have also been developed to assess performance, but these have not developed the same status as graded examinations.

For high achievers, competitions can provide an important source of motivation. For some children, winning and taking part in them is important and stimulating (Howe and Sloboda, 1991). However, research on the effects of school bands entering competitions in the USA has shown no clear pattern of effects on attitudes towards music or student achievement. Most of the benefits of marching-band competitions as perceived by students, directors, parents and administrators are extra-musical (Humphreys *et al.*, 1992).

Reliability in assessing performance

Assessment of musical performance is inevitably subjective. As we saw in relation to composition, experts may be the least reliable judges. Elliott, D. (1987) investigated the perceptions and judgements of performance made by three professional musicians and six young performers. Comments made by the judges were categorised into five groups: context, technique, expressive features, structural features, and value judgements. Assessments of individual performances showed considerable variation, although some performances commanded more consensus than others, but in the area of technical skills – where one might have expected to find the most agreement – there was a large measure of disagreement, even between the three professional judges. Overall, this demonstrates the complexities of assessing performance and indicates how individual listeners may attend to and give different weight to diverse elements.

There is frequently disagreement between expert, peer and self-judgements (Fiske, 1975; Bergee, 1993). Judgements can be affected by expectations. Duerksen (1972) found that students rated the technical and musical characteristics of a recorded piano performance lower when told that the performer was a student rather than a famous pianist. J.W. Davidson and Coimbra (2001) found that alongside the possession of musical skills (control and flexibility of timbre, range and intonation), assessors of solo singers evaluated the performing personalities of those being assessed, based on physical appearance, non-verbal communication, artistry (emotional intention, commitment to interact with the audience) and attitude at the start of the performance. To be assessed as a 'good' performer, singers had to be 'public' in presentational style, but also to show something of their individuality and inner state.

Teachers and pupils focus on different aspects of performance. For teachers, a 'competent' instrumental performance is viewed in terms of technical proficiency; a 'good' performance requires technical security with attention to emotion, fluency and style; while at the 'exceptional' level, technique and accuracy are taken for granted, with greater emphasis on communication with the audience, expression of emotion, inspiration, style and fluency. While the teachers seemed to view technical competence as a prerequisite for all performances, their pupils rated technical perfection as only important or quite important, and as unimportant in relation to being able to play expressively (Prince, 1994).

Peer assessment

Peer assessment is becoming increasingly common in higher education (Hunter, D. and Russ, 1996; Hunter, D., 1999; Searby and Ewers, 1996). It enhances students' critical thinking skills, supporting the development of self-evaluation. Students are usually issued with guidelines and agreed criteria for assessment. Hunter, D. and Ross (1996) suggest that performance can be evaluated as to the extent it is convincing, technically assured, informed by a sense of style, communicates the music in a way that demonstrates an understanding of the performance, and displays individuality. Formative peer assessment is an extremely valuable teaching resource. It supports the development of self-assessment, develops critical thinking skills, enables students to think about the criteria used in assessing work, and through these processes improves attainment (Hallam *et al.*, 2004).

Assessing intellectual development

The assessment procedures outlined above focus on musical skills. In other domains, schemes have been developed which assess the quality of intellectual development (Perry, 1970; Biggs and Collis, 1982). These have been adapted for use in music (see Table 10.1). Level 5 is considered as a turning point. At this level, the musician becomes aware that there are many alternative ways of interpreting,

Table 10.1: *Quality of intellectual development*

Level	Phase of intellectual development
Level 1	There is a perception that there is a single correct way of playing, improvising or composing, which is determined by those in 'authority'.
Level 2	Other styles of playing, improvising or composing are observed but not considered legitimate.
Level 3	Other styles of playing, improvising or composing are observed and seen as legitimate but temporary in status.
Level 4	Other styles of playing, improvising and composing are perceived as acceptable but only within certain defined limits.
Level 5	All styles of playing, improvising and composing are accepted as legitimate and possible.
Level 6	There is a perceived need to develop a personal style in performing, improvising and composition.
Level 7	An initial commitment to a personal style is made perhaps by deliberate imitation of the work of individuals eminent in the field.
Level 8	The implications of personal commitment are experienced.
Level 9	A personal style of performance, improvising or composition is developed.

improvising and composing music, which are different but equally valid. After level 5, the musician gradually develops their own personal style. Adopting this approach, research with performing musicians ranging in age from 6 to 60, professional and novice, found varying levels of development. Some students aged 15 years had attained the highest level, whereas some of the professionals had only achieved level 7 (Hallam, 2001a, 2001b)

Implications for education

To optimise learning, aims, processes and assessment need to be aligned. To increase motivation, assessment needs to be seen by students as authentic – a real-life context. Within society there are many opportunities for performance in a range of widely differing settings, from playing in cafes, places of worship, schools and hospitals to large concert halls. Teachers can draw on these to provide opportunities best suited to the needs of particular groups of students. The essence of performance is communication between composer, performer and audience. A focus on this can reduce anxiety and enhance expressiveness and musicality. Where performance is appropriately contextualised, it can act to increase motivation; raise self-awareness, self-esteem and confidence; satisfy the internal needs of pupils; and raise standards of listening and musical awareness.

The process of learning requires constant, ongoing assessment. In the early stages of musical engagement, the feedback provided by the sounds themselves will need to be augmented by teacher feedback, but as students develop a wide range of aural schemata they will be more able to evaluate their own work. This process can be enhanced through encouraging peer assessment and using video recordings to provide learners with an audience perspective on their work. The value of this cannot be overstated. If musical engagement is to continue throughout the life span, the development of appropriate critical, evaluative skills is crucial.

Further Reading

Colwell, R. (2002) 'Assessment's potential in music education'. In R. Colwell and C. Richardson (eds) *The New Handbook of Research on Music Teaching and Learning.* Oxford: Oxford University Press (pp. 1128–1158).

Hallam, S. (1998a) *Instrumental Teaching: A practical guide to better teaching and learning.* Oxford: Heinemann.

11 Teachers and teaching

Teachers teach, learners learn. Teachers cannot learn for their students (Hallam and Ireson, 1999). Effective teaching can be assessed only in relation to its impact on student learning. Most research on effective teaching has not been directly related to student attainment, but focuses on student attitudes and time on task. The research on teaching in music is no exception.

How teachers conceptualise teaching and their beliefs about it can affect the way that they teach. At the simplest level, teaching can be viewed as either the transmission of knowledge or the facilitation of learning (Kember and Gow, 1994). A more complex formulation, emphasising the facilitation of learning rather than the transmission of knowledge, describes four dimensions: structuring learning, motivating learning, encouraging activity and independence, and establishing interpersonal relations conducive to teaching (Dunkin, 1990). Pratt (1992) developed five conceptions based on evidence from several hundreds of teachers: the engineering conception (transmission of knowledge, delivery of content, passive learners); the apprenticeship conception (the development of knowledge and ways of being); the developmental conception (facilitation of the development of intellect, autonomy and independence); the nurturing conception (facilitating learning in a caring environment); and the social reform concept (developing an ideal based on a particular set of beliefs). These are seen as decreasing in the degree of teacher domination from the engineering concept, which is strongly teacher dominated, through to the social reform concept, where the emphasis is on the individual. There is overlap between conceptions; they are not mutually exclusive. Much music teaching, as we shall see, is based on the transmission of knowledge.

Music teachers' philosophical orientations, whether articulated or not, influence their teaching practices (Swanwick, 1988; Jorgensen, E.R., 1990; Reimer, 1991, 1992), as do their beliefs about teaching. Beliefs are formed through training, experiences in school, and direct experiences with teachers (Andrews, 1991; Dolloff, 1999; Hennessy, 2000). In the actual practice of teaching, the methods adopted are constrained by the context (e.g. school, college, university), the nature of the subject, the assessment system, and the curriculum (Hallam and Ireson, 1999). Particular teaching strategies may be adopted for particular curricula activities. Evidence from all areas of music education indicates that much learning is teacher directed, with little emphasis on the facilitation of learning, although for musical creativity this is essential.

Music teaching effectiveness

Research on music teacher effectiveness has largely been based on classroom observations in the USA. Most does not directly consider learning outcomes (Duke, 1999/2000). In a review, Rosenshine *et al.* (2002) suggested six teaching functions: review, presentation of new material, guided practice, feedback and corrections, independent practice, and weekly and monthly reviews. Effective music teachers, teaching well-defined concepts and skills, begin the lesson with a short review of previous prerequisite material; present material in small steps; guide students during initial practice; give clear and detailed instructions and explanations; provide a high level of active practice for all students; give systematic feedback, corrections, instruction and practice during seatwork; monitor work; and continue practice until students are independent and confident. Such systematic instruction is perceived to be successful when the material to be taught is new and hierarchical. Sink (2002) further suggests that teachers must have knowledge of the subject matter, be able to model behaviour and techniques to pupils, and have mastery of verbal and non-verbal rehearsal, presentation and analytic skills. Each lesson should also have a clear single focus (Colprit, 2000).

Music teaching activity in the USA is often related to ensemble work, where more effective teachers allow more time for warm-up, spend a high percentage of time on performance, use non-verbal modelling extensively, get ensembles on task quickly, and focus comments so that talk is minimised (Goolsby, 1996). The sequential pattern consists of: presentation of the learning task, interactions between students and teacher-conductor through performance and verbal communication, and corrective feedback specific to the task in hand (Price, 1989, 1992; Yarborough and Price, 1989). Analysis of the instructional time of experienced teachers showed that they stopped more frequently, addressing several performance issues during a single stop; rehearsed short passages more often; designed questions to reinforce musically appropriate answers; spent more time on attaining high-level standards through demonstration and modelling and through verbal explanations as well as guided listening; focused on difficult sections; and spent more time on guided practice rather than verbal instructions (Goolsby, 1996, 1997, 1999). On-task behaviour is greater when students are engaged in playing (Forsythe, 1975, 1977; Madsen and Geringer, 1983), a high percentage of off-task behaviour occurring when teachers are preparing activities. Madsen and Madsen (1981) maintain that academic learning suffers when off-task behaviours in classrooms exceed 20 per cent. Frequent use of feedback leads to better performance and more positive attitudes towards learning (Hendel, 1995; Dunn, 1997).

Most music tuition is teacher directed. Even in individual instrumental tuition, the teacher usually dictates the curriculum and selects the repertoire – and how it is to be played, technically and musically (Hepler, 1986). Pupil activity in lessons is mainly playing, but much time is taken up with teacher talk (Tait, 1992; Kostka, 1984). This is almost exclusively uni-directional from teacher to student, although there is evidence that the ratio of teacher talk to student performance varies according to the lesson activity (Albrecht, 1991). Technique is often emphasised at the expense of musical considerations (Thompson, 1984), and questioning represents a small proportion of time (Hepler, 1986). In higher education, the apprenticeship model is perceived to underlie music teaching practice (Persson, 1994), but the evidence suggests that teachers may demand total compliance to suggestions and solutions that they offer, allowing students little opportunity to express their opinions and ideas. This can mean that students become dependent on their teachers. L'Hommidieu (1992), in case studies of three master teachers, attributed their success to student selection, a high level of subject expertise, intuitively effective management of the quality of instruction, and consistency in maintaining that quality.

Comparisons of the effectiveness of group as opposed to individual instrumental music-tuition instruction are inconclusive (Brandt, 1986). A combination of individual and group tuition may be best (Kennell, 2002). Class instruction offers advantages in the utilisation of time and money and may encourage competition, social development and ensemble performance, while individual tuition allows the teacher to focus in detail on every aspect of the individual student's performance (Brandt, 1986).

Providing models and examples
Having a clear internalised representation of what is to be learnt is important for effective learning to take place (Hallam, 1997a). Teacher modelling, vocal or instrumental, plays an important role in this. However, the evidence suggests that teachers spend little time modelling, despite its potential effectiveness (Dickey, 1991, 1992; Sang, 1987; Kostka, 1984; Gonzo and Forsythe, 1976; Rosenthal, 1984). Teachers can usefully model processes as well as the end-products of learning – for instance, how to identify difficulties in a piece of music, how to solve problems, how to set about learning a new piece of music, and how to develop improvisation or composition skills. Models can also be provided through videos

and recordings which students can use at home to support their learning. Model-supported practice – where beginning instrumentalists are provided with cassette tapes containing instructions, reminders, and model 'play along' performances of the music – are highly effective in developing pitch discrimination, pitch matching and rhythmic discrimination, and in enhancing time spent in practice (Zurcher, 1972). Other studies have supported the use of such aural models (Dickey, 1992; Kendall, 1990), although not all the evidence is positive (Anderson, 1981). Effectiveness seems to depend on how the tape is listened to, whether it is designed for playing with, and how easy it is to play with it. Videotape models are useful for assisting in the development of technical skills and improving the quality of performance (Linklater, 1997).

Supported skill learning

Learning to play an instrument requires the learning of aural, cognitive, technical, musical, communication and performing skills. Particularly in the early stages of learning, pupils need teachers to provide scaffolding in the development of these skills. The teacher provides the scaffold, and then gradually removes it as the learner is able to proceed unaided. Six different teacher stages in the process have been suggested (Wood *et al.*, 1976): recruitment (encourages the learner's interest and commitment to the task), reduction of degrees of freedom (reducing the level of complexity of the task to make it manageable), direction maintenance (keeping the student focused on the goal), marking critical features (highlighting details of the task), frustration control (reducing anxiety in the learner), and demonstration (teacher models the solution to a task). Observation of instrumental music lessons using these criteria found that the strategy most often adopted was the marking of critical features (Kennell, 1989, 1992). Demonstration and reducing degrees of freedom followed, with recruitment, direction maintenance and frustration control rarely used. Teachers marked critical features four times more often than they reduced degrees of freedom or offered demonstration. This confirms the view of the teacher as being directive mainly through the use of verbal statements. Four kinds of communication were identified in the critical features category (declarative, commands, questions, and non-verbal gestures). These assisted the teacher in identifying the student's level of understanding while also shaping their behaviour.

Intensity and pace of teaching

Teaching intensity is a global entity which involves sustained control of the teacher–student interaction, efficient accurate presentation of subject matter, enthusiasm and pacing (Madsen, 1990). Appropriate pace and intensity help to maintain pupil attention (Humphreys *et al.*, 1992). Both verbal and non-verbal behaviours contribute to teaching intensity (Yarborough and Price, 1989; Witt, 1986; Madsen *et al.*, 1989). Generally, students are more attentive when the pace and intensity of lessons are high (Seibenaler, 1997; Buckner, 1997). Some research has suggested that faster-paced, more familiar activities should be placed at the beginning and end of rehearsals, while slower-paced, less familiar and more difficult activities should be placed in the middle portion (Pascoe, 1973).

Experienced elementary teachers change behaviours quickly – including body movements, voice loudness, pitch, pace, type of activity, eye contact, gestures and facial expressions – and spend 91 per cent of instructional time in eye contact with individual students or the entire class. Proximity is varied by circling the perimeter of the class, moving to the centre, and approaching individual students or groups of students (Hendel, 1995). In musical conducting, teaching intensity magnitude is similarly determined by body movement, voice loudness, voice pitch, speed, activity, eye contact, gestures, and facial expression. Student performance itself is not affected by high or low magnitude behaviours, but their behaviour is. Increased student attention is attributable to high levels of group and individual eye contact, approving body movements, and approving feedback (Yarborough, 1975). Typically, conductors spend up to

80 per cent of their time in critical evaluation. Where efforts were made to increase approval to 80 per cent, there were significant gains in the quality of performance (Humphreys *et al.*, 1992). Praise rather than criticism engenders motivation and increased effort.

Use of praise

An important element in teaching is the use of praise. Music teachers are often critical in their teaching although praise is more effective in motivating pupils and improving achievement (Price, 1989; Carpenter, 1988). When positive reinforcement which is contingent on particular behaviours is used, achievement, attitudes and attention are improved (Forsythe, 1975, 1977; Madsen and Geringer, 1983; Wagner and Strul, 1979), inappropriate social behaviours are reduced (Madsen and Alley, 1979), and positive attitudes towards music are enhanced (Greer *et al.*, 1973). Students can achieve significantly more accurate intonation when contingent reinforcement is used (Madsen and Madsen, 1972), and positive feedback is most effective for encouraging students to follow classroom rules (Kuhn, 1975). Students can distinguish between praise which is deserved and directed to good performance and that which is used to provide encouragement and gain student co-operation (Taylor, 1997). Teachers need to be honest in their appraisals of performance for them to have meaningful impact.

Working in groups

Playing in chamber music groups is beneficial because it encourages listening skills, working together and independence, and has benefits for cognitive skills (Weerts, 1992). Peer teaching is extremely effective for those acting as teachers and learners (McKeachie *et al.*, 1986). Tutor and tutored benefit in academic terms. Tutors also show more positive attitudes towards school and enhanced self-concepts (Biggs and Moore, 1993). Teachers should not under-estimate the extent to which students can learn from each other.

Teaching composition

Music teachers are often ambivalent about teaching creative activities in the classroom (Davies, 1986; Odam, 2000; Kratus, 1989, 1994). They tend to adopt one of two approaches to teaching composition: an instructional approach, providing information and knowledge about music (Paynter, 1977; Ross, M., 1999); or a resourcing, facilitative approach (Ross, M., 1999; Ross, M. and Kamba, 1997). At primary level, Dogani (2004) found that, typically, creative music lessons were practical, participatory lessons in which musical conventions, understandings and skills were taught through an exercise in musical composition, an extra-musical theme providing the model for a structured arrangement of sound effects based on a narrative. Students worked in small groups, culminating in a shared class performance and reflection. Overall, lessons were firmly craft based and teacher-directed and dominated. Creativity was understood as a constructive act involving an element of children's choice and decision making to which the teacher deferred, while taking final responsibility for the production of an appropriate outcome. The compositions were rich in their use of instrumentation, musical texture, structure and elements, but in performance the emphasis was on demonstrating musical understanding of composing rather than their feelings. It was rare for teachers to allow pupils to approach musical creation in a meaningful way and to allow sufficient time for engagement and support rather than instruction.

The greatest benefits from composition seem to be derived when the teacher views music as an empowering agent rather than as knowledge or accomplishment (Hogg, 1994). This includes providing opportunities for students to compose, ensuring that every task has the potential for a musical outcome, keeping tasks simple, allowing students to work in friendship groups, keeping groups small, allowing exceptional students to work on their own, setting clear boundaries, reviewing progress regularly, learning to ask questions rather than provide answers, allowing time for ideas to be brought to fruition, not worrying if students go off-task, expecting that each group will perform but not insisting upon it, letting each new task emerge from the previous one, questioning the process if the product is unmusical, learning to trust the students, and reflecting on values and work practices. The emphasis on reflection seems particularly important (Van Ernst, 1993). Overall, these findings are consistent with those set out in Chapter 6 relating to the students' needs in undertaking composition tasks.

Technology and teaching

The use of digital media can facilitate musical expression and creativity without the need for students to have highly developed technical musical skills. Computer packages can be useful in teaching aural skills, general musicianship and history of music, and can support instrumental tuition. However, teachers do not always feel that they have appropriate skills to make use of new technologies (Austin, 1993) and in some cases using multi-media packages is no more effective than traditional methods.

Keyboard programmes and those used for implementing general musical curricula have been successfully adopted in middle and secondary schools (Chamberlin *et al.*, 1993; Nelson, 1991; Rogers, K., 1997; Busen-Smith, 1999). Positive findings in relation to attainment have been reported for the use of multi-media in relation to learning to read music and composition (Forest, 1995); understanding musical fundamentals in middle-school instrumental students (McCord, 1993); developing basic listening skills (Goodson, 1992); using computer-based song-writing to support ability to sight sing (Prasso, 1997); improving the identification of musical instruments (Lin, 1994); improving music appreciation (Placek, 1992); enhancing the identification of core repertoire in music (Hughes, 1991); the teaching of beginning saxophonists (Orman, 1998); and teaching student singers about voice anatomy (Ester, 1997). Positive attitudes to learning through technology have been found in relation to learning the basic aural and theoretical elements of jazz improvisation (Fern, 1996); using a game to help note identification in piano playing, although students avoided the more difficult levels (Simms, 1997); using the computer to learn basic historical and theoretical information about music being studied in violin lessons (Kim, 1996); and where they provided accompaniment support for instrumental playing (Tseng, 1996).

Comparisons made with traditional teaching methods have not consistently shown superiority for multi-media methods (Arms, 1997). Bush (2000) compared retention of factual information presented with hypermedia or by the teacher. Those working with the teacher did better. Parrish (1997) found no difference in learning music fundamentals between groups using software or receiving teacher-based tuition, although use of the software freed teacher time for less routine topics. Duitman (1993), using commercially available software to encourage exploration of musical master-works, found no advantage for the software over traditional lecturing; and, in a study of learning style and mode of instruction, Bauer (1994) found that students seemed better able to adapt their learning styles to their lecturers than to a software package. Fortney (1995) also found no difference in attainment between traditional and CD-ROM presentation of information relating to Stravinsky's *Rite of Spring*. Computer-assisted drill and practice on internal identification of sound and sight singing was less beneficial for weaker students than teacher instruction (Ozeas, 1992). Similarly, there were no differences in a study of the development of pitch accuracy between technology- and teacher-led instruction (Simpson, 1996). Seeing graphic representations of their tone did not help young clarinettists to improve (Malave, 1990), and music education majors learning a new instrument with technological support did no better than those receiving only traditional tuition (Sheldon *et al.*, 1999). Teachers using technology as an integral aspect of presentation in the classroom found it problematic, although their students enjoyed having access to the technology outside lesson time

(Repp, 1999). We can conclude from this brief overview that technology can be a useful element in the learning toolkit, but may best be used in addition to traditional teaching rather than as a substitute for it.

Teacher characteristics

Successful music teachers have considerable musical expertise (L'Hommidieu, 1992), in addition to leadership and control skills (Teachout, 1997). As pupils become more advanced, the teacher's level of expertise becomes more important (Davidson, J.W. *et al.*, 1998). Reviewing the extensive literature on the characteristics of successful music teachers, Pembrook and Craig (2002) identified three broad categories: internal qualities, relating to others, and social control/group management. Internal qualities included broad interests; confidence, security, strong ego strength and tough-mindedness; conscientiousness and responsibility; creativity and imagination; emotional stability; energy, enthusiasm and enthusiasm about music; being happy and optimistic; independence and self-sufficiency; neatness; not being compulsive; being restrained and reserved; and self-control and self-discipline. The category relating to others included being caring and empathetic; chatty; encouraging; extroverted; friendly, gregarious, and people oriented; gentle; humble; interested in students; relaxed; sober; trusting; having emotional sensitivity; and a sense of humour. The social control category related to issues of classroom management and included good group management; being authoritative, co-operative, dramatic, expressive, fair, flexible, patient, persistent, realistic and strong in relation to discipline; and exhibiting leadership skills, including being proactive. These attributes need to be utilised at different times in relation to different learning and discipline situations and with different groups of students.

Individual personality characteristics can affect teacher behaviour (Hepler, 1986). Field-dependent teachers spend more time interacting with their students than field-independent teachers. Pace, the amount of praise and criticism given, and the extent of demonstration also depend on personality characteristics (Schmidt, C.P., 1989a). Students with extroverted teachers tend to make more progress than those with introverted teachers (Donovan, 1994). Negative personality traits common in music teachers include high anxiety, hysteria and paranoia. These seem to be caused by the extremely high standards which music teachers set for themselves (Slack, 1977). Music teachers are amongst the most stressed, and are particularly susceptible to burnout (Wilder and Plutchik, 1982; Hodge *et al.*, 1994). Those affected are often the most productive, dedicated and committed (Hamann *et al.*, 1987). Stressors include inappropriate student behaviour and attitudes, heavy teaching loads and ensuing physical exhaustion, anxiety, unclear goals, paperwork, low salaries, lack of recognition, aspects of the teaching environment (interruptions, demands for high standards, out-of-date material, poor resources) and lack of variety in the teaching situation (Pembrook and Craig, 2002). A range of coping strategies have been suggested, including religion, reading, diet, sports, muscle-tension relaxation techniques, peer networks, and additional classroom management training (Brown, P.A., 1987; Hodge *et al.*, 1994).

Teacher–pupil relations

In instrumental tuition, pupil–teacher relationships are crucial in determining the level of musical expertise which the individual is able to attain (Howe and Sloboda, 1991; Sosniak, 1990; Manturzewska, 1990). The principles identified in one-to-one tuition apply in other teaching situations. The development of early motivation to engage with music requires teachers to be relatively uncritical, encouraging and enthusiastic. As students progress, the relationship with the teacher changes from one of liking and admiration to respect for their expertise. While at this point constructive criticism is valued, sarcasm or biting criticism does not engender good, positive working relationships and can demotivate pupils. Teacher–pupil relationships, particularly in instrumental lessons, are heavily influenced by the teacher's own life history, and in particular past relationships with their own teachers (Morgan, 1998). Student personality characteristics determine the way that teacher behaviours are perceived (Schmidt, C.P., 1989b; Schmidt, C.P. and Stephans, 1991). There may also be interpersonal dynamics operating in lessons between teachers and pupils of which teachers are not consciously aware (Gustafson, 1986). Defence mechanisms of projection and turning passive into active may be adopted by teachers to ward off unpleasant memories relating to their own experience as learners. Past problems of the teacher in relation to their own learning can be projected onto the pupil. Inevitably, some teacher–pupil matches will be better than others, but as professionals teachers should set minimum standards of behaviour which they apply consistently, whatever the circumstances.

Developing effective teaching

Music teachers as a group tend to adopt directive approaches in their teaching, dominating pupil–teacher discourse. While this promotes on-task behaviour and is effective in producing positive learning outcomes in many areas of musical development, it is not beneficial for promoting creativity or the ability of students to learn to learn. The creative process takes time and the learning environment provided needs to take account of this. Students need to be given opportunities to develop their ideas and reflect, question and constructively criticise as their work progresses. Teachers can help students to improve their learning skills by:

(i) modelling learning processes across a range of tasks;
(ii) discussing alternative strategies which may be available;
(iii) assisting students in evaluating their strengths and weaknesses;

(iv) supporting students in evaluating their work;
(v) getting students to explain things to each other and evaluate each other's work;
(vi) demonstrating;
(vii) allowing students to make mistakes;
(viii) developing students' problem-solving skills;
(ix) allowing students to learn unaided;
(x) promoting motivation through allowing choice;
(xi) routinely setting aside time for discussion and reflection on work in progress and completed work.

Teachers can assist in the development of support strategies by allowing opportunities to discuss issues relating to planning, goal setting, monitoring of work, time management, promoting concentration, managing motivation and ensuring that the working environment is optimal.

Further Reading

Hallam, S. (1998a) *Instrumental Teaching: A practical guide to better teaching and learning.* Oxford: Heinemann.
Rosenshine, B., Froehlich, H. and Fakhouri, I. (2002) 'Systematic instruction'. In R. Colwell and C. Richardson (eds) *The New Handbook of Research on Music Teaching and Learning.* Oxford: Oxford University Press (pp. 299–314).
Sink, P.E. (2002) 'Behavioural research on direct music instruction'. In R. Colwell and C. Richardson (eds) *The New Handbook of Research on Music Teaching and Learning.* Oxford: Oxford University Press (pp. 315–326).

12 The impact of music through life

In the developed world, music is in evidence in almost every aspect of our lives. We hear music in supermarkets, shopping precincts, restaurants, places of worship, schools, on the radio and television, and through the medium of recordings. Music also plays an important role in the theatre, television, films, video and advertising. Never before in the history of humanity have so many different kinds of music been so easily available to so many people. The development of electronic media in the latter part of the twentieth century revolutionised access to and use of music in our everyday lives. We can turn on the radio, play a CD or tape, or listen to music on video or television with very little effort. This has not always been the case. Prior to these developments, music was accessible for most people only if they made it themselves or attended particular religious or social events.

A reflection of the extent to which people engage with music in the developed world is the size of the music industry worldwide. In the USA and the UK music is amongst the top economic generators of income (Hodges and Haack, 1996; KPMG/National Music Council, 1999). In 2000, the Recording Industry Association of America reported sales of 942.5 million CDs, 76 million music cassettes, 18 million music videos, and 3 million DVDs. Worldwide there are thousands of radio stations dedicated to the playing of music, television programmes and advertisements regularly include music, and the internet has increased consumption further. In the USA, in 1989 the American Medical Association reported that the average high-school student heard over 30 hours of pop music a week, while 98.5 per cent of American teenagers claimed to listen to music in 1993 (Hodges and Haack, 1996). In the UK, teenagers typically report listening to music for three hours a day (North *et al.*, 2000a), in the region of 70 per cent reporting listening to music while studying (Kotsopoulou, 1997). Adolescents are not alone in listening to and enjoying music. A US survey of musical tastes indicated that 75 per cent of mature citizens listened to music for at least one hour every day (Cole, 1999). In the UK, recent figures suggest that in the order of 13.6 million people listen regularly to BBC Radio 1, 10 million to BBC Radio 2, 6.9 million to Classic FM, and 2 million to Radio 3. In addition there are over 300 commercial stations and almost 40 BBC local stations which spend a considerable amount of air time playing music.

Music in everyday life

Nowadays people can use music to manipulate personal moods, arousal and feelings, and to create environments which may manipulate the ways other people feel and behave. Individuals can and do use music as an aid to relaxation, to overcome powerful emotions, to generate the right mood for going to a party, to stimulate concentration – in short, to promote their well-being. It has become a tool to be used to enhance our self-presentation and promote our development (DeNora, 2000; Sloboda *et al.*, 2001; Sloboda and O'Neill, 2002). Music tends to be listened to while individuals are involved in leisure and maintenance activities – for example, housework and shopping – inducing positive mood change and increased arousal and attention. The effects are greater when participants exercise a high level of choice over the music that they hear. Many people listen to music while driving and value the privacy this offers (Oblad, 2000). It appears to improve driving concentration, particularly when it is moderately complex and played at a moderate volume (Turner *et al.*, 1996; Beh and Hirst, 1999). Music that is too stimulating distracts attention. In older people music assists in developing self-identity, connecting with others, maintaining well-being, and experiencing and expressing spirituality, providing ways for people to maintain positive self-esteem, feel competent and independent, and avoid feelings of isolation or loneliness (Hays and Minichiello, in press). In adolescence it is seen to be a source of support when young people are feeling troubled or lonely, acting as a mood regulator, and helping to maintain a sense of belonging and community (Zillman and Gan, 1997). However, music which we have not personally chosen to listen to can have a powerful negative effect on our emotions and subsequent behaviour. Depending on its level of intrusiveness, it may be merely irritating or create great distress. It can lead to complaints, legal proceedings and in some cases violence.

Effects of music in infancy

There is considerable evidence that the foetus can perceive and is stimulated by sounds that can then be recognised after birth (see Chapter 3). In one study, a group of mothers exposed their unborn babies to the sounds of the violin. After birth, the onset of behaviours from 0 to 6 months was charted. The exposed group were significantly more advanced in gross and fine motor activities, linguistic development, aspects of somato-sensory co-ordination and some cognitive behaviours (Lafuente *et al.*, 1997). Other studies indicate that musical stimulation can enhance development, encourage sucking and promote weight gain (Standley, 1998). When exposed to music, babies born prematurely or underweight gain weight, increase food intake and reduce their length of stay in hospital in comparison with controls, (Caine, 1991; Cassidy and Standley, 1995).

Research on the impact of music on children

In addition to its role in developing musical skills, many claims have been made regarding the benefits of music education in relation to a range of transferable skills. One strand of research has explored the effects of music on general intellectual skills. This has been extremely controversial. Research which claimed that listening to Mozart could improve spatial reasoning (Rauscher *et al.*, 1995) has proved difficult to replicate (Chabris, 1999; Hetland, 2000). Studies of the effects of using the Kodaly music teaching method on other skills have had mixed results (Hurwitz *et al.*, 1975), although music lessons designed to develop auditory, visual and motor skills have benefited reading skills (Douglas and Willatts, 1994). The evidence from studies examining the impact of learning to play a musical instrument on IQ is mixed. Some studies have shown positive results (Gardiner *et al.*, 1996; Hetland, 2000), while others have found transitory improvement which was not sustained over time (Costa-Giomi, 1999). Schellenberg (2004) randomly assigned a large sample of children to four different groups, two of which received music lessons (standard keyboard, Kodaly voice) for a year. The other two were control groups that received instruction in a non-musical artistic activity (drama) or no lessons. All four groups exhibited increases in IQ, as would be expected over the time period, but the music groups had reliably larger increases in full-scale IQ with an effect size of 0.35. Children in the control groups had average increases of 4.3 points, while the music groups had increases of 7 points. On all but 2 of the 12 subtests, the music group had larger increases than control groups. In a similar study, considering attainment rather than IQ, Gardiner *et al.* (1996) compared two classes of first-grade children receiving a 'test' arts programme that included Kodaly instruction in vocal music, with two other classes receiving standard arts programmes. After seven months the experimental group performed better on tests of reading and arithmetic.

Studies exploring the effects of increasing the amount of classroom music within the curriculum have found that children receiving extra music lessons kept up with their peers in language and reading skills despite having fewer lessons, although there were differences between high- and low-ability groups (Spychiger, *et al.*, 1993; Zulauf, 1993). The children receiving the additional classroom music lessons showed increased social cohesion within class, greater self-reliance, better social adjustment, and more positive attitudes. These effects were particularly marked in low-ability, disaffected pupils (Spychiger *et al.*, 1993; Hanshumaker, 1980). Further indications of the potential of music for supporting social cohesion come from a project using music to reduce anti-dark-skinned stereotyping among light-skinned Portuguese children. Positive outcomes were seen for children aged 9–10 but not 7–8 (Sousa *et al.*, 2005). Active engagement with music can also increase self-esteem compared with controls in children of low economic status (Costa-Giomi, 1999) and increase social inclusion (Ings *et al.*, 2000). Harland *et al.* (2000) showed that the most frequent overall influences on pupils derived from engagement with the arts were related to personal and social development. In music there were perceived effects relating to awareness of others, social skills, well-being and transfer effects. Variations in response between schools related to the degree of musical knowledge and experience that the pupils brought to the school curriculum. Some students perceived the benefits of music classes as being listening to music and the development of musical skills, while others referred to the sheer fun and therapeutic nature of music, how it gave them confidence to perform in front of others, how it facilitated group work and how it enabled them to learn to express themselves. Those who played instruments mentioned an increase in self-esteem and sense of identity.

Instrumental teachers believe that the benefits of learning to play an instrument include the development of social skills; gaining love and enjoyment of music; developing team work; developing a sense of achievement, confidence and self-discipline; and developing physical co-ordination (Hallam and Prince, 2000). Other major national reports on the arts have emphasised their importance in developing a range of transferable skills, including those related to creativity and critical thinking (NACCCE, 1999). Playing an instrument also enables the pursuit of interesting and rewarding social and leisure activities. Given the importance and range of these benefits, it is important that as many children as possible are provided with the opportunity to engage actively with music making at an early age.

Adolescence

In adolescence music makes a major contribution to the development of self-identity. Teenagers listen to a great deal of music (Hodges and Haack, 1996) – in the UK, typically almost three hours a day (North et al., 2000). They do this to pass time, alleviate boredom, relieve tension, and distract themselves from worries (North et al., 2000a; Zillman and Gan, 1997). Sometimes they use music as a wedge to drive between themselves and their parents (Tolfree, in press). Its effect on moods at this time can be profound (Goldstein, 1980). It is also used in relation to impression management needs. By engaging in social comparisons, adolescents are able to portray their own peer groups more positively than other groups in their network and are thus able to sustain positive self-evaluations. Music facilitates this process (Tarrant et al., 2000).

Much homework is undertaken accompanied by music or by the television playing (Patton et al., 1983; Kotsopoulou, 1997; Hallam, 2004a). What is not clear is the effect this may have on concentration and the quality of the work produced. The evidence to date suggests that the relationships are complex (see Hallam, 2000). Early research on the effects of music on studying began when radio became commonplace in the home. Much was unsystematic. Models have now been developed which enable the effects to be better understood (Hallam, 2000). Generally, studying is enhanced by the playing of calming, relaxing music, although the negative effects of loud, stimulating music can be mediated by the adoption of particular strategies on the part of the listener. In young children and those with emotional and behavioural difficulties, there are clear effects of music on task performance (Hallam and Price, 1998; Hallam and Godwin, 2000; Hallam et al., 2002b; Savan, 1999). Factors that we know may be important mediators of the effects include personality

(Furnham and Bradley, 1997) and the nature of the particular task to be undertaken (Bryan *et al.*, 1998; Salame and Baddeley, 1989; Kotsopoulou and Hallam, 2004). Tasks involving rote memorisation tend to be particularly disrupted. While more research needs to be undertaken, it is clear that young people are increasingly using music as a tool to assist them in achieving their studying goals.

Active participation in music making in adulthood

People not only listen to music; they actively take part in making it. For instance, in 1993 in the USA, 62 million people said that they sang or played a musical instrument. In the UK, millions of people sing or play instruments for the love of it (Everitt, 1997). In 1999, 49 per cent of children reported taking instrumental music lessons, while approximately half of the children who played had a friend or family member who was also actively engaged in music making. Estimates of the percentage of adults playing an instrument have varied between 24 and 30 per cent. (ABRSM, 2000). Music is also important in developing cultures. Werner (1984) described the way that the Mekranoti Indians, primarily hunter gatherers living in the Amazon rain forest in Brazil, spent up to two hours each day making music, the women singing for one to two hours in the morning and evening, the men singing very early each day (e.g. at 4.30 a.m.), typically for two hours, and also often for half an hour or so before sunset. While some of this activity was related to the need for vigilance in case of attack, active music making appears to be intrinsically rewarding.

In the Western world the reasons for adults' participation in music have been grouped into three categories: personal motivations (self-expression, recreation, self-improvement, and use of leisure time), musical motivations (love of music, performing for oneself and others, learning more about music), and social motivations (meeting new people, being with friends, and having a sense of belonging). No single reason consistently emerges as the most important (Coffman,

2002). Hinkle (1988) suggests a further category: spirituality. Several studies have concluded that adult participation is an extension of engagement with active music making in childhood in the home or at school (Belz, 1995; Holmquist, 1995; Chiodo, 1998; Conda, 1997). The pattern of engagement seems to change over the life course, diminishing in the middle years and increasing in retirement (Larson, 1983), life-changing events sometimes providing an impetus for re-engagement (Conda, 1997). Different levels of participation have been identified: participants, spectators and those not involved. People appear to be socialised into one of these groups and few change group over their lifetime. Participants can be dabblers, recreationists, hobbyists, amateurs, apprentices or professionals (Gates, 1991). Community music ensembles largely consist of amateurs, apprentices and professionals – people who are validated by performance.

The possible benefits of adult participation in music, in a professional or amateur capacity, are many and varied. Choral singing seems to have positive emotional, social, physical and creative outcomes (Beck *et al.*, 2000) which may also be spiritual (Clift and Hancox, 2001). Bailey and Davidson (2002, 2003, in press) researching members of choirs for homeless men and middle-class participants, found that group singing and performance, even at low levels of musicality, yielded considerable emotional, social and cognitive benefits to participants. The emotional effects were similar regardless of training or socio-economic status, but interpersonal and cognitive components had different meanings for marginalised and middle-class singers. The marginalised individuals appeared to embrace all aspects of the group singing experience, while the middle-class choristers were inhibited by prevalent social expecta-tions of musicianship. Irish (1993) also found commonality in meaning constructions of participation in adults with similar education patterns. Social and musical components appear to contribute equally to commitment to and enjoyment of membership of amateur operatic societies, the musical and acting components providing challenge, achievement and opportunity to escape temporarily the frustrations of everyday living (Pitts, 2004).

Music ensembles can provide senior citizens with a venue to make friends, and intergenerational music activities between children, teenagers and senior citizens have particular social value (Bowers, 1998; Darrow *et al.*, 1994; Leitner, 1982). Music, through community education programmes, can also help adults move toward socio-political transformation (Kaltoft, 1990). Engaging with music has a range of positive personal and social outcomes that do not seem to diminish with age. Although older adults require more time to encode and select information (Cavanaugh, 1997) and have slower reaction times (Bee, 1996), these can be minimised through task familiarity, sufficient structuring of information and regular exercise (Cavanaugh, 1997). Primary mental abilities decline with age, but higher order mental activities do not; adults may maintain or even increase mental abilities in areas of expertise including music (Pieters, 1996).

There are direct health benefits for musical participation. Choral performance increases secretory immunoglobulin A and reduces cortisol levels of professional (Beck *et al.*, 2000) and amateur choristers (Kreutz *et al.*, in press) before and after singing. Active group singing enhances the immune system. Playing the piano exercises the heart as much as a brisk walk (Parr, 1985) and there are lower mortality rates in those who attend cultural events, read books or periodicals, make music, or sing in a choir (Bygren *et al.*, 1996). Music making contributes to perceived good health, quality of life and mental well-being (Coffman and Adamek, 1999; Vanderark *et al.*, 1983; Wise *et al.*, 1992; Kahn, 1998).

In the USA a number of curricula have been developed for elderly adults (see Coffman, 2002, for a review). These have been successful in that participants have enjoyed them and musical skills have improved. However, there has been little consideration of learning and teaching per se. Where adults attend classes they often defer to the teacher's expertise and rely on teacher evaluation. Self-esteem does not automatically improve with increasing musical attainment (Alperson, 1995; Chen, 1996), although Rybak (1996) found evidence of clear goals, concentration and absence of self-consciousness in groups with intermediate to advanced skills. It may be that absolute levels of expertise are important in determining learner autonomy. In self-created chamber music groups, with high levels of expertise, there is emphasis on fun and conversation and it is rehearsal rather than performance that is pleasurable (Blank and Davidson, 2003). Familiar works are played to provide rewarding experiences, in addition to time being spent on new and difficult works. For such amateur groups the social is as important as the musical (Booth, 1999).

Music for all

Music can enhance the quality of the lives of those who have aural impairments or learning difficulties. Approximately 14 per cent of the population has some significant hearing impairment. This figure rises to about 25 per cent among older people. New technological developments have made it possible for most hearing-impaired people to access music. Technology is now available which enables deaf people to play electronic keyboards, and a range of multi-media techniques using colour and vibration have been developed to help deaf people appreciate music (see Hallam, 1998a). There are choirs where songs are performed through hand signing. Ways of signing which signify musical notes have also been developed.

Music therapy can help children with learning difficulties to focus their attention, to increase their concentration span and, over time, to improve vocalisations, looking behaviour, imitation, and initiation of ideas (Bunt, 1994). Music therapy is often used to develop communication skills (Braithwaite *et al.*, 1998) and can enhance personal relationships (Aldridge *et al.*, 1995). Improvised musical play using music and lyrics has been used to facilitate social play between developmentally delayed and non-developmentally delayed children in mainstream settings (Gunsberg, 1988, 1991), and there is a substantial body of research showing that music can be effective with children with learning difficulties when it is offered as a reward for particular behaviours (Bunt, 1997). Using sound beams, it is now possible for children and adults with severe and profound learning difficulties to take part in active music making (Ellis, 1995).

There is indication from various sources that music making may help dyslexics (Thomson, 1993; Overy, 2000). The concentration of children with emotional and behavioural difficulties can be improved with background music (Hallam and Price, 1998; Savan, 1999), active and passive music therapy can reduce reported aggression (Montello and Coons, 1998), and music can be used in play therapy (Carmichael and Atchinson, 1997). Improvisational music therapy can lead to substantial improvements in the communicative behaviours of autistic children (Edgerton, 1994), learning words to music can assist with language skills (Buday, 1995), and music therapy can play a role in the assessment and differential diagnosis of autism (Wigram, 1995).

Background music has been effective in improving work-oriented behaviour in adults with developmental handicaps (Groeneweg *et al.*, 1988), reducing the extent of teeth grinding (Caron *et al.*, 1986) and reducing some aspects of self-injurious behaviour (Ford, 1999). Participating in gamelan workshops has improved musical ability, self-confidence and attention in adults with learning difficulties (MacDonald *et al.*, 1999a; 1999b; O'Donnell *et al.*, 1999) and impacted on participants' identity and perceived position within society (MacDonald and Miell, 2002).

Music and medicine

The value of music in medicine is increasingly being recognised. Music is used for preventative work (Messmer and Jones, 1998; Stephens et al., 1998; Fukado, 2000), and to reduce anxiety, for instance, in waiting areas before surgery (Winter *et al.*, 1994; Robb *et al.*, 1995) and calming patients after they have been given details of their operations (Miluk-Kolasa et al., 1994). It has proved very effective in maintaining the motivation, psychological well-being, physical comfort and exercise endurance of bone-marrow transplant patients (Boldt, S., 1996); and anxiety has been reduced in patients who have had heart attacks (White, 1992), those receiving chemotherapy (Sabo and Michael, 1996), patients with tumours (Johnston and Rohaly-Davis, 1996) and those undergoing treatment for addiction (Hammer, 1996). It is effective in promoting muscle relaxation (Robb, 2000; Strauser, 1997) and has proved useful in assisting in the reduction of anxiety in children (Edwards, 1999; Klein and Winkelstein, 1996) and across a range of patients in dentistry (Standley, 1986, 1991). A number of hospitals have instigated arts projects with which to promote the more speedy recovery of patients.

Music can assist in pain reduction in medicine and dentistry (Standley, 1986), and recent research suggests a role relating to the immune system. Although this is a relatively new field of study and the findings need to be interpreted with caution, most but not all are positive (Rider, 1987; Bartlett *et al.*, 1993). Listening to music seems to be able to elicit changes in biochemicals such as endorphins, cortisol, ACTH (adrenocorticotropic hormone), interleukin-1 and secretory immunoglobin A (Maranto and Scartelli, 1992; Scartelli, 1992; McCraty *et al.*, 1996). The effects may be stronger when the music is live, improvised and paired with an imagery technique (Rider and Weldin, 1990), but positive effects have been found using Muzak (Charnetski and Brennan, 1998).

As people live longer there is a greater need for developing ways of caring for the elderly. Music can be useful in ameliorating some of the effects of Alzheimer's disease (Koger *et al.*, 1999; Brotons *et al.*, 1997). It can improve social behaviours (Pollack and Namazi, 1992) and vocalising, reduce restlessness during meals, reduce agitated behaviour, and improve reality orientation (Clair and Bernstein,

1990; Smith-Marchese, 1994) and face recognition (Carruth, 1997). Autobiographical and general memory can be stimulated through music – for instance, using familiar songs from the past (Foster and Valentine, 1998). Music can also have a positive effect on carers of the elderly. This has been explored specifically in relation to music therapy that included dance (Clair and Ebberts, 1997). Music, paired with relaxation techniques, has also been used to alleviate depression in elderly patients living at home (Hanser, 1990; Hanser and Thompson, 1994).

Music has been used to ameliorate symptoms in psychiatric hospitals (Harris *et al.*, 1992), and reduce lunch-time violence (Hunter and Love, 1996). Some of the negative effects of schizophrenia have been alleviated by music therapy (Chambliss *et al.*, 1996; John, 1995), and children with psychotic symptoms have benefited from music playing in the background when they were engaged in learning (Burleson *et al.*, 1989).

Music, commerce, advertising and work

Music has always played a major part in work activities and continues to do so. It has been used to co-ordinate movement, alleviate boredom, develop team spirit and speed up the pace of work. Nowadays, singing to accompany work is much less common in the developed world, but recorded music is played extensively in workplaces, shops, airports, restaurants and hotels. The commercial and industrial uses of music constitute major industries (Bruner, 1990). One of the largest providers of recorded music for consumption in public places is Muzak. In 1994 they claimed to be serving 80 million people. Research undertaken by Muzak suggests that when music is playing workers perform better, with improved attitudes and communication, increased efficiency and concentration, and a reduction in errors. There is some recent independent evidence to support this (North and MacKenzie, 2000). Subjective reports of working with music playing are generally positive

(Wentworth, 1991; Newman *et al.*, 1966; North *et al.*, 2000b; Lesuik 2005).

Our shopping, eating and drinking habits can be manipulated through music. It affects speed of consumption and the kinds of behaviour exhibited in cafes (Milliman, 1982, 1986; McElrea and Standing, 1982; North and Hargreaves, 1998; North *et al.*, 1999). The type of music playing can influence what is bought in super-markets – for example, German or French wine (North *et al.*, 1999) – and music perceived as attractive by particular groups may encourage them to approach particular commercial environments (North and Hargreaves, 1996). The type of music played when we are put on hold on the telephone influences waiting time, callers being more likely to hold if they like the music (Ramos, 1993; North *et al.*, 1999). In advertising, music is used to encourage consumers to buy particular products. It is perceived to enhance the attitudes of potential customers if it fits with or conforms to their conception of the nature of the product – for instance, exciting classical music in an advert for an expensive sports car. Effects may be mediated by the familiarity of the music, how much it is liked and prior mood. If the music is liked, it is anticipated that this positive response will be associated with the product (Bruner, 1990; Gorn, 1982). Whatever the underlying principles, there is no doubt that music is effective in enhancing the appeal of products (Groenland and Schoormans, 1994). It is also very successful in promoting memory for them. One study demonstrated that 99 per cent of the participants successfully recognised the music to selected brand-name commercials (Hodges and Haack, 1996).

Music in education

Music has benefits throughout our lives, literally from birth to death. All kinds of music are available to most people 24 hours a day. It pervades our everyday lives and influences our behaviour. The downside of the easy availability of music in the developed world is that there is a tendency for it to be taken for granted. Educators frequently are called upon to justify the place of music in the curriculum and often have to battle for sufficient time allocation for appropriate engagement with music to take place. The demand for music is likely to continue to increase in the future, with the music industries requiring a musically skilled workforce to sustain development. To fulfil this need, a time investment is required in early years and primary music education to ensure opportunities are available for all children to develop general musical skills for a richer and fuller life, and for some to take these forward and develop the high levels of skill needed to pursue a range of careers in the music industry.

Further Reading

Hallam, S. (2001d) *The Power of Music*. London: Performing Right Society. *www.thepowerofmusic.co.uk*.

References

Abel, J.L. and Larkin, K.T. (1990) 'Anticipation of performance among musicians: physiological arousal, confidence and state-anxiety'. *Psychology of Music*, 18(2) (pp. 171–182).

Abeles, H.F. and Chung, J.W. (1996) 'Responses to music'. In D.A. Hodges (ed.) *Handbook of Music Psychology*. San Antonio, TX: IMR Press.

Abeles, H.F. and Porter, S.Y. (1978) 'The sex-stereotyping of musical instruments'. *Journal of Research in Music Education*, 26(2) (pp. 65–75).

ABRSM (2000) *Making Music 2000*. London: Associated Board of the Royal Schools of Music.

Adams, J.A. (1987) 'Historical review and appraisal of research on the learning, retention and transfer of human motor skills'. *Psychological Bulletin*, 101(1) (pp. 41–74).

Adler, T. (1980) 'The acquisition of a traditional competence: folk-musical and folk-cultural learning among bluegrass banjo players'. Doctoral dissertation, Indiana University, *Dissertation Abstracts International*, 41(3) (1165A).

Aiello, R. and Sloboda, J.A. (eds) (1994) *Musical Perceptions*. Oxford and New York: Oxford University Press.

Aiello, R., Tanaka, J. and Winborne, W. (1990) 'Listening to Mozart: perceptual differences among musicians'. *Journal of Music Theory Pedagogy*, 4(2) (pp. 269–293).

Albrecht, K. (1991) Reported in C.P. Schmidt, 'Systematic research in applied music instruction: a review of the literature'. *The Quarterly Journal of Music Teaching and Learning*, 3(2) (pp. 32–45).

Aldridge, D., Gustroff, G. and Neugebauer, L. (1995) 'A pilot study of music therapy in the treatment of children with developmental delay'. *Complementary Therapeutic Medicine*, 3(4) (pp. 197–205).

Allen, B.A. and Boykin, A.W. (1992) 'African American children and the educational process: alleviating cultural discontinuity through prescriptive pedagogy'. *School Psychology Review*, 21 (pp. 586–596).

Alperson, R. (1995) 'A qualitative study of Dalcroze Eurhythmics classes for adults'. *Dissertation Abstracts International*, 56(10) (3875A) (University Microfilms No. AAT96–03274).

Altenmuller, E.O. (1989) 'Cortical DC-potentials as electrophysiological correlates of hemisphere dominance of higher cognitive functions'. *International Journal of Neuroscience*, 47 (pp. 1–14).

Altenmuller, E.O. (2003) 'How many music centres are in the brain?' In I. Peretz and R.J.A. Zatorre (eds) *The Cognitive Neuroscience of Music*. Oxford: Oxford University Press (pp. 346–356).

Altenmuller, E.O., Gruhn, W., Parlitz, D. *et al.* (1997) 'Music learning produces changes in brain activation patterns: a longitudinal DC-EEG-study unit'. *International Journal of Arts Medicine*, 5 (pp. 28–34).

Amabile, T.M. (1996) *Creativity in Context*. Boulder, CO: Westview Press.

Amchin, R.A. (1996) 'Creative musical response: the effects of teacher–student interaction on the improvisation abilities of fourth and fifth grade students'. Doctoral dissertation, University of Michigan, 1995. *Dissertation Abstracts International*, 56(8) (3044A).

Ames, C. and Archer, J. (1988) 'Achievement goals in the classroom: students' learning strategies and motivational processes'. *Journal of Educational Psychology*, 80 (pp. 260–267).

Amunts, K., Schlaug, G., Jaencke, L. *et al.* (1997) 'Motor cortex and hand motor skills: structural compliance in the human brain'. *Human Brain Mapping*, 5 (pp. 206–215).

Anderson, J.N. (1981) 'Effects of tape recorded aural models on sight-reading and performance skills'. *Journal of Research in Music Education*, 29(1) (pp. 23–30).

Andrews, B.W. (1991) 'Re-shaping music teacher education for the 1990s'. *The Recorder*, 33(4) (pp. 129–132).

Anon. (1997) 'Neanderthal notes: did ancient humans play modern scales?' *Scientific American*, 277 (pp. 28–30).

Anshel, M.H. and Marisi, D.Q. (1978) 'Effect of music and rhythm on physical performance'. *Research Quarterly*, 49(2) (pp. 109–113).

Appel, S.S. (1976) 'Modifying solo performance anxiety in adult pianists'. *Journal of Music Therapy*, 13 (pp. 2–16).

Arikan, M.K., Devrim, M., Oran, O. *et al.* (1999) 'Music effects on event-related potentials of humans on the basis of cultural environment'. *Neuroscience Letters*, 268 (pp. 21–24).

Arms, L. (1997) The effects of computer-assisted keyboard instruction on meter discrimination and rhythm discrimination of general music education students in the elementary school. Unpublished doctoral dissertation, Tennessee State University, Memphis.

Asmus, E.P. (1994) 'Motivation in music teaching and learning'. *The Quarterly Journal of Music Teaching and Learning*, 5(4) (pp. 5–32).

Atik, Y. (1994) 'The conductor and the orchestra: interactive aspects of the leadership process'. *Leadership and Organisation Development Journal*, 13 (pp. 22–28).

Atkinson, J. (1964) *An Introduction to Motivation*. New York: D. Van Nostrand.

Austin, J.R. (1991) 'Competitive and non-competitive goal structures: an analysis of motivation and achievement among elementary band students'. *Psychology of Music*, 19(2) (pp. 142–158).

Austin, J.R. (1993) 'Technocentrism and technophobia: finding a middle ground for music educators in the next millennium'. In D. Sebald (ed.) *Technological Directions in Music Education*. San Antonio, TX: IMR Press (pp. 1–10).

Austin, J.R. and Berg, M.H. (in press) 'Exploring music practice among 6th grade band and orchestra students'. *Psychology of Music*.

Avanzini, G., Faienza, C., Minciacchi, D., Lopez, L. and Majno, M. (eds) (2003) *The Neurosciences and Music*. New York: New York Academy of Sciences.

Azzara, C.D. (1992) 'The effect of audiation-based improvisation techniques on the music achievement of elementary instrumental music students'. Doctoral dissertation, Eastman School of Music, University of Rochester. *Dissertation Abstracts International*, 53(4) (1088A).

Azzara, C.D. (1999) 'An aural approach to improvisation'. *Music Educators Journal*, 86(3) (pp. 21–25).

Azzara, C.D. (2002) 'Improvisation'. In R. Colwell and C. Richardson (eds) *The New Handbook of Research on Music Teaching and Learning*. Oxford: Oxford University Press (pp. 171–187).

Bachem, A. (1937) 'Various types of absolute pitch'. *Journal of the Acoustical Society of America*, 9 (pp. 146–151).

Bachem, A. (1940) 'The genesis of absolute pitch'. *Journal of the Acoustical Society of America*, 11 (pp. 434–439).

Bacher, L.F. and Robertson, S.S. (2001) 'Stability of coupled fluctuations in movement and visual attention in infants'. *Developmental Psychobiology*, 39 (pp. 99–106).

Bachman, M.-L. (1991) *Dalcroze Today: An education through and into music*. Oxford: Oxford University Press.

Baharaloo, S., Johnston, P.A., Service, S.K., Gitschier, J. and Freimer, N.B. (1998) 'Absolute pitch: an approach for identification of genetic and nongenetic components'. *American Journal of Human Genetics*, 62 (pp. 224–231).

Baharaloo, S., Service, S.K., Risch, N., Gitschier, J. and Freimer, N.B. (2000) 'Familial aggregation of absolute pitch'. *American Journal of Human Genetics*, 67 (pp. 755–758).

Bahr, N., Christensen, C.A. and Bahr, M. (2005) 'Diversity of accuracy profiles for absolute pitch recognition'. *Psychology of Music*, 33(1) (pp. 58–93).

Bailey, B.A. and Davidson, J.W. (2002) 'Adaptive characteristics of group singing: perceptions from members of a choir for homeless men'. *Musicae Scientiae*, 6(2) (pp. 221–256).

Bailey, B.A. and Davidson, J.W. (2003) 'Amateur group singing as a therapeutic instrument'. *Nordic Journal of Music Therapy*, 12(1) (pp. 18–32).

Bailey, B.A. and Davidson, J.W. (in press) 'Effects of group singing and performance for marginalized and middle class singers'. *Psychology of Music*.

Bamberger, J. (1977) 'In search of a tune'. In D. Perkins and B. Leondar (eds) *The Arts and Cognition*, Baltimore, MD: Johns Hopkins University Press (pp. 284–389).

Bamberger, J. (1982) 'Revisiting children's drawings of simple rhythms: a function for reflection-in-action'. In S. Strauss and R. Stavy (eds) *U-shaped Behavioural Growth*. New York: Academic Press (pp. 191–226).

Bamberger, J. (1986) 'Cognitive issues in the development of musically gifted children'. In R. Sternberg and J.W. Davidson (eds) *Conceptions of Giftedness*. Cambridge: Cambridge University Press (pp. 388–413).

Bamberger, J. (1991) *The Mind behind the Musical Ear: How children develop musical intelligence*. Harvard: Harvard University Press.

Bamberger, J. (1994) 'Coming to hear in a new way'. In R. Aiello and J.A. Sloboda (eds) *Musical Perceptions*. Oxford and New York: Oxford University Press (pp. 131–151).

Bandura, A. (1977) 'Self-efficacy: toward a unifying theory of behavioural change'. *Psychological Review*, 84 (pp. 191–215).

Bandura, A. (1989) 'Self-regulation of motivation and action through internal standards and goal systems'. In L.A. Pervin (ed.) *Goal Concepts in Personality and Social Psychology*. Hillsdale, NJ: Laurence Erlbaum Associates (pp. 19–86).

Bangs, R.L. (1992) An application of Amabile's model of creativity to music instruction: a comparison of motivational strategies. Unpublished doctoral dissertation, University of Miami, Coral Gables, Florida.

Banton, L. (1995) 'The role of visual and auditory feedback during the sightreading of music'. *Psychology of Music*, 23(1) (pp. 3–16).

Barrett, M.S. (1997) 'Invented notations: a view of young children's musical thinking'. *Research Studies in Music Education*, 8 (pp. 2–14).

Barrett, M.S. (1999) 'Modal dissonance: an analysis of children's invented notations of known songs, original songs, and instrumental compositions'. *Bulletin of the Council for Research in Music Education*, 141 (pp. 14–22).

Barrett, M.S. (2000) 'Windows, mirrors and reflections: a case study of adult constructions of children's musical thinking'. *Bulletin of the Council for Research in Music Education*, 145 (pp. 43–61).

Barrett, M.S. (2001) 'Constructing a view of children's meaning making as notators: a case study of a five-year old's descriptions and explanations of invented notations'. *Research Studies in Music Education*, 16 (pp. 33–45).

Barrett, M.S. (2003) 'Invented notations and mediated memory: a case-study of two children's use of invented notations'. *Bulletin of the Council for Research in Music Education*, 153/154 (pp. 55–62).

Barrow, J.D. (1995) *The Artful Universe*. Oxford: Clarendon Press..

Barry, N.H. (1992) 'The effects of practice strategies, individual differences in cognitive style, and gender upon technical accuracy and musicality of student instrumental performance'. *Psychology of Music*, 20 (pp. 112–123).

Barry, N.H. and Hallam, S. (2002) 'Practising'. In R. Parncutt and G.E. McPherson (eds) *The Science and Psychology of Music Performance: Creative strategies for teaching and learning*. Oxford: Oxford University Press (pp. 151–166).

Barry, N.H. and McArthur, V. (1994) 'Teaching practice strategies in the music studio: a survey of applied music teachers'. *Psychology of Music*, 22 (pp. 44–55).

Bartel, L.R. and Thompson, E.G. (1994) 'Coping with performance stress: a study of professional orchestral musicians in Canada'. *The Quarterly Journal of Music Teaching and Learning*, 5(4) (pp. 70–78).

Bartlett, D.L. (1996) 'Physiological responses to music and sound stimuli'. In D.A. Hodges (ed.) *Handbook of Music Psychology*. San Antonio, TX: IMR Press (pp. 343–386).

Bartlett, D.L., Kaufman, D. and Smeltekop, R. (1993) 'The effects of music listening and perceived sensory experiences on the immune system as measured by Interleukin-1 and Cortisol'. *Journal of Music Therapy*, 30(4) (pp. 194–209).

Baruch, C. and Drake, C. (1997) 'Tempo discrimination in infants'. *Infant Behavioral Development*, 20 (pp. 573–577).

Bash, L. (1984) 'The effectiveness of three instructional methods on the acquisition of jazz improvisation skills'. Doctoral dissertation, State University of New York at Buffalo. *Dissertation Abstracts International*, 44(7) (2079A).

Basmajian, J.V. and Newton, W.J. (1974) 'Feedback training of parts of buccinator muscle in man'. *Psychophysiology*, 11(1) (p. 92).

Basmajian, J.V. and White, E.R. (1973) 'Neuromuscular control of trumpeters' lips'. *Nature*, 241 (p. 70).

Bastian, H.G. (1989) *Leben fur Musik. Eine Biographie-Studie uber usikalische (Hoch)- Begabungen*. Mainz, Germany: Schott.

Bauer, W. (1994) The relationships among elements of learning style, mode of instruction, and achievement of college music appreciation students. Unpublished doctoral dissertation, Kent State University, Kent, Ohio.

Beck, R., Cesario, T., Yousefi, S. and Enamoto, H. (2000) 'Choral singing, performance perception and immune system changes in salivary immunoglobulin and cortisol'. *Music Perception*, 18(1) (pp. 87–106).

Bee, H.L. (1996) *Journey of Adulthood*. (3rd edition) Englewood Cliffs, NJ: Prentice-Hall.

Beh, H.C. and Hirst, R. (1999) 'Performance on driving-related tasks during music'. *Ergonomics*, 42(8) (pp. 1087–1098).

Behne, K.E. (1997) 'The development of "Musikerleben" in adolescence: how and why young people listen to music'. In I. Deliege and J.A. Sloboda (eds) *Perception and Cognition of Music*. Hove: Psychology Press.

Belz, M.J.D. (1995) 'The German Gesangverein as a model of life long participation in music'. Doctoral dissertation, University of Minnesota, 1994. *Dissertation Abstracts International*, 56 (485A).

Bennett, S. (1976) 'The process of musical creation: interviews with eight composers'. *Journal of Research in Music Education*, 24(1) (pp. 3–13).

Benton, A.L. (1977) 'The amusias'. In M. Critchley and R.A. Henson (eds) *Music and the Brain*. London: Heinemann.

Ben-Tovim, A. and Boyd, D. (1990) *The Right Instrument for your Child*. London: Victor Gollancz.

Berg, M.H. (2000) 'Thinking for yourself: the social construction of chamber music experience'. In R.R. Rideout and S.J. Paul (eds) *On the Sociology of Music: Vol 2. Papers from the Music Education Symposium at the University of Oklahom.* Amherst, MA: University of Massachusetts Press (pp. 91–112).

Bergee, M.J. (1993) 'Certain attitudes toward occupational status held by music education majors'. *Journal of Research in Music Education*, 40 (pp. 104–113).

Bergeson, T.R. and Trehub, S.E. (1999) 'Mothers' singing to infants and preschool children'. *Infant Behavior and Development*, 22 (pp. 51–64).

Berglas, S. and Jones, E.E. (1978) 'Drug choice as a self-handicapping strategy in response to non-contingent success'. *Journal of Personality and Social Psychology*, 36 (pp. 405–417).

Berkaak, O.A. and Ruud, E. (1994) *Sunwheels: Fortellinger om et rockeband (Sunwheels: Tales of a rock group)*. Oslo: Universitetsforlaget.

Berliner, P. (1994) *Thinking in Jazz: The infinite art of improvisation*, Chicago: University of Chicago Press.

Berlyne, D.E. (1971) *Aesthetics and Psychobiology*. New York: Appleton-Century-Crofts.

Bever, T. and Chiarello, G. (1974) 'Cerebral dominance in musicians and nonmusicians'. *Science*, 185 (pp. 537–539).

Bigand, E. (2003) 'More about the musical expertise of musical untrained listeners'. In G. Avanzini, C. Faienza, D. Minciacchi, L. Lopez and M. Majno (eds) *The Neurosciences and Music*. New York: New York Academy of Sciences (pp. 304–312).

Biggs, J.B. (1996) 'Enhancing teaching through constructive alignment'. *Higher Education*, 32 (pp. 1–18).

Biggs, J.B. and Collis, K.F. (1982) *Evaluating the Quality of Learning: The SOLO taxonomy*. New York: Academic Press.

Biggs, J.B. and Moore, P.J. (1993) *The Process of Learning*. Englewood Cliffs, NJ: Prentice-Hall.

Blacking, J.A.R. (1971) 'Towards a theory of musical competence'. In E. DeJager (ed.) *Man: Anthropological essays in honour of O.F. Raum*. Cape Town: Struik.

Blacking, J.A.R. (1995) *Music, Culture, and Experience*. London: University of Chicago Press.

Blaine, Jr., J.R. (1976) 'Adaptation of the Suzuki-Kendall method to the teaching of a heterogeneous brass wind instrumental class of trumpets and trombones'. *Bulletin of the Council for Research in Music Education*, 56 (pp. 55–60).

Blank, M. and Davidson, J.W. (submitted) A consideration of the effect of gender on co-performer communication in piano duos.

Blood, A.J. and Zatorre, R.J.A. (2001) 'Intensely pleasurable responses to music correlate with activity in brain regions implicated in reward and emotion'. *Proceedings of the National Academy of the Sciences*, 98 (pp. 11818–11823).

Blood, A.J., Zatorre, R.J.A., Bermudez, P. *et al.* (1999) 'Emotional responses to pleasant and unpleasant music correlated with activity in the paralimbic brain regions'. *Nature Neuroscience*, 2 (pp. 382–387).

Bloom, B.S. (1985) *Developing Talent in Young People*. New York: Ballantine.

Bochkaryov, L.L. (1975) 'The psychological aspects of musicians' public performance'. *Voprosy Psikhologii*, 21 (pp. 68–79).

Boldt, S. (1996) 'The effects of music therapy on motivation, psychological well-being, physical comfort and exercise endurance of bone marrow transplant patients'. *Journal of Music Therapy*, 33(3) (pp. 164–188).

Booth, W. (1999) *For the Love of it: Amateuring and its rivals*. Chicago: University of Chicago Press.

Borthwick, S.J. and Davidson, J.W. (2002) 'Developing a child's identity as a musician: a family "script" perspective'. In R.A.R. MacDonald, D.J. Hargreaves and D.E. Miell (eds) *Musical Identities*. Oxford: Oxford University Press (pp. 60–78).

Bouillaud, J. (1865) 'Sur la faculte du language articule'. *Bulletin of the Academy National of Medecine*, 30 (pp. 752–768).

Bowers, J. (1998) 'Effects of an intergenerational choir for community-based seniors and college students on age-related attitudes'. *Journal of Music Therapy*, 35 (pp. 2–18).

Boyle, J.D. (1970) 'The effect of prescribed rhythmical movements on the ability to read music at sight'. *Journal of Research in Music Education*, 18 (pp. 307–318).

Bradley, I..L. (1974) 'Developments of aural and visual perception through creative processes'. *Journal of Research in Music Education*, 22 (pp. 234–240).

Brady, P.T. (1970) 'Fixed-scale mechanism of absolute pitch'. *Journal of the Acoustical Society of America*, 48 (pp. 883–887).

Braithwaite, M., Sigafoos, J., Schonell, F. and Schonell, E. (1998) 'Effects of social versus musical antecedents on communication responsiveness in five children with developmental disabilities'. *Journal of Music Therapy*, 35(2) (pp. 88–104).

Brand, M. (1982) 'Relationship between musical environment and musical aptitude among sixth grade children'. *Bulletin of Research in Music Education*, 13 (pp. 13–19).

Brand, M. (1985) 'Development and validation of the home-musical environment scale for use at the early elementary level'. *Psychology of Music*, 13(1) (pp. 40–48).

Brand, M. (1986) 'Relationship between home musical environment and selected musical attributes of second grade children'. *Journal of Research in Music Education*, 34 (pp. 111–120).

Brandfonbrener, A.G. (1990) 'Beta blockers in the treatment of performance anxiety'. *Medical Problems of Performing Artists*, 5(1) (pp. 23–26).

Brandstrom, S. (1995–6) 'Self-formulated goals and self-evaluation in music education'. *Bulletin of the Council for Research in Music Education*, 127 (pp. 16–21).

Brandstrom, S. (1999) 'Music teachers' everyday conceptions of musicality'. *Bulletin of the Council for Research in Music Education*, 141 (pp. 21–25).

Brandt, T. (1986) 'A review of research and literature concerned with private and class instruction in instrumental music'. *Journal of Band Research*, 22(1) (pp. 48–55).

Breamer, S. (1985) 'The parent–child relationship: the right kind of nurturing will aid in promoting practice'. *Suzuki World*, 4(1) (pp. 2–3).

Bregman, A.S. (1990) *Auditory Scene Analysis*. Cambridge, MA: The MIT Press.

Bregman, A.S. and Campbell, J. (1971) 'Primary auditory stream segregation and perception of order in rapid sequences of tones'. *Journal of Experimental Psychology*, 89 (pp. 244–249).

Brick, J.S. (1984) 'An exploratory study of the effects of a self-instructional programme utilizing the Pitch Master on pitch discrimination and pitch accuracy in performance of young trombonists'. *Psychology of Music*, 12 (pp. 119–125).

Brinkman, D.J. (1999) 'Problem finding, creativity style and musical compositions of high school students'. *Journal of Creative Behaviour*, 33(1) (pp. 62–68).

Brinner, B. (1986) 'Competence and interaction in the performance of "Pathetan" in central Java Indonesia Gamelan, improvisation'. Doctoral dissertation, University of California, Berkeley. *Dissertation Abstracts International*, 47(3) (704A).

Brokaw, J.P. (1983) The extent to which parental supervision and other selected factors are related to achievement of musical and technical-physical characteristics by beginning instrumental students. Unpublished PhD thesis, University of Michigan.

Brophy, T.S. (1999) 'The melodic improvisations of children ages 6 through 12: a developmental perspective'. Doctoral dissertation, University of Kentucky, 1998. *Dissertation Abstracts International*, 59(9) (3386A).

Brotons, M. (1994) 'Effects of performing conditions on music performance anxiety and performance quality'. *Journal of Music Therapy*, 31 (pp. 63–81).

Brotons, M., Koger, S.M. and Pickett-Cooper, P. (1997) 'Music and dementias: a review of the literature'. *Journal of Music Therapy*, 34 (pp. 204–245).

Brown, D. (1991) *Human Universals*. New York: McGraw-Hill.

Brown, P.A. (1987) 'An investigation of problems which cause stress among music teachers in Tennessee'. *Dissertation Abstracts International*, 48(3) (0521A).

Brown, R.A. (1928) 'A comparison of the whole, part, and combination methods of learning piano music'. *Journal of Experimental Psychology*, 12 (pp. 235–248).

Bruner, G.C., II (1990) 'Music, mood and marketing'. *Journal of Marketing*, October (pp. 94–104).

Brust, J.C.M. (2003) 'Music and the neurologist: a historical perspective'. In I. Peretz and R.J.A. Zatorre (eds) *The Cognitive Neuroscience of Music*. Oxford: Oxford University Press (pp. 181–191).

Bryan, T., Sullivan-Burstein, K. and Mathur, S. (1998) 'The influence of affect on social-information processing'. *Journal of Learning Disabilities*, 31(5) (pp. 418–427).

Buckner, J.L. (1997) Assessment of teacher and student behaviour in relation to the accomplishment of performance goals. Unpublished doctoral dissertation, University of Texas at Austin.

Buday, E.M. (1995) 'The effects of signed and spoken words taught with music on sign and speech imitation by children with autism'. *Journal of Music Therapy*, 32 (3) (pp. 189–202).

Bundra, J. (1993) 'A study of music listening processes through the verbal reports of school-aged children'. *Dissertation Abstracts International* (University Microfilms No. 9415701).

Bunt, L. (1994) *Music Therapy: An art beyond words*. London: Routledge.

Bunt, L. (1997) 'Clinical and therapeutic uses of music'. In D.J. Hargreaves and A.C. North (eds) *The Social Psychology of Music*. Oxford: Oxford University Press (pp. 249–267).

Burland, K. and Davidson, J.W. (2002) 'Training the talented'. *Music Education Research*, 4(1) (pp. 123–142).

Burleson, S., Center, D.B. and Reeves, H. (1989) 'The effect of background music on task performance in psychotic children'. *Journal of Music Therapy*, 25(4) (pp. 198–205).

Burnard, P. (1995) 'Task design and experience in composition'. *Psychology of Music*, 5 (pp. 32–46).

Burnard, P. and Younker, B.A. (2002) 'Mapping pathways: fostering creativity in composition'. *Music Education Research*, 4(2) (pp. 245–261).

Burns, E.M. and Campbell, S.L. (1994) 'Frequency and frequency-ratio resolution by possessors of relative and absolute pitch: a most excellent case of categorical perception'. *Journal of the Acoustical Society of America*, 96(5) (pp. 2704–2719).

Busen-Smith, M. (1999) 'Developing strategies for delivering music technology in secondary PGCE courses'. *British Journal of Music Education*, 16(2) (pp. 197–213).

Bush, J.E. (2000) 'The effects of a hypermedia program, cognitive style, and gender on middle school students' music achievement'. *Contributions to Music Education*, 27(1) (pp. 9–26).

Bygren, L.A., Konlaan, B.B. and Johnasson, S.-E. (1996) 'Attendance at cultural events, reading books or periodicals, and making music or singing in a choir as determinants for survival: Swedish interview survey of living conditions'. *British Medical Journal*, 313 (pp. 1577–1580).

Byrne, C. and Sheridan, M. (1998) 'Music: a source of deep imaginative satisfaction?' *British Journal of Music Education*, 15(3) (pp. 295–301).

Caine, J. (1991) 'The effects of music on the selected stress behaviours, weight, caloric and formula intake, and length of hospital stay of premature and low birth weight neonates in a newborn intensive care unit'. *Journal of Music Therapy*, 28(4) (pp. 180–192).

Caldwell, R. (1990) *The Performer Prepares*. Dallas, TX: PST Inc.

Cantor, N. and Kihlstrom, J.F. (1985) 'Social intelligence: the cognitive basis of personality'. In P. Shaver (ed.) *Review of Personality and Social Psychology (Vol. 6)*. Beverly Hills, CA: Sage (pp. 15–33).

Cantor, N. and Kihlstrom, J.F. (1987) *Personality and Social Intelligence*. Englewood Cliffs, NJ: Erlbaum.

Cantwell, R.H. and Millard, Y. (1994) 'The relationship between approach to learning and learning strategies in learning music'. *British Journal of Educational Psychology*, 64 (pp. 45–63).

Carmichael, K.D. and Atchinson, D.H. (1997) 'Music in play therapy: playing my feelings'. *International Journal of Play Therapy*, 6(1) (pp. 63–72).

Caron, J.R., Donnell, N.E. and Friedman, M. (1996) 'The reduction of bruxism using passive music listening with persons having developmental disabilities'. *Canadian Journal of Music Therapy*, 4(1) (pp. 58–73).

Carpenter, R. (1988) 'A description of relationships between verbal behaviours of teacher-conductors and ratings of selected junior and senior high school band rehearsals'. *Update*, 7 (pp. 37–40).

Carruth, E.K. (1997) 'The effects of singing and the spaced retrieval technique on improving face-name recognition in nursing home residents with memory loss'. *Journal of Music Therapy*, 34(3) (pp. 165–186).

Carterette, E.C. and Kendall, R. (1999) 'Comparative music perception and cognition'. In D. Deustch (ed.) *The Psychology of Music*. (2nd edition) London: Academic Press (pp. 725–792).

Cassidy, J.W. and Standley, J.M. (1995) 'The effect of music listening on physiological responses of premature infants in the MCU'. *Journal of Music Therapy*, 32(4) (pp. 208–227).

Cavanaugh, J.C. (1997) *Adult Development and Aging*. (3rd edition) Pacific Grove, CA: Brooks/Cole.

Ceci, S.J. (1990) *On Intelligence ... More or Less: A bio-ecological treatise on intellectual development*. Englewood Cliffs, NJ: Prentice-Hall.

Chabris, C. (1999) 'Brief exposure to music does not increase intelligence'. *Nature*, 400 (p. 826).

Chaffin, R. and Imreh, G. (1994) Memorizing for piano performance: a case study of expert memory. Paper presented at 3rd Practical Aspects of Memory Conference, July/August, University of Maryland, Washington, DC.

Chaffin, R. and Imreh, G. (1997) 'Pulling teeth and torture: musical memory and problem solving'. *Thinking and Reasoning*, 3 (pp. 315–336).

Chaffin, R. and Lemieux, A.F. (2004) 'General perspectives on achieving musical excellence'. In A. Williamon (ed.) *Musical Excellence: Strategies and techniques to enhance performance*. Oxford: Oxford University Press (pp. 19–40).

Chaffin, R., Imreh, G. and Crawford, M. (2002) *Practicing Perfection: Memory and piano performance*. Mahwah, NJ: Erlbaum.

Chamberlin, L.L., Clark, R.W. and Svengalis, J.N. (1993) 'Success with keyboards in middle school'. *Music Educators Journal*, 79(9) (pp. 31–36).

Chambliss, C., McMichael, H., Tyson, K., Monaco, C. and Tracy, J. (1996) 'Motor performance of schizophrenics after mellow and frenetic antecedent music'. *Perceptual and Motor Skills*, 82 (pp. 153–154).

Chandler, T.A., Chiarella, D. and Auria, C. (1987) 'Performance expectancy, success, satisfaction, and attributions as variables in band challenges'. *Journal of Research in Music Education*, 35(4) (pp. 249–258).

Chang, H.W. and Trehub, S.E. (1977) 'Auditory processing of relational information by young infants'. *Journal of Experimental Child Psychology*, 24 (pp. 324–331).

Charnetski, C.F. and Brennan, F.X. Jr. (1998) 'Effect of music and auditory stimuli on secretory immunoglobulin A (IgA)'. *Perceptual Motor Skills*, 87 (pp. 1163–1170).

Chen, H. (1996) 'An investigation of self-directed learning among non-music major adult piano learners in one-to-one piano instruction'. *Dissertation Abstracts International*, 57(7) (2929A) (University Microfilms No. AAT96–35962).

Chin, C.S. (2003) 'The development of absolute pitch: a theory concerning the roles of music training at an early developmental age and individual cognitive style'. *Psychology of Music*, 31(2) (pp. 155–171).

Chiodo, P.A. (1998) 'The development of lifelong commitment: a qualitative study of adult instrumental music participation'. Doctoral dissertation, State University of New York at Buffalo, 1997. *Dissertation Abstracts International*, 58(7) (2578A).

Clair, A.A. and Bernstein, B. (1990) 'A preliminary study of music therapy programming for severely regressed persons with Alzheimer's-type dementia'. *The Journal of Applied Gerontology*, 9(3) (pp. 299–311).

Clair, A.A. and Ebberts, A.G. (1997) 'The effects of music therapy on interactions between family caregivers and their care receivers with late stage dementia'. *Journal of Music Therapy*, 34(3) (pp. 148–164).

Clark, D.B. and Agras, W.S. (1991) 'The assessment and treatment of performance anxiety in musicians'. *American Journal of Psychiatry*, 148 (pp. 598–605).

Clarkson, M.G. and Clifton, R.K. (1985) 'Infant pitch perception: evidence for responding to pitch categories and the missing fundamental'. *Journal of the Acoustical Society of America*, 77 (pp. 1521–1528).

Clarkson, M.G., Clifton, R.K. and Perris, E.E. (1988) 'Infant timbre perception: discrimination of spectral envelopes'. *Perception and Psychophysics*, 43(1) (pp. 15–20).

Cleveland, T. (1988) 'Viewing the voice: a picture is worth a thousand words'. *The NATS Journal*, November/December (pp. 31–32).

Clifford, M.M. (1986) 'The comparative effects of strategy and effort attributions'. *British Journal of Educational Psychology*, 56 (pp. 75–83).

Clift, S. and Hancox, G. (2001) 'The perceived benefits of singing: findings from preliminary surveys of a university college choral society'. *The Journal of the Royal Society for the Promotion of Health*, 121(4) (pp. 248–256).

Cobes, C.J. (1972) 'The conditioning of a pitch response using uncertain singers'. *Bulletin of the Council for Research in Music Education*, 30 (pp. 29–39).

Coffman, D.D. (2002) 'Adult education'. In R. Colwell and C. Richardson (eds) *The New Handbook of Research on Music Teaching and Learning*. Oxford: Oxford University Press.

Coffman, D.D. and Adamek, M. (1999) 'The contribution of wind band participation to quality of life of senior adult band members'. *Dialogue in Instrumental Music Education*, 20(1) (pp. 25–34).

Cohen, A.J. and Baird, K. (1990) 'Acquisition of absolute pitch: the question of critical periods'. *Psychomusicology*, 9(1) (pp. 31–37).

Cohen, S. (1991) *Rock Culture in Liverpool: Popular music in the making*. Oxford: Clarendon Press.

Cole, A. (1999) 'Play it again, man'. *Modern Maturity*, 42(4) (pp. 10–12).

Colley, A., Banton, L. and Down, J. (1992) 'An expert–novice comparison in musical composition'. *Psychology of Music*, 20(2) (pp. 124–137).

Collier, J.L. (1983) *Louis Armstrong: An American genius*. Oxford: Oxford University Press.

Collins, D. (2005) 'A synthesis process model of creative thinking in composition'. *Psychology of Music* 33(2) (pp. 193–216).

Colprit, E.J. (2000) 'Observation and analysis of Suzuki string teaching'. *Journal of Research in Music Education*, 48(3) (pp. 206–221).

Colwell, R. (ed.) 1992 *Handbook of Research on Music Teaching and Learning: Music Educators National Conference*. New York: Schirmer Books.

Colwell, R. (2002) 'Assessment's potential in music education'. In R. Colwell and C. Richardson (eds) *The New Handbook of Research on Music Teaching and Learning*. Oxford: Oxford University Press (pp. 1128–1158).

Colwell, R. and Richardson, C. (eds) (2002) *The New Handbook of Research on Music Teaching and Learning*. Oxford: Oxford University Press.

Conda, J.M. (1997) 'The late bloomers piano club: a case study of a group in progress'. Doctoral dissertation, University of Oklahoma, 1997. *Dissertation Abstracts International*, 58 (409A).

Cope, P. (2002) 'Informal learning of musical instruments: the importance of social context'. *Music Education Research*, 4(1) (pp. 93–104).

Costa-Giomi, E. (1999) 'The effects of three years of piano instruction on children's cognitive development'. *Journal of Research in Music Education*, 47(5) (pp. 198–212).

Costa-Giomi, E., Gilmour, R., Siddell, J. and Levebre, E. (2001) 'Absolute pitch, early music training, and spatial abilities'. In R.J.A. Zatorre and I. Peretz (eds) *The Biological Foundations of Music, Vol. 930*. New York: Annals of the New York Academy of Science (pp. 3294–3296).

Covington, M. (1984) 'The motive for self-worth'. In R. Ames and C. Ames (eds) *Research on Motivation in Education: Student motivation*. New York: Academic Press (pp. 77–111).

Cox, J. (1989) 'Rehearsal organisational structures used by successful high school choral directors'. *Journal of Research in Music Education*, 37 (pp. 201–218).

Coy, D. (1990) 'A multi-sensory approach to teaching jazz improvisation to middle school band students'. Doctoral dissertation, University of Oregon. *Dissertation Abstracts International*, 50(11) (13508A).

Craske, M. and Craig, K. (1984) 'Musical performance anxiety: the three systems model and self-efficacy theory'. *Behaviour Research and Therapy*, 22 (pp. 267–280).

Creech, A. (2001) Play for me: an exploration into motivations, issues and outcomes related to parental involvement in their children's violin study. Unpublished MA dissertation, University of Sheffield.

Creech, A. and Hallam, S. (2003) 'Parent–teacher–pupil interactions in instrumental music tuition: a literature review'. *British Journal of Music Education*, 20(1) (pp. 29–44).

Cross, I. (2003) 'Music, cognition, culture and evolution'. In I. Peretz and R.J.A. Zatorre (eds) *The Cognitive Neuroscience of Music*. Oxford: Oxford University Press (pp. 42–56).

Crozier, W.R. (1997) 'Music and social influence'. In D.J. Hargreaves and A.C. North (eds) *The Social Psychology of Music*. Oxford: Oxford University Press (pp. 67–83).

Csikszentmihalyi, M. (1975) *Beyond Boredom and Anxiety: The experience of play in work and games*. San Francisco, CA: Jossey-Bass.

Csikszentmihalyi, M. (1988) 'Society, culture and person: a systems view of creativity'. In R.J. Sternberg (ed.) *The Nature of Creativity: Contemporary psychological perspectives*. New York: Cambridge University Press (pp. 325–339).

Csikszentmihalyi, M. (1996) *Creativity*. New York: HarperCollins.

Csikszentmihalyi, M. and Rich, G. (1997) 'Musical improvisation: a systems approach'. In R.K. Sawyer (ed.) *Creativity in Performance*. Greenwich, CT: Ablex (pp. 43–66).

Csikszentmihalyi, M., Rathunde, K. and Whalen, S. (1993) *Talented Teenagers: The roots of success and failure*. Cambridge: Cambridge University Press.

Cuddy, L.L. and Cohen, A.J. (1976) 'Recognition of transposed melodic sequences'. *Quarterly of Experimental Psychology*, 28 (pp. 255–270).

Cunningham, J.G. and Sterling, R.S. (1988) 'Developmental change in the understanding of affective meaning in music'. *Motivation and Emotion*, 12(4) (pp. 399–413).

Cusack, R. and Roberts, B. (2000) 'Effects of differences in timbre on sequential grouping'. *Perceptual Psychophysiology*, 62 (pp. 1112–1120).

Cutietta, R. (1986) 'Biofeedback training in music: from experimental to clinical applications'. *Bulletin of the Council for Research in Music Education*, 87 (pp. 35–42).

Daignault, L. (1997) 'Children's creative musical thinking within the context of a computer-supported improvisational approach to composition'. *Dissertation Abstracts International*, 57(11) (4681A).

Dalla Bella, S. and Peretz, I. (2003) 'Congenital amusia interferes with the ability to synchronise with music'. In G. Avanzini, C. Faienza, D. Minciacchi, L. Lopez and M. Majno (eds) *The Neurosciences and Music*. New York: New York Academy of Sciences (pp. 166–169).

Darrow, A.A., Johnson, C.M. and Ollenberger, T. (1994) 'The effect of participation in an intergenerational choir on teens' and older persons' cross age attitudes'. *Journal of Music Therapy*, 31 (pp. 119–134).

Davidson, J.W. (1993) 'Visual perception of performance manner in the movement of solo musicians'. *Psychology of Music*, 21(2) (pp. 103–113).

Davidson, J.W. (1994) 'Which areas of a pianist's body convey information about expressive intention to an audience?' *Journal of Human Movement Studies*, 26 (pp. 279–301).

Davidson, J.W. (1995) 'What does the visual information contained in music performances offer the observer? Some preliminary thoughts'. In R. Steinberg (ed.) *The Music Machine: Psychophysiology and psychopathology of the sense of music*. Heidelberg: Springer-Verlag (pp. 103–115).

Davidson, J.W. (2001) 'The role of the body in the production and perception of solo vocal performance: a case study of Annie Lennox'. *Musicae Scientiea*, 5 (pp. 235–256).

Davidson, J.W. (2002a) 'Understanding the expressive movements of a solo pianist'. *Musik-psychologie*, 5 (pp. 235–256).

Davidson, J.W. (2002b) 'The solo performer's identity'. In R.A.R. MacDonald, D.J. Hargreaves and D.E. Miell (eds) *Musical Identities.* Oxford: Oxford University Press (pp. 97–116).

Davidson, J.W. and Borthwick, S. (2002) 'Family dynamics and family scripts: a case study of musical development'. *Psychology of Music*, 20(1) (pp. 121–136).

Davidson, J.W. and Coimbra, D.C.C. (2001) 'Investigating performance evaluation by assessors of singers in a music college setting'. *Musicae Scientiae*, 5 (pp. 33–54).

Davidson, J.W. and Good, J.M.M. (2002) 'Social and musical co-ordination between members of a string quartet: an exploratory study'. *Psychology of Music*, 30 (pp. 186–201).

Davidson, J.W. and King, E.C. (2004) 'Strategies for ensemble practice'. In A. Williamon (ed.) *Musical Excellence: Strategies and techniques to enhance performance.* Oxford: Oxford University Press (pp. 105–122).

Davidson, J.W., Sloboda, J.A. and Howe, M.J.A. (1995/6) 'The role of parents and teachers in the success and failure of instrumental learners.' *Bulletin of the Council for Research in Music Education*, 127 (pp. 40–44).

Davidson, J.W., Howe, M.J.A., Moore, D.G. and Sloboda, J.A. (1996) 'The role of family influences in the development of musical ability'. *British Journal of Developmental Psychology*, 14 (pp. 399–412).

Davidson, J.W., Howe, M.J.A. and Sloboda, J.A. (1997) 'Environmental factors in the development of musical performance skill over the lifespan'. In D.J. Hargreaves and A.C. North (eds) *The Social Psychology of Music*. Oxford: Oxford University Press (pp. 188–208).

Davidson, J.W., Moore, D.G., Sloboda, J.A. and Howe, M.J.A. (1998) 'Characteristics of music teachers and the progress of young instrumentalists'. *Journal of Research in Music Education*, 46 (pp. 141–160).

Davidson, L. and Scripp, L. (1988) 'Young children's musical representations: windows of music cognition'. In J.A. Sloboda (ed.) *Generative Processes in Music: The psychology of performance, improvisation and composition*. New York: Oxford University Press (pp. 195–230).

Davidson, L. and Scripp, L. (1992) 'Surveying the co-ordinates of cognitive skills in music'. In R. Colwell (ed.) *Handbook of Research on Music Teaching and Learning: Music Educators National Conference*. New York: Schirmer Books (pp. 392–413).

Davidson, L. and Welsh, P. (1988) 'From collections to structure: the developmental path of tonal thinking'. In J.A. Sloboda (ed.) *Generative Processes in Music: The psychology of performance, improvisation and composition*. Oxford: Oxford University Press (pp. 260–285).

Davidson, L., McKernon, P. and Gardner, H. (1981) 'The acquisition of song: a developmental approach'. *Documentary Report of the Ann Arbor Symposium*. Reston, VA: Music Educators National Conference (pp. 301–315).

Davies, C.D. (1986) 'Say it until a song comes (reflections on songs invented by children 3–13)'. *British Journal of Music Education*, 3(3) (pp. 279–293).

Davis, L.P. (1981) 'The effects of structured singing activities and self-evaluation practice on elementary band students' instrumental music performance, melodic tonal imagery, self-evaluation and attitude'. Doctoral dissertation, Ohio State University. *Dissertation Abstracts International*, 1982, 42 (3051–A) (University Microfilms No. 8128981).

Davis, M. (1994) 'Folk music psychology'. *The Psychologist*, 7(12) (p. 537).

Deffenbacher, J.L. (1980) 'Worry and emotionality in test anxiety'. In I.G. Sarason (ed.) *Test Anxiety: Theory, research and applications*. Hillsdale, NJ: Laurence Erlbaum Associates (pp. 111–124).

Deffenbacher, J.L. and Hazaleus, S.L. (1985) 'Cognitive, emotional and physiological components of test anxiety'. *Cognitive Therapy and Research*, 9 (pp. 169–180).

Delzell, J.K. and Leppla, D.A. (1992) 'Gender association of musical instruments and preferences of fourth-grade students for selected instruments'. *Journal of Research in Music Education*, 40 (pp. 93–103).

Demany, L. (1982) 'Auditory stream segregation in infancy'. *Infant Behaviour and Development*, 5 (pp. 261–276).

Demany, L. and Arnaud, F. (1984) 'The perceptual reality of tone chroma in early infancy'. *Journal of the Acoustical Society of America*, 76 (pp. 57–66).

Demany, L., McKenzie, B. and Vurpillot, E. (1977) 'Rhythm perception in early infancy'. *Nature*, 266 (pp. 718–719).

Demorest, S. and Morrison, S.J. (2003) 'Exploring the influence of cultural familiarity and expertise on neurological responses to music'. In G. Avanzini, C. Faienza, D. Minciacchi, L. Lopez and M. Majno (eds) *The Neurosciences and Music*. New York: New York Academy of Sciences (pp. 112–117).

DeNicola, D.N. (1990) The development and evaluation of a twelve step sequential method to teach class piano sight reading. Paper presented at November meeting of Southern Division of the Music Educators National Conference, Winston-Salem, North Carolina.

DeNora, T. (2000) *Music in Everyday Life*. Cambridge: Cambridge University Press.

Deutsch, D. (1999) 'Grouping mechanisms in music'. In D. Deutsch (ed.) *The Psychology of Music*. (2nd edition) London: Academic Press (pp. 299–348).

Deutscher Musikrat (1993) *Gute Noten mit kritischen Anmerkungen. Erste ergebnisse einer Umfrage unter den Teilnehmern der regionalwettbewerbe 'Jungend musiziert' 1992*. Augsburg, Germany.

DeWitt, L.A. and Crowder, R.G. (1986) 'Recognition of novel memories after brief delays'. *Music Perception*, 3 (pp. 259–274).

Dickey, M.R. (1991) 'A comparison of verbal instruction and nonverbal teacher–student modelling in instrumental ensembles'. *Journal of Research in Music Education*, 16(1) (pp. 65–77).

Dickey, M.R. (1992) 'A review of research on modeling in music teaching and learning'. *Bulletin of the Council for Research in Music Education*, 113 (pp. 27–40).

Diener, C.I. and Dweck, C.S. (1978) 'An analysis of learned helplessness: continuous changes in performance, strategy and achievement cognitions following failure'. *Journal of Personality and Social Psychology*, 36 (pp. 451–462).

Diener, C.I. and Dweck, C.S. (1980) 'An analysis of learned helplessness: (II) The processing of success'. *Journal of Personality and Social Psychology*, 39 (pp. 940–952).

Dissanayake, E. (1988) *What is Art for?* Seattle: University of Washington Press.

Doan, G.R. (1973) An investigation of the relationships between parental involvement and the performance ability of violin students. Unpublished doctoral dissertation, Ohio State University, Columbus.

Dogani, K. (2004) 'Teachers' understanding of composing in the primary classroom'. *Music Education Research*, 6(3) (pp. 263–280).

Dolgin, K.G. and Adelson, E.H. (1990) 'Age changes in the ability to interpret affect in sung and instrumentally presented melodies'. *Psychology of Music*, 18 (pp. 87–98).

Dolloff, L.A. (1999) 'Imagining ourselves as teachers, the development of teacher identity in music teacher education'. *Music Education Research*, 1(2) (pp. 191–207).

Donald, L.S. (1997) The organisation of rehearsal tempos and efficiency of motor skill acquisition in piano performance. Unpublished doctoral dissertation, University of Texas at Austin.

Donner, N. (1987) 'The effect of daily practice'. *Suzuki World*, 6(5/6) (p. 5).

Donovan, A.J. (1994) 'The interaction of personality traits in applied music teaching'. Doctoral dissertation, University of Southern Mississipi, 1994. *Dissertation Abstracts International*, 55 (1499A).

Douglas, S. and Willatts, P. (1994) 'The relationship between musical ability and literacy skill'. *Journal of Research in Reading*, 17 (pp. 99–107).

Dowling, W.J. (1973) 'The perception of interleaved melodies'. *Cognitive Psychology*, 5 (pp. 322–337).

Dowling, W.J. (1978) 'Scale and contour: two components of a theory for memory for melodies'. *Psychological Review*, 85 (pp. 341–354).

Dowling, W.J. (1982) 'Melodic information processing and its development'. In D. Deutsch (ed.) *The Psychology of Music*. (2nd edition) London: Academic Press (pp. 413–429).

Dowling, W.J. (1984) 'Development of musical schemata in children's spontaneous singing'. In W.R. Crozier and A.J. Chapman (eds) *Cognitive Processes in the Perception of Art*. Amsterdam: North-Holland (pp. 145–163).

Dowling, W.J. (1986) 'Context effects on melody recognition: scale-step versus interval representation'. *Music Perception*, 3 (pp. 281–296).

Dowling, W.J. (1988) 'Tonal structure and children's early learning of music'. In J.A. Sloboda (ed.) *Generative Processes in Music: The psychology of performance, improvisation and composition*. Oxford: Clarendon Press (pp. 113–128).

Dowling, W.J. (1991) Tonal strength and melody recognition after long and short delays'. *Perception and Psychophysics*, 50 (pp. 305–313).

Dowling, W.J. (1992) 'Perceptual grouping, attention and expectancy in listening to music'. In J. Sundberg (ed.) *Gluing Tones: Grouping in music composition, performance and listening*. Stockholm: Publications of the Royal Swedish Academy (pp. 77–98).

Dowling, W.J. (1993) 'Procedural and declarative knowledge in music cognition and education'. In T.J. Tighe and W.J. Wilding (eds) *Psychology and Music: The understanding of melody and rhythm*. Hillsdale, NJ: Erlbaum (pp. 5–18).

Dowling, W.J. (1994) 'The development of melodic perception and production'. In I. Deliege (ed.) *Proceedings of the 3rd International Conference on Music Perception and Cognition*. Liege. Belgium: European Society for the Cognitive Sciences of Music (pp. 253–254).

Dowling, W.J. (1999) 'The development of music perception and cognition'. In D. Deutsch (ed.) *The Psychology of Music*. (2nd edition) London: Academic Press (pp. 603–625).

Dowling, W.J. and Harwood, D. (1986) *Music Cognition*. New York: Academic Press.

Doxey, C. and Wright, C. (1990) 'An exploratory study of children's music ability'. *Early Childhood Research Quarterly*, 5 (pp. 425–440).

Drake, C. (1993) 'Reproduction of musical rhythms by children, adult musicians, and adult nonmusicians'. *Perception and Psychophysics*, 53 (pp. 25–33).

Drake, C. and Bertrand, D. (2003) 'The quest for universals in temporal processing in music'. In I. Peretz and R.J.A. Zatorre (eds) *The Cognitive Neuroscience of Music*. Oxford: Oxford University Press (pp. 21–31).

Drake, C. and Gerard, C. (1989) 'A psychological pulse train: how young children use this cognitive framework to structure simple rhythms'. *Psychological Research*, 51 (pp. 16–22).

Drake, C., Dowling, W.J. and Palmer, C. (1991) 'Accent structures in the reproduction of simple tunes by children and adult pianists'. *Music Perception*, 8 (pp. 315–334).

Drake, C., Jones, M.R. and Baruch, C. (2000) 'The development of rhythmic attending in auditory sequences: attunement, reference period, focal attending'. *Cognition*, 77 (pp. 251–288).

Dregalla, H.E. (1983) 'A study of predictors of music achievement among students from selected high schools of Nebraska'. *Dissertation Abstracts International*, 44 (5420).

Duitman, H.E. (1993) Using hypermedia to enrich the learning experience of college students in a music appreciation course. Unpublished doctoral dissertation, Ohio State University, Columbus.

Duke, R.A. (1999/2000) 'Measures of instructional effectiveness in music research'. *Bulletin of the Council for Research in Music Education*, 143 (pp. 1–49).

Duke, R.A. and Pierce, M.A. (1990) Effects of tempo and context on transfer of performance skills. Paper presented at the Music Educators National Conference national convention, Washington.

Duke, R.A., Flowers, P.J. and Wolfe, D.E. (1997) 'Children who study with piano with excellent teachers in the United States'. *Bulletin of the Council for Research in Music Education*, 132 (pp. 51–84).

Duncker, K. (1945) 'On problem solving'. *Psychological Monographs*, 58. Washington, DC: American Psychological Association.

Dunkin, M.J. (1990) 'The induction of academic staff to a university: processes and products'. *Higher Education*, 20 (pp. 47–66).

Dunn, D.E. (1997) 'Effect of rehearsal hierarchy and reinforcement on attention, achievement, and attitude of selected choirs'. *Journal of Research in Music Education*, 45(4) (pp. 547–567).

Dweck, C.S. (1975) 'The role of expectations and attributions in the alleviation of learned helplessness'. *Journal of Personality and Social Psychology*, 31 (pp. 674–685).

Dweck, C.S. (1999) *Self-theories: Their role in motivation personality and development*. Philadelphia, PA: Psychology Press.

Dweck, C.S. and Elliott, E.S. (1983) 'Achievement motivation'. In P. Mussen and E.M. Hetherington (eds) *Handbook of Child Psychology*. New York: Wiley (pp. 643–691).

Dweck, C.S. and Leggett, E.L. (1988) 'A social cognitive approach to motivation and personality'. *Psychological Review*, 95(2) (pp. 256–373).

Eccles, J. (1983) 'Expectancies, values and academic behaviours'. In J.T. Spence (ed.) *Achievement and Achievement Motives*. San Francisco, CA: Freeman (pp. 75–146).

Edgerton, C.L. (1994) 'The effect of improvisational music therapy on the communicative behaviours of autistic children'. *Journal of Music Therapy*, 31(1) (pp. 31–62).

Edlund, B. (2000) 'Listening to oneself at a distance'. In C. Woods, G. Luck, R. Brochard, F. Seddon and J.A. Sloboda (eds) *Proceedings of the 6th International Conference on Music Perception and Cognition*, 5–10 August, Keele, UK: Keele University.

Edwards, J. (1999) 'Music therapy with children hospitalised for severe injury or illness'. *British Journal of Music Therapy*, 13(1) (pp. 21–27).

Ekstrom (1974) (private communication) cited in Welch, G.F. 'A schema theory of how children learn to sing'. *Psychology of Music*, 13(1) (pp. 3–18).

Elbert, T., Pantev, C., Wienbruch, C., Rockstroh, B. and Taub, E. (1995) 'Increased cortical representation of the fingers of the left hand in string players'. *Science*, 270 (pp. 305–306).

Elliot, A.J. and Church, M. (1997) 'A hierarchical model of approach and avoidance achievement motivation'. *Journal of Personality and Social Psychology*, 72 (pp. 218–232).

Elliott, C.A. (1982) 'The relationship among instrumental sightreading ability and seven selected predictor variables'. *Journal of Research in Music Education*, 30(1) (pp. 5–14).

Elliott, D. (1987) 'Assessing musical performance'. *British Journal of Music Education*, 4(2) (pp. 157–184).

Elliott, E.S. and Dweck, C.S. (1988) 'Goals: an approach to motivation and achievement'. *Journal of Personality and Social Psychology*, 54 (pp. 5–12).

Ellis, P. (1995) 'Incidental music: case study in the development of sound therapy'. *British Journal of Music Education*, 12 (pp. 59–70).

Elton, L.B.R. and Laurillard, D. (1979) 'Trends in student learning'. *Studies in Higher Education*, 4 (pp. 87–102).

Ely, M.C. (1991) 'Stop performance anxiety!' *Music Educators Journal*, 79(2) (pp. 35–39).

Emmons, R.A. (1989) 'The personal striving approach to personality'. In L.A. Pervin (ed.) *Goal Concepts in Personality and Social Psychology*. Hillsdale, NJ: Laurence Erlbaum Associates (pp. 87–126).

Ericsson, K.A., Tesch-Romer, C. and Krampe, R. (1990) 'The role of practice and motivation in the acquisition of expert-level performance in real life'. In M.J.A. Howe (ed.) *Encouraging the Development of Exceptional Skills and Talents*. Leicester: British Psychological Society (pp. 109–130).

Ericsson, K.A., Krampe, R.T. and Tesch-Romer, C. (1993) 'The role of deliberate practice in the acquisition of expert performance'. *Psychological Review*, 100(3) (pp. 363–406).

Ester, D.P. (1997) 'Teaching vocal anatomy and function via HyperCard technology'. *Contributions to Music Education*, 24(1) (pp. 91–99).

Everitt, A. (1997) *Joining In: An investigation into participatory music*. London: Calouste Gulbenkian Foundation.

Evoskevich, P. (1979) 'Biofeedback and its use in the treatment of musical performance anxiety'. *Saxophone Symposium*, 4 (pp. 31–32).

Feather, N. (ed.) (1982) *Expectations and Actions*. Hillsdale, NJ: Erlbaum.

Feijoo, J. (1981) 'Le feotus, Pierre et le Coup'. In E. Herbinet and M.-C. Busnel (eds) *L'aube des sens*. Cahiers du Nouveau-ne, Paris: Stock.

Ferguson, A.R., Carbonneau, M.R. and Chambliss, C. (1994) 'Effects of positive and negative music on performance of a karate drill'. *Perceptual and Motor Skills*, 78 (pp. 1217–1218).

Fern, J. (1996) 'The effectiveness of a computer-based courseware program for teaching jazz improvisation'. Doctoral dissertation, University of Southern California. *Dissertation Abstracts International*, 57(1) (144A).

Field, T., Martinez, A., Nawrocki, T., Pickens, J., Fox, N.A. and Schanberg, S. (1998) 'Music shifts frontal EEG in depressed adolescents'. *Adolescence*, 33(129) (pp. 109–116).

Fine, P.A. and Moore, B.J.C. (1993) 'Frequency analysis and musical ability'. *Music Perception*, 11 (pp. 39–54).

Finnas, L. (1987) 'Do young people misjudge each other's musical taste?' *Psychology of Music*, 15 (pp. 152–166).

Finnas, L. (1989) 'A comparison between young people's privately and publicly expressed musical preferences'. *Psychology of Music*, 17 (pp. 132–145).

Fishbein, M. and Middlestadt, S. (1988) 'Medical problems among ICSOM musicians: overview of a national survey'. *Medical Problems of Performing Artists*, 3 (pp. 1–8).

Fiske, H.E. (1975) 'Judge group differences in the rating of high school trumpet performances'. *Journal of Research in Music Education*, 23 (pp. 22–29).

Fitts, P.M. and Posner, M.I. (1967) *Human Performance*. Belmont, CA: Brooks Cole.

Flavell, J.H., Beach, D.R. and Chinsky, J.M. (1966) 'Spontaneous verbal rehearsal in a memory task as a function of age'. *Child Development*, 37 (pp. 283–299).

Flohr, J. (1985) 'Young children's improvisations: emerging creative thought'. *Creative Child and Adult Quarterly*, 10(2) (pp. 79–85).

Fogle, D.O. (1982) 'Toward effective treatment for music performance anxiety'.*Psychotherapy: Theory, research, and practice*, 19(3) (pp. 368–375).

Folkestad, G. (1996) *Computer Based Creative Music Making: Young people's music in the digital age. Goteborg Studies in Educational Sciences* (104). Gothenburg: Acta Universitatis Gothoburgensis.

Folkestad, G. (2004) 'A meta-analytic approach to qualitative studies in music education: a new model applied to creativity and composition'. In J. Tafuri (ed.) *Research for Music Education: The 20th Seminar of the ISME Research Commission*, 4–10 July, Las Palmas, Spain.

Folkestad, G. and Hultquist, A. (in press) *Professional Composers Assessment Criteria of Composition*. School of Music and Music Education, Gothenberg University.

Folts, M. (1973) 'The relative aspects of two procedures as followed by flute, clarinet, and trumpet students while practising on the development of tone quality and on selected performance skills'. Doctoral dissertation, New York University. *Dissertation Abstracts International*, 34 (1312–A).

Ford, S.E. (1999) 'The effect of music on the self-injurious behavior of an adult female with severe developmental disabilities'. *Journal of Music Therapy*, 36(4) (pp. 293–313).

Forest, J. (1995) 'Music technology helps students succeed'. *Music Educators Journal*, 81(5) (pp. 35–48).

Fornas, J., Lindberg, U. and Sernhede, O. (1995) *In Garageland: Rock, youth and modernity*. London: Routledge.

Forsythe, J.L. (1975) 'The effect of teacher approval, disapproval, and errors on student attentiveness: music versus classroom teachers'. In C.K. Madsen, R.D. Greer and C.H. Madsen, Jr (eds) *Research in Music Behaviour*. New York: Teachers College Press (pp. 49–55).

Forsythe, J.L. (1977) 'Elementary student attending behaviour as a function of classroom activities'. *Journal of Research in Music Education*, 25 (pp. 228–239).

Fortney, P.M. (1995) 'Learning style and music instruction via an interactive audio CD-ROM: an exploratory study'. *Contributions to Music Education*, 22 (pp. 77–97).

Foster, N.A. and Valentine, E.R. (1998) 'The effect of concurrent music on autobiographical recall in dementia clients'. *Musicae Scientiae*, 2(2) (pp. 143–152).

Founta, O. (2002) Student musicians' performance anxiety and personality. Unpublished MMus thesis, Welsh School of Music and Drama, Cardiff.

Fourcin, A. and Abberton, E. (1971) 'First applications of a new laryngraph'. *Medical and Biological Illustration*, 21 (pp. 172–182).

Frakes, L. (1984) Differences in music achievement, academic achievement and attitude among participants, dropouts and non-participants in secondary school music. Unpublished doctoral thesis, University of Iowa.

Franklin, E. (1977) 'An experimental study of text notation'. *Bulletin of the Council for Research in Music Education*, 50 (pp. 18–20).

Fredrikson, M., Gunnarsson, R. and Klein, K.C. (1986) 'Emotion, attention and autonomic arousal'. *Biological Psychology*, 23 (pp. 96–97).

Freeman, J. (1991) *Gifted Children Growing Up*. Cassell: London.

Freundlich, D. (1978) 'The development of musical thinking: case studies in improvisation'. Doctoral dissertation, Harvard University, *Dissertation Abstracts International*, 39(11) (6617A).

Freyhof, H., Gruber, H. and Ziegler, A. (1993) *Anfange des Expertiseerwerbs bei Berufsund Laienmusikern (Paper 7/1993)*. Munchen, Germany: Max Planck Institut fur psychologische Forschung.

Fukado, S.Y. (2000) Music therapy applied as an alternative method for the treatment of asthma. Paper presented at the Biannual Conference of the International Society for Music Education, Edmonton, Canada.

Furman, C.E. (1978) 'The effect of musical stimuli on the brainwave production of children'. *Journal of Music Therapy*, 15 (pp. 108–117).

Furnham, A. and Bradley, A. (1997) 'Music while you work: the differential distraction of background music on the cognitive test performance of introverts and extraverts'. *Applied Cognitive Psychology*, 11 (pp. 445–455).

Gabbard, G.O. (1980) 'Stage fright: symptoms and causes'. *The Piano Quarterly*, 112 (pp. 11–15).

Gabrielsson, A. (1988) 'Timing in music performance and its relations to music experience'. In J.A. Sloboda (ed.) *Generative Processes in Music: The psychology of performance, improvisation and composition*. Oxford: Oxford University Press (pp. 27–51).

Gabrielsson, A. (1993) 'Emotion and music'. *Newsletter of the European Society for the Cognitive Sciences of Music*, 4 (pp. 4–9).

Gabrielsson, A. (2001) 'Emotions in strong experiences with music'. In P.N. Juslin and J.A. Sloboda (eds) *Music and Emotion: Theory and research*. Oxford: Oxford University Press (pp. 431–452).

Gardiner, M.E., Fox, A., Knowles, F. and Jeffrey, D. (1996) 'Learning improved by arts training'. *Nature*, 381(6580) (p. 284).

Gardner, H. (1999) *Intelligence Reframed: Multiple intelligences for the 21st century*. New York: Basic Books.

Gardner, H., Kornhaber, M.L. and Wake, W.K. (1996) *Intelligence: Multiple perspectives*, New York: Harcourt Brace College Publishers.

Gaston, E.T. (1968) 'Man and music'. In E.T. Gaston (ed.) *Music in Therapy*. New York: Macmillan (pp. 7–29).

Gates, J.T. (1991) 'Music participation: theory, research and policy'. *Bulletin of the Council for Research in Music Education*, 109 (pp. 1–35).

Gellrich, M. (1987) *Ubetechnik im Instrumental spiel, Strategien zur Ausbildung von Selbststeuerung und Selbstkontrolle (Practising Technique:*

Strategies for self-monitoring and self-control). Diplomarbeit, Psychologie, Technische universitet, Berlin.

Gellrich, M., Osterwold, M. and Schulz, J. (1986) 'Leistungsmotivation bei Kindern im Instumentalunterricht. Bericht uber eine erkundungsstudie' ('Children's performance motivation in instrumental teaching'). *Musikpsychologie*, 3 (pp. 33–69).

Genc, B.O., Genc, E., Tastkin, G. *et al.* (2001) 'Musicogenic epilepsy with actal single photon emission computed cosmography (SPECT): could these cases contribute to our knowledge of music processing?' *European Journal of Neurology*, 8 (pp. 191–194).

Gentile, D. (1998) 'An ecological approach to the development of perception of emotion in music'. *Dissertation Abstracts International*, 59(5–B) (2454), University of Minnesota.

Gerardi, G.M. and Gerken, L. (1995) 'The development of affective responses to modality and melodic contour'. *Music Perception*, 12 (pp. 279–290).

Gerrard, L.E., Poteat, G.M. and Ironsmith, M. (1996) 'Promoting children's creativity: effects of competition, self-esteem, and immunization'. *Creativity Research Journal*, 9(4) (pp. 339–346).

Ghent, P. (1989) Expert learning in music. Master's thesis. University of Toronto, Ontario, Canada.

Gilbert, J.P. (1981) 'Motoric music skill development in young children: a longitudinal investigation'. *Psychology of Music*, 9(1) (pp. 21–25).

Gilhooly, K.J. (1996) *Thinking: Directed, undirected and creative*. London: Academic Press.

Ginsborg, J. (2000) 'Off by heart: expert singers' memorisation strategies and recall for the words and music for songs'. In C. Woods, G. Luck, R. Brochard, F. Seddon and J.A. Sloboda (eds) *Proceedings of the 6th International Conference on Music Perception and Cognition*, 5–10 August, Keele, UK: Keele University.

Ginsborg, J. (2002) 'Classical singers learning and memorising a new song: an observational study'. *Psychology of Music*, 30 (pp. 58–101).

Goldstein, A. (1980) 'Thrills in response to music and other stimuli'. *Physiological Psychology*, 8(1) (pp. 126–129).

Goleman, D. (1996) *Emotional Intelligence: Why it can matter more than IQ*. London: Bloomsbury.

Gonzo, D. and Forsythe, J. (1976) 'Developing and using videotapes to teach rehearsal techniques and principles'. *Journal of Research in Music Education*, 24(1) (pp. 32–41).

Goode, D.J. and Knight, S.P. (1991) 'Identification, retrieval, and analysis of arts medicine literature'. *Medical Problems of Performing Artists*, 6(1) (pp. 3–7).

Goodman, E. (2000) Analysing the ensemble in music rehearsal and performance: the nature and effects of interaction in cello–piano duos. Unpublished doctoral dissertation, University of London.

Goodman, E. (2002) 'Ensemble performance'. In J. Rink (ed.) *Musical Performance: A guide to understanding*. Cambridge: Cambridge University Press (pp. 153–167).

Goodson, C.A. (1992) Intelligent music listening: an interactive hypermedia program for basic music listening skills. Unpublished doctoral dissertation, University of Utah, Salt Lake City.

Goolsby, T.W. (1994) 'Profiles of processing: eye movements during sightreading'. *Music Perception*, 12 (pp. 97–123).

Goolsby, T.W. (1996) 'Time use in instrumental rehearsals: a comparison of experienced, novice, and student teachers'. *Journal of Research in Music Education*, 44(4) (pp. 286–303).

Goolsby, T.W. (1997) 'Verbal instruction in instrumental rehearsals: a comparison of three career levels in pre-service teachers'. *Journal of Research in Music Education*, 45(1) (pp. 21–40).

Goolsby, T.W. (1999) 'A comparison of expert and novice music teachers' preparing identical band compositions: an operational replication'. *Journal of Research in Music Education*, 47(2) (pp. 174–187).

Gorder, W. (1980) 'Divergent production abilities as constructs of musical creativity'. *Journal of Research in Music Education*, 28(1) (pp. 34–42).

Gordon, E.E. (1965) *Musical Aptitude Profile Manual*. Boston: Houghton Mifflin.

Gordon, E.E. (1979) *Primary Measures of Music Audiation*. Chicago: GIA Publications.

Gordon, E.E. (1982) *Intermediate Measures of Music Audiation*. Chicago: GIA Publications.

Gordon, E.E. (1989a) *Advanced Measures of Music Audiation*. Chicago: GIA Publications.

Gordon, E.E. (1989b) *Audie: A game for understanding and analysing your child's musical potential*. Chicago: GIA Publications.

Gordon, E.E. (1993) *Learning Sequences in Music: Skills, contents, and patterns. A music learning theory*. Chicago: GIA Publications.

Gordon, E.E. (1997) *Learning Sequences in Music: Skill, content and patterns*. Chicago: GIA.

Gorn, G.J. (1982) 'The effect of music in advertising on choice behaviour: a classical conditioning approach'. *Journal of Marketing*, 46 (pp. 94–101).

Gourlay, K.A. (1984) 'The non-universality of music and the universality of non-music'. *World Music*, 26 (pp. 25–36).

Greco, V. (1997) 'Investigation of the effects of student-selected repertoire on the practice habits of instrumental music students'. MA action research project, St Xavier University (ERIC Document Reproduction Service No. ED 418 049).

Green, L. (2001) *How Popular Musicians Learn: A way ahead for music education*. London and New York: Ashgate.

Greennagel, D. (1995) 'A study of selected predictors of jazz vocal improvisation skills'. Doctoral dissertation, University of Miami. *Dissertation Abstracts International*, 55(8) (2201A).

Greer, R.D., Dorow, L.G., Wachhaus, G. and White, E.R. (1973) 'Adult approval and student music selection behaviour'. *Journal of Research in Music Education*, 21 (pp. 345–354).

Gregersen, P.K., Kowalsky, E., Kohn, E. and Marvin, E.W. (1999) 'Absolute pitch: prevalence, ethnic variation and estimation of the genetic component'. *American Journal of Human Genetics*, 65(3) (pp. 911–913).

Gregory, A.H. (1997) 'The roles of music in society'. In D.J. Hargreaves and A.C. North (eds) *The Social Psychology of Music*. Oxford: Oxford University Press (pp. 123–140).

Gregory, A.H., Worrall, L. and Sarge, A. (1996) 'The development of emotional responses to music in young children'. *Motivation and Emotion*, 20(4) (pp. 341–349).

Griffiths, T.D. (2003) 'The neural processing of complex sounds'. In I. Peretz and R.J.A. Zatorre (eds) *The Cognitive Neuroscience of Music*. Oxford: Oxford University Press (pp. 168–180).

Griswold, P.A. and Chroback, D.A. (1981) 'Sex role associations of music instruments and occupations by gender and major'. *Journal of Research in Music Education*, 29(1) (pp. 57–62).

Groeneweg, G., Stan, E.A., Celser A., MacBeth, L. and Vrbancic, M.I. (1988) 'The effect of background music on the vocational behavior of mentally handicapped adults'. *Journal of Music Therapy*, 3(3) (pp. 118–134).

Groenland, E.A.G. and Schoormans, J.P.L. (1994) 'Comparing mood-induction and affective conditioning as mechanisms influencing product evaluation and product choice'. *Psychology and Marketing*, 11(2) (pp. 183–197).

Gromko, J. (1993) 'Perceptual differences between expert and novice music listeners: a multidimensional scaling analysis'. *Psychology of Music*, 21(1) (pp. 34–47).

Grondahl, D. (1987) *Thinking Processes and Structures used by Professional Pianists in Keyboard Learning*. Hovedfagsewksamen in Music Education, The Norwegian State Academy of Music, Oslo.

Gruber, H.E. (1980) *Darwin on Man: A psychological study of scientific creativity*. Chicago: University of Chicago Press.

Gruber, H.E. and Davis, S. (1988) 'Inching our way up Mount Olympus: the evolving systems approach to creative thinking'. In R. Sternberg (ed.) *The Nature of Creativity: Contemporary psychological perspectives*. Cambridge: Cambridge University Press (pp. 243–270).

Gruson, L.M. (1988) 'Rehearsal skill and musical competence: does practice make perfect?' In Sloboda, J.A. (ed.) *Generative Processes in Music: The psychology of performance, improvisation, and composition*. Oxford: Clarendon Press (pp. 91–112).

Gruzelier, J.H. and Egner, T. (2004) 'Physiological self-regulation: biofeedback and neurofeedback'. In A. Williamon (ed.) *Musical Excellence: Strategies and techniques to enhance performance*. Oxford: Oxford University Press (pp. 197–220).

Gunsberg, A.S. (1988) 'Improvised musical play: a strategy for fostering social play between developmentally delayed and non-delayed preschool children'. *Journal of Music Therapy*, 15(4) (pp. 178–191).

Gunsberg, A.S. (1991) 'Play as improvisation: the benefits of music for developmentally delayed young children's social play'. *Early Child Development and Care*, 66 (pp. 85–91).

Gustafson, R.I. (1986) 'Effects of interpersonal dynamics in the student-teacher dyads in diagnostic and remedial content of four private violin lessons'. *Psychology of Music*, 14(2) (pp. 130–139).

Hallam, S. (1992) Approaches to learning and performance of expert and novice musicians. Unpublished PhD thesis. University of London.

Hallam. S, (1995a) 'Professional musicians' approaches to the learning and interpretation of music'. *Psychology of Music*, 23(2) (pp. 111–128).

Hallam, S. (1995b) 'Professional musicians' orientations to practice: implications for teaching'. *British Journal of Music Education*, 12(1) (pp. 3–19).

Hallam, S. (1997a) 'Approaches to instrumental music practice of experts and novices: implications for education'. In H. Jorgensen and A. Lehman (eds) *Does Practice Make Perfect? Current theory and research* on instrumental music practice. NMH-publikasjoner 1997:1, Oslo, Norway: Norges Musikkhgskole (Norwegian Academy of Music) (pp. 89–108).

Hallam, S. (1997b) 'The development of memorisation strategies in musicians: implications for instrumental teaching'. *British Journal of Music Education*, 14(1) (pp. 87–97).

Hallam, S. (1997c) 'What do we know about practising? Towards a model synthesising the research literature'. In H. Jorgensen and A. Lehman (eds) *Does Practice Make Perfect? Current theory and research on instrumental music practice*. NMH-publikasjoner 1997:1, Oslo, Norway: Norges musikkhgskole (Norwegian Academy of Music) (pp. 179–231).

Hallam, S. (1998a) *Instrumental Teaching: A practical guide to better teaching and learning*. Oxford: Heinemann.

Hallam, S. (1998b) Personality, practice and performance: problems and possibilities. Keynote presentation at Conference of the Deutsche Gesellschaft for Musikpsychologie (German Society for Music Psychology), 4–6 September, Dortmund.

Hallam, S. (1998c) 'Predictors of achievement and drop out in instrumental tuition'. *Psychology of Music*, 26(2) (pp. 116–132).

Hallam, S. (2000) The effects of background music on studying. Invited presentation given at Conference of the Society for Research in Psychology of Music and Music Education, 8–9 April, University of Leicester.

Hallam, S. (2001a) 'The development of expertise in young musicians: strategy use, knowledge acquisition and individual diversity'. *Music Education Research*, 3(1) (pp. 7–23).

Hallam, S. (2001b) 'The development of metacognition in musicians: implications for education'. *The British Journal of Music Education*, 18(1) (pp. 27–39).

Hallam, S. (2001c) 'Learning in music'. In C. Philpott and C. Plummeridge (eds) *Issues in the Teaching of Music*. London: Routledge (pp. 61–76).

Hallam, S. (2001d) *The Power of Music*. London: Performing Right Society. *www.thepowerofmusic.co.uk*.

Hallam, S. (2002) 'Musical motivation: towards a model synthesising the research'. *Music Education Research*, 4(2) (pp. 225–244).

Hallam, S. (2003) 'Supporting students in learning to perform'. In I.M. Hanken, S.G. Nielsen and M. Nerland (eds) *Research in and for Higher Music Education. Festschrift for Harald Jorgensen*. NMH-publikasjoner 2002:2, Oslo, Norway: Norges Musikkhgskole (Norwegian Academy of Music) (pp. 23–44).

Hallam, S. (2004a) *Homework: The evidence*. London: Institute of Education, University of London.

Hallam, S. (2004b) 'How important is practicing as a predictor of learning outcomes in instrumental music?' In S.D. Lipscomb, R. Ashley, R.O. Gjerdingen and P. Webster (eds) *Proceedings of the 8th International Conference on Music Perception and Cognition*, 3–7 August 2004, Northwestern University, Evanston, Illinois (pp. 165–168).

Hallam, S. (in press, a) 'Gender differences in the factors which predict musical attainment in school aged students'. *Bulletin of the Council for Research in Music Education*.

Hallam, S. (in press, b) 'Musicality'. In G.E. McPherson (ed.) *The Child as Musician: A handbook of musical development*. Oxford: Oxford University Press.

Hallam, S. and Godwin, C. (2000) The effects of background music on primary school pupils' performance on a writing task. Paper presented at annual conference of the British Educational Research Association, 7–9 September 2000, University of Wales, Cardiff.

Hallam, S. and Ireson, J. (1999) 'Pedagogy in the secondary school'. In P. Mortimore (ed.) *Pedagogy and its Impact on Learning*. London: Sage (pp. 68–97).

Hallam, S. and Price, J. (1998) 'Can the use of background music improve the behaviour and academic performance of children with emotional and behavioural difficulties?' *British Journal of Special Education*, 25(2) (pp. 87–90).

Hallam, S. and Prince, V. (2000) *Research into Instrumental Music Services*. London: Department for Education and Employment.

Hallam, S. and Prince, V. (2003) 'Conceptions of musical ability'. *Research Studies in Music Education*, 20 (pp. 2–22).

Hallam, S. and Shaw, J. (2003). 'Constructions of musical ability'. *Bulletin of the Council for Research in Music Education*. Special Issue, 19th International Society for Music Education Research Seminar, 3–9 August 2002, School of Music, University of Gothenberg, Gothenburg, Sweden, 153/4 (pp. 102–107).

Hallam, S. and Stainthorp, R. (1995) 'Learning processes'. In A. Kemp (ed.) *Principles and Processes of Private Music Teaching. Module 2, Unit 2B*. Reading: International Centre for Research in Music Education, University of Reading (pp. 1–39).

Hallam, S. and Woods, C. (2003) Instrumental music teachers' perceptions of musical ability. Paper presented at 3rd International Research in Music Education Conference, 8–12 April, University of Exeter.

Hallam, S., Ireson, J. and Davies, J. (2002a) *Effective Pupil Grouping in the Primary School – a Practical Guide*. London: Fulton.

Hallam, S., Price, J. and Katsarou, G. (2002b) 'The effects of background music on primary school pupils' task performance'. *Educational Studies*, 28(2) (pp. 111–122).

Hallam, S., Kirton. A., Peffers, J., Robertson, P. and Stobart, G. (2004) *Final Report of the Evaluation of Project 1 of the Assessment is for Learning Development Programme: Support for professional practice in formative assessment*. Edinburgh: Scottish Executive.

Halpern, A.R. (1989) 'Memory for the absolute pitch of familiar songs'. *Memory and Cognition*, 17 (pp. 572–581).

Halpern, A.R. (2003) 'Cerebral substrates for musical temporal processes'. In I. Peretz and R.J.A. Zatorre (eds) *The Cognitive Neuroscience of Music*. Oxford: Oxford University Press (pp. 217–230).

Hamann, D.L. (1982) 'An assessment of anxiety in instrumental and vocal performances'. *Journal of Research in Music Education*, 30 (pp. 77–90).

Hamann, D.L. and Sobaje, M. (1983) 'Anxiety and the college musician: a study of performance conditions and subject variables'. *Psychology of Music*, 11 (pp. 37–50).

Hamann, D.L., Daugherty, E.D. and Mills, C.R. (1987) 'An investigation of burnout assessment and potential job related variables among public school music educators'. *Psychology of Music*, 15(2) (pp. 128–140).

Hamilton, R.H., Pascuel-Leone, A., Rodriguez, D. and Schlaug, G. (2000) 'Increased prevalence of absolute pitch in blind musicians'. *Society for Neuroscience Abstracts*, 26(1–2) (Abstract no. 739.13).

Hammer, S.E. (1996) 'The effects of guided imagery through music on state and trait anxiety'. *Journal of Music Therapy*, 33(1) (pp. 47–70).

Hanser, S.B. (1990) 'A music strategy for depressed older adults in the community'. *The Journal of Applied Gerontology*, 9(3) (pp. 283–298).

Hanser, S.B. and Thompson, L.W. (1994) 'Effects of a music therapy strategy on depressed older adults'. *Journal of Gerontology: Psychological Sciences*, 49(6) (pp. 265–269).

Hanshumaker, J. (1980) 'The effects of arts education on intellectual and social development: a review of selected research'. *Bulletin of the Council for Research in Music Education*, 61 (pp. 10–27).

Hardy, L. and Parfitt, G. (1991) 'A catastrophe model of anxiety and performance'. *British Journal of Psychology*, 82 (pp. 163–178).

Hargreaves, D.J. (1986) *The Developmental Psychology of Music.* Cambridge: Cambridge University Press.

Hargreaves, D.J. and North, A.C. (eds) (2001) *Musical Development and Learning: An international perspective.* London: Continuum.

Hargreaves, D.J., Cork, C.A. and Setton, T. (1991) 'Cognitive strategies in jazz improvisation: an exploratory study'. *Canadian Journal of Research in Music Education,* 33 (pp. 47–54).

Harland, J., Kinder, K., Lord, P., Stott, A., Schagen, I. and Haynes, J. (2000) *Arts Education in Secondary Schools: Effects and effectiveness.* London: NFER/The Arts Council of England/Royal Society of Arts.

Harnischmacher, C. (1993) *Instrumentales Uben und Aspekte de Personlichkeit. Eine grundlagenstudie zur Erforschung physicher und psychischer Abweichungen durch Instrumentalspiels.* Frankfurt am Main: Peter Lang.

Harnischmacher, C. (1995) 'Spiel oder Arbeit? Eine Pilotstudie zu, instrumentalen Ubeverhalten von Kindern und Jugendlichen'. In H. Gembris, R.D. Kraemer and G. Maas (eds) *Musikpadagogosche Forschungsberichte 1994.* Augsburg: Wisner (S.41–56).

Haroutounian, J. (2000) 'Perspectives of musical talent: a study of identification criteria and procedures'. *High Ability Studies,* 11(2) (pp. 137–160).

Harris, C.S., Bradley, R. and Titus, S.K. (1992) 'Comparison of the effects of hard rock and easy listening on the frequency of observed inappropriate behaviors: control of environmental antecedents in a large public area'. *Journal of Music Therapy,* 29(1) (pp. 6–17).

Harvey, N., Garwood, J. and Palencia, M. (1987) 'Vocal matching of pitch intervals: learning and transfer effects'. *Psychology of Music,* 15 (pp. 90–106).

Hassler, M. and Feil, A. (1986) 'A study of the relationship of composition improvisation to selected personality variables'. *Bulletin of the Council for Research in Music Education,* 87 (pp. 26–34).

Hays, T. and Minichiello, V. (2005) 'The meaning of music in the lives of older people: a qualitative study'. *Psychology of Music,* 33(4) (pp. 437–452).

Heaney, M.F. (1994) The components of a string education: a qualitative study of selected members of the Philadelphia Orchestra String Section. Unpublished doctoral dissertation, Florida State University, Tallahassee.

Hebb, D.O. (1949) *The Organization of Behaviour*. Chichester, UK: John Wiley and Sons.

Hendel, C. (1995) 'Behavioural characteristics and instructional patterns of selected music teachers'. *Journal of Research in Music Education*, 47 (pp. 174–187).

Henderson, V. and Dweck, C.S. (1990) 'Achievement and motivation in adolescence: a new model and data'. In S. Feldman and G. Elliott (eds) *At the Threshold: The developing adolescent*. Cambridge, MA: Harvard University Press (pp. 308–329).

Hennessey, S. (2000) 'Overcoming the red feeling: the development of confidence to teach music in primary school amongst student teachers'. *British Journal of Music Education*, 17(2) (pp. 183–196).

Hepler, L.E. (1986) 'The measurement of teacher/student interaction in private music lessons and its relation to teacher field dependence/independence'. *Dissertation Abstracts International*, 47 (2939–A) (University Microfilms No. 86–27848).

Hepper, P.G. (1988) 'Fetal "soap" addiction'. *Lancet*, 1 (pp. 1147–1148).

Hetland, L. (2000) 'Listening to music enhances spatial-temporal reasoning: evidence for the Mozart effect'. *The Journal of Aesthetic Education*, 34(3–4) (pp. 105–148).

Hevner, K. (1936) 'Experimental studies of the elements of expression in music'. *American Journal of Psychology*, 48 (pp. 246–268).

Hewson, A.T. (1966) 'Music reading in the classroom'. *Journal of Research in Music Education*, 14(4) (p. 289).

Hickey, M. (1995) Qualitative and quantitative relationships between children's creative musical thinking processes and products. Unpublished doctoral dissertation, Northwestern University, Evanston, Illinois.

Hickey, M. (2000) 'The use of consensual assessment in the evaluation of children's music composition'. In C. Woods, G. Luck, R. Brochard, F. Seddon and J.A. Sloboda (eds) *Proceedings of the 6th International Conference on Music Perception and Cognition*, 5–10 August, Keele, UK: Keele University.

Hickey, M. (2001) 'An application of Amabile's consensual assessment technique for rating the creativity of children's musical compositions'. *Journal of Research in Music Education*, 49 (pp. 234–244).

Hickey, M. (2002) 'Creativity research in music, visual art, theatre and dance'. In R. Colwell and C. Richardson (eds) *The New Handbook of Research of Music Teaching and Learning*. Oxford: Oxford University Press (pp. 398–415).

Hickey, M. (2003) *Why and How to Teach Music Composition: A new horizon for music education.* Reston, VA: MENC, The National Association for Music Education.

Hinkle, L.B. (1988) 'The meaning of choral experience to the adult membership of the German singing societies comprising the United Singers Federation of Pennsylvania'. Doctoral dissertation, Pennsylvania State University, 1987. *Dissertation Abstracts International,* 48 (2568A).

Hirata, Y., Kuriki, S. and Pantev, C. (1999) 'Musicians with absolute pitch show distinct neural activities in the auditory cortex'. *NeuroReport,* 10(5) (pp. 999–1002).

Hodge, G., Jupp, J. and Taylor, A. (1994) 'Work stress, distress and burnout in music and mathematics teachers'. *British Journal of Educational Psychology,* 64(1) (pp. 65–76).

Hodges, D.A. (1975) 'The effects of recorded aural models on the performance achievement of students in beginning band classes'. *Journal of Band Research,* 12 (pp. 30–34).

Hodges, D.A. (1992) 'The acquisition of music reading skills'. In R. Colwell (ed.) *Handbook of Research on Music Teaching and Learning: Music Educators National Conference.* New York: Schirmer Books (pp. 466–471).

Hodges, D.A. (ed.) (1996a) *Handbook of Music Psychology.* (2nd edition) San Antonio, TX: IMR Press.

Hodges, D.A. (1996b) 'Human musicality'. In D.A. Hodges (ed.) *Handbook of Music Psychology.* San Antonio, TX: IMR Press (pp. 29–68).

Hodges, D.A. and Haack, P.A. (1996) 'The influence of music on behaviour'. In D.A. Hodges (ed.) *Handbook of Music Psychology,* San Antonio, TX: IMR Press (pp. 469–555).

Hogg, N. (1994) 'Strategies to facilitate student composing'. *Research Studies in Music Education,* 2 (pp. 15–24).

Holmquist, S.P. (1995) 'A study of community choir members' school experiences'. Doctoral dissertation, University of Oregan, 1995. *Dissertation Abstracts International,* 56 (1699A).

Horowitz, R. (1995) 'The development of a rating scale for jazz guitar improvisation performance'. Doctoral dissertation, Columbia University Teachers College. *Dissertation Abstracts International,* 55(11) (3443A).

Howard, D.M. and Welch, G.F. (1987) 'A new microcomputer system for the assessment and development of singing ability, Institute of Acoustics', *Proceedings of Day Conference on New Developments in Instrumentation and Computing in Acoustics,* May, London, 9(4).

Howe, M.J.A. (1989) *Fragments of Genius: The strange feats of idiot savants*. London: Routledge.

Howe, M.J.A. (1990) *The Origins of Exceptional Ability*. Blackwell: Oxford.

Howe, M.J.A. and Sloboda, J. (1991) 'Young musicians' accounts of significant influences in their early lives. 2. Teachers, practising and performing'. *British Journal of Music Education*, 8(1) (pp. 53–63).

Howe, M.J.A. and Sloboda, J. (1992) 'Problems experienced by talented young musicians as a result of the failure of other children to value musical accomplishments'. *Gifted Education*, 8 (pp. 16–18).

Howe, M.J.A., Davidson, J.W., Moore, D.M. and Sloboda, J.A. (1995) 'Are there early childhood signs of musical ability?' *Psychology of Music*, 23 (pp. 162–176).

Hughes, T.H. (1991) A hypermedia listening station for the college music literature class. Unpublished doctoral dissertation, University of Arizona, Tucson.

Humphreys, J.T., May, W.V. and Nelson, D.J. (1992) 'Research on music ensembles'. In R. Colwell (ed.) *Handbook of Research on Music Teaching and Learning: Music Education National Conference*, New York: Schirmer Books (pp. 651–668).

Hunter, D. (1999) 'Developing peer-learning programmes in music: group presentations and peer assessment'. *British Journal of Music Education*, 16(1) (pp. 51–63).

Hunter, D. and Russ, M. (1996) 'Peer assessment in performance studies'. *British Journal of Music Education*, 13(1) (pp. 67–78).

Hunter, M.E. and Love, C.C. (1996) 'Total quality management and the reduction of inpatient violence and costs in a forensic psychiatric hospital'. *Psychiatric-Services*, 47(7) (pp. 751–754).

Hurley, C.G. (1995) 'Student motivations for beginning and continuing/discontinuing string music tuition'. *The Quarterly Journal of Music Teaching and Learning*, 6(1) (pp. 44–55).

Huron, D. (2003) 'Is music an evolutionary adaptation?' In I. Peretz and R.J.A. Zatorre (eds) *The Cognitive Neuroscience of Music*. Oxford: Oxford University Press (pp. 57–77).

Hurwitz, I., Wolff, P.H., Bortnick, B.D. and Kokas, K. (1975) 'Non-musical effects of the Kodaly music curriculum in primary grade children'. *Journal of Learning Disabilities*, 8 (pp. 45–52).

Hutton, D. (1953) 'A comparative study of two methods of teaching sight singing in the fourth grade'. *Journal of Research in Music Education*, 1 (pp. 119–126).

Hykin, J., Moore, R., Duncan, K., Clare, S., Baker, P., Johnson, I., Bowtell, R., Mansfield, P. and Gowland, P. (1999) 'Fetal brain activity demonstrated by functional magnetic resonance imaging'. *Lancet*, 354 (pp. 645–646).

Ings, R., Jones, R. and Randell, N. (2000) *Mapping Hidden Talent*. London: The Prince's Trust/National Youth Agency/Youth Work Press.

Irish, B.M. (1993) 'Meaning in music: cognitive and affective response in adults'. Doctoral dissertation, Cornell University, 1993. *Dissertation Abstracts International*, 54 (1198A).

Irvine, J.K. and LeVine, W.R. (1981) 'The use of biofeedback to reduce the left hand tension for string players'. *American String Teacher*, 31 (pp. 10–12).

Iwanaga, M. and Moroki, Y. (1999) 'Subjective and physiological responses to music stimuli controlled over activity and preference'. *Journal of Music Therapy*, 36(1) (pp. 26–38).

James, A. (1988) 'Medicine and performing arts. The stage fright syndrome'. *Transactions of the Medical Society of London*, 105 (pp. 5–9).

James, I. and Savage, I. (1984) Beneficial effect of nadolol on anxiety-induced disturbances of musical performance in musicians: a comparison with diazepam and placebo. *American Heart Journal*, 108 (pp. 1150–1155).

Jenkins, J.M.D. (1976) 'The relationship between maternal parents' musical experience and the musical development of two and three year old girls'. *Dissertation Abstracts International*, 37(11) (7325A) (University Microfilms No. 77–11111, 150).

John, D. (1995) 'The therapeutic relationship in music therapy as a tool in the treatment of psychosis'. In T. Wigram, B. Saperston and R. West (eds) *The Art and Science of Music Therapy: A handbook*. Langhorne: Harwood Academic Publishers/Gordon and Breach Science Publishers.

Johnson-Laird, P.N. (1988) 'Reasoning, imagining and creating'. *Bulletin of the Council for Research in Music Education*, 95 (pp. 71–87).

Johnson-Laird, P.N. (1991) 'Jazz improvisation: a theory at the computational level'. In P. Howell, R. West and I. Cross (eds) *Representing Musical Structure*. London: Academic Press (pp. 291–325).

Johnson-Laird, P.N. (1993) *Human and Machine Thinking*. Hillsdale, NJ: Lawrence Erlbaum.

Johnson-Laird, P.N. (2002) 'How jazz musicians improvise'. *Music Perception*, 19 (pp. 415–442).

Johnston, K. and Rohaly-Davis J. (1996) 'An introduction to music therapy: helping the oncology patient in the ICU'. *Critical Care Nursing Quarterly*, 18(4) (pp. 54–60).

Johnstone, H. (1993) 'The use of video self-assessment, peer assessment and instructor feedback in evaluating conducting skills in music student teachers'. *British Journal of Music Education*, 10(1) (pp. 57–63).

Jones, M. (1971) 'A pilot study in the use of a vertically arranged keyboard instrument with the uncertain singer'. *Journal of Research in Music Education*, 19 (pp. 183–194).

Jones, M. (1979) 'Using a vertical-keyboard instrument with the uncertain singer, *Journal of Research in Music Education'*. 27 (pp. 173–184).

Jorgensen, E.R. (1990) 'Philosophy and the music teacher'. *Music Educators Journal*, 76(5) (pp. 17–23).

Jorgensen, H. (1995) Teaching/learning strategies in instrumental practice: a report on research in progress. Paper presented at 3rd Research Alliance of Institutes for Music Education Symposium, Florida State University, 6–10 April, Tallahassee, Florida.

Jorgensen, H. (1996) *Tid til oving? Studentenes bruk av tid til oving ved Norges musikkhogskole 1* (*Time to Practise*) Oslo: Norges Musikkhgskole (Norwegian Academy of Music).

Jorgensen, H. (1997) 'Time for practicing? Higher level students' use of time for instrumental practicing'. In H. Jorgensen and A.C. Lehmann (eds) *Does Practice Make Perfect? Current theory and research on instrumental music practice*. Oslo: Norges Musikkhgskole (Norwegian Academy of Music) (pp. 123–140).

Jorgensen, H. (1998) *Planlegges oving?* (*Is Practice Planned?*) Oslo: Norges Musikkhgskole (Norwegian Academy of Music).

Jorgensen, H. (2000) 'Student learning in higher instrumental education: who is responsible?' *British Journal of Music Education*, 17 (pp. 67–77).

Jorgensen, H. (2002) 'Instrumental performance expertise and amount of practice among instrumental students in a conservatoire'. *Music Education Research*, 4 (pp. 105–119).

Jorgensen, H. (2004) 'Strategies for individual practice'. In A. Williamon (ed.) *Musical Excellence: Strategies and techniques to enhance performance*. Oxford: Oxford University Press (pp. 85–104).

Joyner, D.R. (1969) 'The monotone problem'. *Journal of Research in Music Education*, 17 (pp. 115–124).

Jusczyk, P.W. and Krumhansl, C.L. (1993) 'Pitch and rhythmic patterns affecting infants' sensitivity to musical phrase structure'. *Journal of*

Experimental Psychology: Human perception and performance, 19 (pp. 627–640).

Juslin, P.N. and Sloboda, J.A. (eds) *Music and Emotion: Theory and research*. Oxford: Oxford University Press.

Kafer, H.A. (1982) The structured border lesson: the effectiveness of controlling the entry and exit environment of the private music lesson. Unpublished doctoral dissertation, North Texas State University.

Kahn, A.P. (1998) 'Healthy aging: a study of self-perceptions of well-being'. *Dissertation Abstracts International*, 58 (4740B) (University Microfilms No. AAT98–10054).

Kalmar, M. and Balasko, G. (1987) 'Musical mother tongue and creativity in preschool children's melody improvisations'. *Bulletin of the Council for Research in Music Education*, 91 (pp. 77–86).

Kaltoft, G. (1990) 'Music and emancipatory learning in three community education programs'. *Dissertation Abstracts International*, 51(7) (2239A) (University Microfilms No. AAT90–33861).

Karmiloff-Smith, A. (1992) *Beyond Modularity: A developmental perspective on cognitive science*. Cambridge, MA: The MIT Press.

Karni, A, Meyer, G., Jezzard, P., Adams, M.M., Turner, R. and Ungerleider, L.G. (1995) 'FMRI evidence for adult motor cortex plasticity during motor skill learning'. *Nature*, 377 (pp. 155–158).

Kastner, M.P. and Crowder, R.G. (1990) 'Perception of the major/minor distinction: IV. Emotional connotation in young children'. *Music Perception*, 8(2) (pp. 189–201).

Keenan, J.V., Thangaraj, A., Halpern, A. *et al.* (2001) 'Absolute pitch and planum temporale'. *NeuroImage*, 14 (pp. 1402–1408).

Kelley, L. and Sutton-Smith, B. (1987) 'A study of infant musical productivity'. In J.C. Peery, I.W. Peery and T.W. Draper (eds) *Music and Child Development*. New York: Springer-Verlag (pp. 35–53).

Kember D. and Gow, L. (1994) 'Orientations to teaching and their effect on the quality of student learning'. *Journal of Higher Education*, 65 (pp. 59–74).

Kemp, A.E. (1981) 'The personality structure of the musician. 1. Identifying a profile of traits for the performer'. *Psychology of Music*, 9(1) (pp. 3–14).

Kemp, A.E. (1994) 'Aspects of upbringing as revealed through the personalities of musicians'. *The Quarterly Journal of Music Teaching and Learning*, 5(4) (pp. 34–41).

Kemp, A.E. (1996) *The Musical Temperament: Psychology and personality of musicians*. Oxford: Oxford University Press.

Kendall, M.J. (1990) 'A review of selected research literature in elementary instrumental music education with implication for teaching'. *Journal of Band Research*, 25 (pp. 64–82).

Kendrick, M.J., Craig, K.D., Lawson, D.W. and Davidson, P.O. (1982) 'Cognitive and behavioural therapy for musical-performance anxiety'. *Journal of Consulting and Clinical Psychology*, 50 (pp. 353–362).

Kennell, R. (1989) 'Three teacher scaffolding strategies in college applied music instruction'. *Dissertation Abstracts International*, 50 (2822–A) (University Microfilms No. 89–17656).

Kennell, R. (1992) 'Toward a theory of applied music instruction'. *The Quarterly Journal of Music Teaching and Learning*, 3(2) (pp. 5–16).

Kennell, R. (2002) 'Systematic research in studio instruction in music'. In R. Colwell and C. Richardson (eds) *The New Handbook of Research on Music Teaching and Learning*. Oxford: Oxford University Press.

Kenny, B.J. and Gellrich, M. (2002) 'Improvisation'. In R. Parncutt and G.E. McPherson (eds) *The Science and Psychology of Music Performance: Creative strategies for teaching and learning*. Oxford: Oxford University Press (pp. 117–134).

Kenny, W.E. (1992) The effect of metacognitive strategy instruction on the performance proficiency and attitude toward practice of beginning band students. Unpublished doctoral dissertation, University of Illinois, Urbana-Champaign, Illinois.

Kessen, W., Levine, J. and Wendrich, K.A. (1979) 'The imitation of pitch in infants'. *Infant Behaviour and Development*, 2 (pp. 93–99).

Kim, S. (1996) An exploratory study to incorporate supplementary computer-assisted historical and theoretical studies into applied music instruction. Unpublished doctoral dissertation, Columbia University Teachers College, New York.

Klein, S.A. and Winkelstein, M.L. (1996) 'Enhancing paediatric health care with music'. *Journal of Paediatric Health Care*, 10(2) (pp. 74–81).

Klinedinst, R.E. (1991) 'Predicting performance achievement and retention of fifth-grade instrumental students'. *Journal of Research in Music Education*, 39(3) (pp. 225–238).

Klinger, E. (1975) 'Consequences of commitment to and disengagement from incentives'. *Psychological Review*, 82(1) (pp. 1–25).

Klinger, E. (1977) *Meaning and Void: Inner experience and the incentives in people's lives*. Minneapolis, University of Minneapolis Press.

Klinger, E. (1987) 'Current concerns and disengagement from incentives'. In F. Halisch and J. Kuhl (eds) *Motivation, Intention and Volition*. New York: Springer-Verlag (pp. 337–347).

Knieter, G.L. (1971) 'The nature of aesthetic education'. *Toward an Aesthetic Education*. Washington, DC: Music Educators National Conference.

Koelsch, S. and Friederici, A.D. (2003) 'Toward the neural basis of processing structure in music, comparative results of different neurophysicological investigation methods'. In G. Avanzini, C. Faienza, D. Minciacchi, L. Lopez and M. Majno (eds) *The Neurosciences and Music*. New York: New York Academy of Sciences (pp. 15–28).

Koelsch, S., Gunter, T. and Friederici, A.D. *et al.* (2000) 'Brain indices of music processing: non-musicians are musical'. *Journal of Cognitive Neuroscience*, 12 (pp. 520–541).

Koestner, R. and McClelland, D.C. (1990) 'Perspectives on competence motivation'. In L.A. Pervin (ed.) *Handbook of Personality: Theory and research*. New York: Guilford Press (pp. 527–548).

Kogan, N. (1997) 'Reflections on aesthetics and evolution'. *Critical Review*, 11 (pp. 193–240).

Koger, S., Chapin, K. and Brotons, M. (1999) 'Is music therapy an effective intervention for dementia? A meta-analytic review of literature'. *Journal of Music Therapy*, 36(1) (pp. 2–15).

Kopiez, R. (1990) *Der Einfluss kognitiver Strukturne auf das Erlernen eines Musikstucks am Instrument (The Influence of Cognitive Structures on the Learning of Instrumental Music)*. Frankfurt: Peter Lang.

Kopiez, R. (1991) 'Structural aids to the cognitive practice of music: graphic or verbal analysis'. *Psychologica Belgica*, 31(2) (pp. 163–171).

Kopiez, R., Weihs, C., Ligges, U. and Lee, J.I. (in press) 'Classification of high and low achievers in a music sight reading task'. *Psychology of Music*.

Kornicke, L.E. (1992) 'An exploratory study of individual difference variables in piano sight-reading achievement'. Doctoral dissertation, Indiana University. *Dissertation Abstracts International*, 53 (12A) (University Microfilms No. 9301458).

Kornicke, L.E. (1995) 'An exploratory study of individual difference variables in piano sight-reading achievement'. *Quarterly Journal of Music Teaching and Learning*, 6 (pp. 56–79).

Kostka, M.J. (1984) 'An investigation of reinforcements, time use and student attention in piano lessons'. *Journal of Research in Music Education*, 32 (pp. 113–122).

Kotsopoulou, A. (1997) Music in students' lives. Unpublished MA dissertation, University of London.

Kotsopoulou, A. (2001) A cross cultural study of the use and perceived effects of background music in studying. Unpublished PhD thesis, University of London.

Kotsopoulou, A. and Hallam, S. (2004) 'Cross cultural differences in listening to music while studying'. In S.D. Lipscomb, R. Ashley, R.O. Gjerdingen and P. Webster (eds) *Proceedings of the 8th International Conference on Music Perception and Cognition*, 3–7 August, Northwestern University, Evanston, Illinois (pp. 397–400).

Kovacs, S. (1916) 'Untersuchungen uber das musikalische Gedachtnis'. *Zeit f. ang. Psych.*, 11 (pp. 113–135).

KPMG/National Music Council (1999) *A Sound Performance: The economic value of music to the United Kingdom*. London: National Music Council.

Krampe, R.T. (1994) *Maintaining Excellence: Cognitive-motor performance in pianists differing in age and skill level* (Studien und Berichte /MPI fur Bildungsforschung 58). Berlin, Germany: Sigma.

Kratus, J. (1989) 'A time analysis of the compositional processes used by children ages 7–11'. *Journal of Research in Music Education*, 37(1) (pp. 5–20).

Kratus, J. (1991) 'Growing with improvisation'. *Music Educators Journal*, 78(4) (pp. 35–40).

Kratus, J. (1994) 'Relationships among children's music audiation and their compositional processes and products'. *Journal of Research in Music Education*, 42(2) (pp. 115–130).

Kratus, J. (1996) 'A developmental approach to teaching music improvisation'. *International Journal of Music Education*, 26 (pp. 3–13).

Kreutz, G., Bongard, S., Rohrmann, S., Hodapp, V. and Grebe, D. (in press) 'Effects of choir singing or listening on secretory immunoglobulin A, cortisol, and emotional state'. *Journal of Behavioural Medicine*.

Krumhansl, C.L. and Jusczyk, P.W. (1990) 'Infants' perception of phrase structure in music'. *Psychological Science*, 1 (pp. 70–73).

Kuck, H., Grossbach, M., Bangert, M. and Altenmuller, E. (2003) 'Electrophysiological evidence of a common network'. In G. Avanzini, C. Faienza, D. Minciacchi, L. Lopez and M. Majno (eds) *The Neurosciences and Music*. New York: New York Academy of Sciences (pp. 244–253).

Kuhn, T.L. (1975) 'The effect of teacher approval and disapproval on attentiveness, music achievement and attitude of 5th grade students'. In C.K. Madsen, R.D. Greer and C.H. Madsen, Jr (eds) *Research in Music Behaviour*. New York: Teachers College.

Laczo, Z. (1981) 'A psychological investigation of improvisation abilities in the lower and higher classes of the elementary school'. *Bulletin of the Council for Research in Music Education*, 66/67 (pp. 39–45).

Lafuente, M.J., Grifol, R., Segarra, J., Soriano, M., Gorba, A. and Montesinos, A. (1997) 'Effects of the Firstart method of prenatal stimulation on psychomotor development: the first six months'. *Pre and Perinatal Journal*, 11(3) (pp. 151–162).

Lamont, A. (2002) 'Musical identities and the school environment'. In R.A.R. MacDonald, D.J. Hargreaves and D.E. Miell (eds) *Musical Identities*. Oxford: Oxford University Press (pp. 41–59).

Lamont, A. and Cross, I. (1994) 'Children's cognitive representations of musical pitch'. *Music Perception*, 12(1) (pp. 27–55).

Lamp, C. and Keys, N. (1935) 'Can aptitude for specific instruments be predicted?' *American Journal of Educational Psychology*, 26 (pp. 587–596).

Langner, G. (1992) 'Periodicity encoding in the auditory system'. *Hearing Research*, 60 (pp. 115–142).

Larson, P. (1983) 'An exploratory study of lifelong musical interest and activity: case studies of twelve retired adults'. Doctoral dissertation, Temple University, 1982. *Dissertation Abstracts International*, 44 (100A).

Lassiter, D.G. (1981) A survey of parental involvement in the development of professional musicians. Unpublished master's thesis, Florida State University, Tallahassee.

Leavell, B. (1997) 'Making the change: middle school band students' perspectives on the learning of musical-technical skills in jazz performance'. Doctoral dissertation, University of North Texas. *Dissertation Abstracts International*, 57(7) (2931A).

LeBlanc, A. (1980) 'Outline of a proposed model of sources of variation in musical taste'. *Bulletin of the Council for Research in Music Education*, 61 (pp. 29–34).

LeBlanc, A. (1982) 'An interactive theory of musical preference'. *Journal of Music Therapy*, 19 (pp. 28–45).

LeBlanc, A. (1994) 'A theory of music performance anxiety'. *The Quarterly Journal of Music Teaching and Learning*, 5(4) (pp. 60–69).

LeBlanc Corporation (1961) *The Influence of Parents' Attitudes on Children's Musical Activity*. Kenosha, WI: LeBlanc Corporation.

Lecanuet, J.P. (1996) 'Prenatal auditory experience'. In I. Deliege and J.A. Sloboda (eds) *Musical Beginnings: Origins and development of musical competence*. Oxford: Oxford University Press (pp. 3–25).

LeDoux, J.E. (1993) 'Emotional memory systems in the brain'. *Behavioural and Brain Research*, 58 (pp. 69–70).

LeDoux, J.E. (1996) *The Emotional Brain: The mysterious underpinnings of emotional life*. New York: Simon and Schuster.

Lehmann, A.C. (1997a) 'Acquired mental representations'. In H. Jorgensen and A.C. Lehmann (eds) *Does Practice Make Perfect? Current theory and research on instrumental music practice*. Oslo: Norges Musikkhgskole (Norwegian Academy of Music) (pp. 141–164).

Lehmann, A.C. (1997b) 'The acquisition of expertise in music: efficiency of deliberate practice as a moderating variable in accounting for sub-expert performance'. In I. Deliege and J.A. Sloboda (eds) *Perception and Cognition of Music*. Hove: Psychology Press (pp. 161–187).

Lehmann, A.C. and Ericsson, K.A. (1995) 'The relationship between historical constraints of musical practice and increase of musicians' performance skills'. Paper presented at 7th European Conference on Developmental Psychology, 23–27 August, Poland.

Lehmann, A.C. and Ericsson, K.A. (1996) 'Structure and acquisition of expert accompanying and sight-reading performance'. *Psychomusicology*, 15 (pp. 1–29).

Lehmann, A.C. and Ericsson, K.A. (1998) 'Preparation of a public piano performance: the relation between practice and performance'. *Musicae Scientiae*, 2 (pp. 67–94).

Lehrer, P.M. (1987) 'A review of the approaches of the management of tension and stage fright in music performance'. *Journal of Research in Music Education*, 35(3) (pp. 141–154).

Leitner, M.J. (1982) 'The effects of intergenerational music activities on senior day care participant and elementary school children'. *Dissertation Abstracts International*, 42(8) (3752A) (University Microfilms No. AAT82–02620).

Lenhoff, H.M., Perales, O. and Hickok, G. (2001) 'Absolute pitch in Williams Syndrome'. *Music Perception*, 18(4) (p. 491).

Lepper, M. and Greene, D. (1975) 'Turning play into work: effects of adult surveillance and extrinsic rewards on children's intrinsic motivation'. *Journal of Personality and Social Psychology*, 31 (pp. 479–486).

Lerdhal, F. and Jackendoff, R. (1983) *A Generative Theory of Tonal Music*. Cambridge, MA: The MIT Press.

Lesuik, T. (2005) 'The effect of music listening on work performance'. *Psychology of Music*, 33(2) (pp. 173–191).

Levee, J.R., Cohen, M.J. and Rickles, W.H. (1976) 'Electromyographic biofeedback for relief of tension in the facial and throat muscles of a woodwind musician'. *Biofeedback and Self-Regulation*, 1(1) (pp. 113–120).

LeVine, W.R. and Irvine, J.K. (1984) 'In vivo EMG biofeedback in violin and viola pedagogy'. *Biofeedback and Self-Regulation*, 9 (pp. 161–168).

Levitin, D.J. (1994) 'Absolute memory for musical pitch: evidence for the production of learned memories'. *Perception and Psychophysics*, 56 (pp. 414–423).

Levitin, D.J. and Bellugi, U. (1998) 'Musical abilities in individuals with Williams Syndrome'. *Music Perception*, 15(4) (pp. 357–389).

Levitin, D.J. and Cook, P.R. (1996) 'Memory for musical tempo: additional evidence that auditory memory is absolute'. *Perceptual Psychophysics*, 58 (pp. 927–935).

L'Hommidieu, R.L. (1992) The management of selected educational variables by master studio teachers in music performance. Unpublished doctoral dissertation, Northwestern University, Evanston, Illinois.

Liegeois-Chauvel, C., Peretz, I., Babai, M., Laguitton, V. and Chauvel, P. (1998) 'Contribution of different cortical areas in the temporal lobes to music processing'. *Brain*, 121 (pp. 1853–1867).

Liegeois-Chauvel, C., De Graaf, J.B., Laguitton, V. and Chauvel, P. (1999) 'Specialisation of left auditory cortex for speech perception in man depends on temporal coding'. *Cerebral Cortex*, 9 (pp. 484–496).

Liegeois-Chauvel, C., Giraud, K., Badier, J.-M., Marquis, P. and Chavel, P. (2003) 'Intracerebral evoked potentials in pitch perception reveal a functional asummetry of human auditory cortex'. In I. Peretz and R.J.A. Zatorre (eds) *The Cognitive Neuroscience of Music*. Oxford: Oxford University Press (pp. 152–168).

Lim, S. and Lippman, L.G. (1991) 'Mental practice and memorisation of piano music'. *The Journal of General Psychology*, 118(1) (pp. 21–30).

Lin, S. (1994) Investigation of the effect of teacher-developed computer-based music instruction on elementary education majors. Unpublished doctoral dissertation, University of Illinois at Urbana-Champaign.

Linklater, F. (1997) 'Effects of audio- and videotape models on performance achievement of beginning clarinettists'. *Journal of Research in Music Education*, 45(3) (pp. 402–414).

Lipman, F. (1987) 'Personalities in world music education no. 5. Shinichi Suzuki'. *International Journal of Music Education*, 10 (pp. 36–39).

Little, B.R. (1989) 'Personal projects analysis: trivial pursuits, magnificent obsessions and the search for coherence'. In D.M. Buss and N. Cantor (eds) *Personality Psychology: Recent trends and emerging directions*. New York: Springer-Verlag (pp. 15–31).

Lowry, K. and Wolf, C. (1988) 'Arts education in the People's Republic of China: results of interviews with Chinese musicians and visual artists'. *Journal of Aesthetics Education*, 22(1) (pp. 89–98).

McCarthy, J.F. (1980) 'Individualised instruction, student achievement and drop out in an urban elementary instrumental music program'. *Journal of Research in Music Education*, 28 (pp. 59–69).

McClelland, D.C., Atkinson, J.W., Clark, R.W. and Lowell, E.L. (1953) *The Achievement Motive*. New York: Appleton-Century-Crofts.

McCord, K. (1993) 'Teaching music fundamentals through technology in middle school music classes'. In K. Walls (ed.) *The 3rd International Conference on Technological Directions in Music Education*. San Antonio, TX: IMR Press (pp. 68–71).

McCormick, J. and McPherson, G.E. (2003) 'The role of self-efficacy in a musical performance examination: an exploratory structural equation analysis'. *Psychology of Music*, 31(1) (pp. 37–52).

McCraty, R., Atkinson, M., Rein, G. and Watkins, A.D. (1996) 'Music enhances the effect of positive emotional states on salivary IgA'. *Stress Medicine*, 12 (pp. 167–175).

MacDonald, R.A.R. and Miell, D.E. (2000) 'Creativity and music education: the impact of social variables'. *International Journal of Music Education*, 36 (pp. 58–68).

MacDonald, R.A.R. and Miell, D.E. (2002) 'Music for individuals with special needs: a catalyst for developments in identity, communication, and musical ability'. In R.A.R. MacDonald, D.J. Hargreaves, and D.E. Miell (eds) *Musical Identities*. Oxford: Oxford University Press (pp. 163–178).

MacDonald, R.A.R. and Wilson, G. (2005) 'Musical identities of professional jazz musicians: a focus group investigation'. *Psychology of Music*, 33(4) (pp. 395–418).

MacDonald, R.A.R., Murray, J.L. and Levenson, V.L. (1999a) 'Staff attitudes towards individuals with intellectual disabilities and HIV/AIDS'. *Journal of Applied Research in Intellectual Disabilities*, 12 (pp. 348–358).

MacDonald, R.A.R., O'Donnell, P.J. and Davies, J.B. (1999b) 'Structured music workshops for individuals with learning difficulty: an empirical investigation'. *Journal of Applied Research in Intellectual Disabilities*, 12 (pp. 225–241).

MacDonald, R.A.R., Miell, D.E. and Mitchell, L. (2002a) 'An investigation of children's musical collaborations: the effect of friendship and age'. *Psychology of Music*, 30 (pp. 148–163).

MacDonald, R.A.R., Hargreaves, D.J. and Miell, D.E. (2002b) (eds) *Musical Identities*. Oxford: Oxford University Press.

McElrea, H. and Standing, L. (1992) 'Fast music causes fast drinking'. *Perceptual and Motor Skills*, 75 (p. 362).

McKeachie, W.J., Pintrich, P., Lin, Y.G. and Smith, D. (1986) *Teaching and Learning in the College Classroom*. University of Michigan: NCRIP–TAL.

MacKinnon, D.W. (1965) 'Personality and the realization of creative talent'. *American Psychologist*, 20 (pp. 273–281).

MacKnight, C.B. (1975) 'The effects of tonal pattern training of the performance achievement of beginning wind instrumentalists'. *Experimental Research in the Psychology of Music: Studies in the psychology of music*, 10 (pp. 53–76).

McLaughin, D.B. (1985) An investigation of performance problems confronted by multiple woodwind specialists. Unpublished EdD thesis. Columbia University Teachers College.

McPherson, G.E. (1993) 'Evaluating improvisational ability of high school instrumentalists'. *Bulletin of the Council for Research in Music Education*, 119 (pp. 11–20).

McPherson, G.E. (1994) 'Factors and abilities influencing sight-reading skill in music'. *Journal of Research in Music Education*, 42 (pp. 217–231).

McPherson, G.E. (1995/6) 'Five aspects of musical performance and their correlates'. *Bulletin of the Council for Research in Music Education*, Special Issue, 15th International Society for Music Education, 9–15 July, University of Miami, Florida.

McPherson, G.E. and Davidson, J.W. (2002) 'Musical practice: mother and child interactions during the first year of learning an instrument'. *Music Education Research*, 4(1) (pp. 141–156).

McPherson, G.E. and Davidson, J.W. 'Playing an instrument'. In G.E. McPherson (ed.) *The Child as Musician: A handbook of musical development*. Oxford: Oxford University Press.

McPherson, G.E. and McCormick, J. (1999) 'Motivational and self-regulated components of musical practice'. *Bulletin of the Council for Research in Music Education*, 141 (pp. 98–102).

McPherson, G.E. and McCormick, J. (in press) 'Self-efficacy and music performance'. *Psychology of Music.*

McPherson, G.E. and Renwick, J. (2001) 'Longitudinal study of self-regulation in children's music practice'. *Music Education Research*, 3(1) (pp. 169–186).

McPherson, G.E. and Zimmerman, B.J. (2002) 'Self-regulation of musical learning: a social cognitive perspective'. In R. Colwell and C. Richardson (eds) *The New Handbook of Research on Music Teaching and Learning.* Oxford: Oxford University Press (pp. 327–347).

McPherson, G.E., Bailey, M. and Sinclair, K. (1997) 'Path analysis of a model to describe the relationship among five types of musical performance'. *Journal of Research in Music Education*, 45 (pp. 103–129).

Macek, K. (1987) 'The photographic ear'. *Piano Quarterly*, 35(137) (pp. 46–48).

Madsen, C.K. (1974) 'Sharpness and flatness in scalar solo vocal performance'. *Sciences de l'Art – Scientific Aesthetics*, 9(1–2) (pp. 91–97).

Madsen, C.K. (1990) 'Teacher intensity in relationship to music education'. *Bulletin of the Council for Research in Music Education*, 104 (pp. 38–46).

Madsen, C.K. and Alley, J.M. (1979) 'The effect of reinforcement on attentiveness: a comparison of behaviourally trained music therapists and other professionals with implications for competency-based academic preparation'. *Journal of Music Therapy*, 16(2) (pp. 70–82).

Madsen, C.K. and Geringer, J.M. (1981) 'The effect of a distraction index on improving practice attentiveness and musical performance'. *Bulletin of the Council for Research in Music Education*, 66–67 (pp. 46–52).

Madsen, C.K. and Geringer, J.M. (1983) 'Attending behaviour as a function of in-class activity in university music classes'. *Journal of Music Therapy*, 20 (pp. 30–38).

Madsen, C.K. and Madsen, C.H. (1972) 'Selection of music listening or candy as a function of contingent versus non-contingent reinforcement and scale singing'. *Journal of Music Therapy*, 9 (pp. 190–198).

Madsen, C.K. and Madsen, C.H. (1981) *Teaching/discipline: A positive approach for educational development.* (3rd edition) Boston: Allyn and Bacon.

Madsen, C.K., Edmonson, F.A. and Madsen, C.H. (1969) 'Modulated frequency discrimination in relation to age and musical training'. *Journal of the Acoustical Society of America*, 46(6) (pp. 1468–1472).

Madsen, C.K. Standley, J.M. and Cassidy, J.W. (1989) 'Demonstration and recognition of high and low contrasts in teacher intensity'. *Journal of Research in Music Education*, 37 (pp. 85–92).

Maehr, M.L. and Midgely, C. (1996) *Transforming School Cultures*. Boulder, CO: Westview Press.

Maess, B., Koelsch, S., Gunter, T. and Friederici, D. (2001) 'Musical syntax is processed in the Broca's area: an MEG study'. *Nature Neuroscience*, 4 (pp. 540–541).

Malave, J.E. (1990) A computer-assisted aural-visual approach to improve beginning students' clarinet tone quality. Unpublished doctoral dissertation, University of Texas at Austin.

Mansberger, N.B. (1988) The effects of performance anxiety management training on musicians' self-efficacy and musical performance quality. Unpublished masters' thesis, Western Michigan University, Kalamazoo.

Manturzeweska, M. (1969) *Psychologiczne Warunki Osiagniec Pianistycznych (Psychological Conditions and Piano Achievemement)*. Wroclaw: Ossolinieum.

Manturzewska, M. (1990) 'A biographical study of the life-span development of professional musicians'. *Psychology of Music*, 18(2) (pp. 112–139).

Maranto, C.D. and Scartelli, J. (1992) 'Music in the treatment of immune-related disorders'. In R. Spintge and R. Droh (eds) *Music Medicine*. St Louis, MO: MMB Music (pp. 142–154).

Marcoux, C. and Toussaint, R. (1995) 'The training of the parent: a contribution to the development of musical interpretation of the young pianist'. *Newsletter of the European Society for the Cognitive Sciences of Music*, 8 (pp. 17–21).

Markus, H. and Ruvolo, A. (1989) 'Possible selves: personalized representations of goals'. In L.A. Pervin (ed.) *Goal Concepts in Personality and Social Psychology*. Hillsdale, NJ: Lawrence Erlbaum Associates (pp. 211–242).

Marsh, K. (1995) 'Children's singing games: composition in the playground?' *Research Studies in Music Education*, 4 (pp. 2–11).

Martin, L. and Segrave, K. (1988) *Anti-Rock: The opposition to rock 'n' roll*. Connecticut: Archon.

Masataka, N. (1999) 'Preference for infant-directed singing in 2 day old hearing infants of deaf parents'. *Developmental Psychology*, 35 (pp. 1001–1005).

Mawbey, W.E. (1973) 'Wastage from instrumental classes in schools'. *Psychology of Music*, 1 (pp. 33–43).

Mayer, R.E. (1999) 'Fifty years of creativity research'. In R.J. Sternberg (ed.) *Handbook of Creativity*. Cambridge: Cambridge University Press (pp. 449–460).

Mead, G.H. (1934) *Mind, Self and Society*. Chicago: University of Chicago Press.

Meichenbaum, D. (1985) *Stress Inoculation Training*. New York: Pergamon.

Mellor, L. (1999) 'Language and music teaching: the use of personal construct theory to investigate teacher's responses to young people's music compositions'. *Music Education Research*, 1(2) (pp. 147–157).

Merriam, A.P. (1964) *The Anthropology of Music*. Northwestern University Press.

Messenger, J. (1958) 'Esthetic talent'. *Basic College Quarterly*, 4 (pp. 20–24).

Messmer, P.R. and Jones, S.G. (1998) 'Saving lives: an innovative approach for teaching CPR'. *Nursing and Health Care Perspectives*, 19(3) (pp. 108–110).

Meyer, L.B. (1956) *Emotion and Meaning in Music*. Chicago: University of Chicago Press.

Meyer, L.B. (2000) *The Spheres of Music*. Chicago: University of Chicago Press.

Meyer, L.B. (2001) 'Music and emotion: distinctions and uncertainties'. In P.N. Juslin and J.A. Sloboda (eds) *Music and Emotion: Theory and research*. Oxford: Oxford University Press (pp. 341–360).

Meyer, M. (1899) 'Is the memory of absolute pitch capable of development by training?' *Psychological Review*, 6(5) (pp. 514–516).

Mialaret, J.P. (1994) 'La Creativite musicale'. In A. Zenatti (ed.) *Psychologie de la Musique*. Paris: Presses Universitaires de France (pp. 223–258).

Miell, D.E. and MacDonald, R.A.R. (2000) 'Children's creative collaborations: the importance of friendship when working together on musical composition'. *Social Development*, 9(3) (pp. 348–369).

Miell, D.E., MacDonald, R.A.R. and Hargreaves, D.J. (in press) *Musical Communication*. Oxford: Oxford University Press.

Miklaszewski, K. (1989) 'A case study of a pianist preparing a musical performance'. *Psychology of Music*, 17 (pp. 95–109).

Miklaszewski, K. (1995) 'Individual differences in preparing a musical composition for public performance'. In M. Manturzewska,

K. Miklaszewski and A. Biatkowski (eds) *Psychology of Music Today.* Warsaw: Fryderyk Chopin Academy of Music (pp. 138–147).

Miller, G. (2000) 'Evolution of human music through sexual selection'. In N.L. Wallin, B. Merker and S. Brown (eds) *The Origins of Music.* Cambridge, MA: The MIT Press (pp. 329–360).

Milliman, R.E. (1982) 'Using background music to affect the behaviour of supermarket shoppers'. *Journal of Marketing*, 46 (pp. 86–91).

Milliman, R.E. (1986) 'The influence of background music on the behaviour of restaurant patrons'. *Journal of Consumer Research*, 13 (pp. 286–289).

Miluk-Kolasa, B., Obminski, Z., Stupnicki, R. and Golec, L. (1994) 'Effects of music treatment on salivary cortisol in patients exposed to pre-surgical stress'. *Experimental and Clinical Endocrinology*, 102 (pp. 118–120).

Mischel, W. (1973) 'Toward a cognitive social learning reconceptualisation of personality'. *Psychological Review*, 80 (pp. 252–283).

Mitchell, D.H. (1985) 'The influences of preschool musical experiences on the development of tonal memory'. *Dissertation Abstracts International*, 46 (1223A) (Micrographics Department, University of Southern California, Los Angeles, CA, 90089–1082).

Mithen, S. (1996) *The Prehistory of the Mind.* London: Thames and Hudson.

Mito, H. (2004) 'Role of daily musical activity in acquisition of musical skill'. In J. Tafuri (ed.) *Research for Music Education: The 20th Seminar of the ISME Research Commission*, 4–10 July, Las Palmas, Spain.

Miyazaki, K. (1988) 'Musical pitch identification, by absolute pitch possessors'. *Perception and Psychophysics*, 44 (pp. 501–512).

Miyazaki, K. (1989) 'Musical pitch identification: effects of timbre and pitch region'. *Music Perception*, 7 (pp. 1–14).

Miyazaki, K. (1990) 'The speed of musical pitch identification by absolute pitch possessors'. *Music Perception*, 8 (pp. 177–188).

Miyazaki, K. (1992) 'Perception of musical intervals by absolute pitch possessors'. *Music Perception*, 9 (pp. 413–426).

Miyazaki, K. (1993) 'Absolute pitch as an inability: identification of musical intervals in a tonal context'. *Music Perception*, 11 (pp. 55–72).

Miyazaki, K. (1995) 'Perception of relative pitch with different references: some absolute pitch listeners can't tell musical interval names'. *Perception and Psychophysics*, 57 (pp. 962–970).

Monson, I. (1992) *Saying Something: Jazz improvisation and interaction.* Chicago: University of Chicago Press.

Montano, D.R. (1983) 'The effect of improvising in given rhythms on piano students' sight reading rhythmic accuracy achievement'. Doctoral dissertation, University of Missouri-Kansas City. *Dissertation Abstracts International*, 44(6) (1720A).

Montello, L. (1990) 'Utilizing music therapy as a mode of treatment for the performance stress of professional musicians'. Doctoral dissertation, New York University. *Dissertation Abstracts International*, 50(10) (3175A).

Montello, L. and Coons, D.D. (1998) 'Effects of active versus passive group music therapy on preadolescents with emotional, learning and behavioural disorders'. *Journal of Music Therapy*, 35(1) (pp. 49–67).

Moog, H. (1976) *The Musical Experience of the Pre-school Child* (trans. C. Clarke) London: Schott.

Moorhead, G. and Pond, D. (1978) *Music for Young Children.* Santa Barbara, CA: Pillsbury Foundation for the Advancement of Music Education (originally published as four separate papers: 1941, 1942, 1944, 1951).

Moorman, D. (1985) 'An analytic study of jazz improvisation with suggestions for performance'. Doctoral dissertation, New York University. *Dissertation Abstracts International*, 45(7) (2023A).

Morasky, R.L., Reynolds, C. and Clark, G. (1981) 'Using biofeedback to reduce left arm extensor EMG of string players during musical performance'. *Biofeedback and Self-Regulation*, 6 (pp. 565–572).

Morasky, R.L., Reynolds, C. and Sowell, L.E. (1983) 'Generalisation of lowered EMG levels during musical performance following EMG training'. *Biofeedback and Self-Regulation*, 8 (pp. 207–216).

Morgan, C. (1998) Instrumental music teaching and learning: a life history approach. Unpublished doctoral thesis, University of Exeter.

Morrongiello, B.A., Trehub, S.E., Thorpe, L.A. and Capodilupo, S. (1985) 'Children's perception of melodies: the role of contour, frequency, and rate of presentation'. *Journal of Experimental Child Psychology*, 40 (pp. 279–292).

Mueller, C.M. and Dweck, C.S. (1998) 'Intelligence praise can undermine motivation and performance'. *Journal of Personality and Social Psychology*, 75 (pp. 33–52).

Munte, T.F., Nager, W., Beiss, T., Schroeder, C. and Erne, S.N. (2003) 'Specialization of the specialised electrophysiological investigations in professional musicians'. In G. Avanzini, C. Faienza, D. Minciacchi, L. Lopez and M. Majno (eds) *The Neurosciences and Music*. New York: New York Academy of Sciences (pp. 112–117).

Murningham, J.K. and Conlan, D.E. (1991) 'The dynamics of intense work groups: a study of British string quartets'. *Administrative Science Quarterly*, 36 (pp. 165–186).

Murray, H.A. (1938) *Explorations in Personality*. New York: Oxford University Press.

Murray, T., Large, J. and Dalgaard, J. (1979) 'Vocal jitter in sung and spoken vowels'. *Journal of Research and Singing*, 2 (pp. 28–43).

Nagel, J.J. (1990) 'Performance anxiety and the performing musician: a fear of failure or a fear of success?' *Medical Problems of Performing Artists*, 5(1) (pp. 37–40).

National Advisory Committee on Creative and Cultural Education (1999) *All Our Futures: Creativity culture and education*. London: Department for Culture, Media and Sport/Department for Education and Employment.

Nawrot, E.S. (2003) 'The perception of emotional expression in music: evidence from infants, children and adults'. *Psychology of Music*, 31(1) (pp. 75–92).

Neftel, K.A., Adler, R.H., Keppeli, L., Rossi, M., Dolder, M., Kaser, H.E., Bruggesser, H.H. and Vorkauf, H. (1982) 'Stage-fright in musicians: a model illustrating the effects of beta blockers'. *Psychosomatic Medicine*, 44 (pp. 461–469).

Neher, A. (1962) 'A physiological explanation of unusual behaviour in ceremonies involving drums'. *Human Biology*, 34 (pp. 151–160).

Neiman, Z. (1989) 'Teaching specific motor skills for conducting to young music students'. *Perceptual and Motor Skills*, 68 (pp. 847–858).

Nelson, B.J. (1991) 'The development of a middle school general music curriculum: a synthesis of computer-assisted instruction and music learning theory'. *Southeastern Journal of Music Education*, 3 (pp. 141–148).

Nettl, B. (1975) 'Music in primitive cultures: Iran, a recently developed nation'. In C. Hamm, B. Nettl and R. Byrnside (eds) *Contemporary Music and Music Cultures*. Englewood Cliffs, NJ: Prentice-Hall.

Newell, A. and Simon, H.A. (1972) *Human Problem Solving*. Englewood Cliffs, NJ: Prentice-Hall.

Newman, R.I., Hunt, D.I. and Rhodes, F. (1966) 'The effects of music on employee attitude and productivity in a skateboard factory'. *Journal of Applied Psychology*, 50(6) (pp. 493–496).

Nielsen, S.G. (1997) 'Self-regulation of learning strategies during practice: a case study of a church organ student preparing a musical work for performance'. In H. Jorgensen and A.C. Lehmann (eds) *Does Practice Make Perfect? Current theory and research on instrumental music practice*. Oslo, Norway: Norges Musikkhgskole (Norwegian Academy of Music) (pp. 109–122).

Nielsen, S.G. (1999a) 'Learning strategies in instrumental music practice'. *British Journal of Music Education*, 16(3) (pp. 275–291).

Nielsen, S.G. (1999b) 'Regulation of learning strategies during practice: a case study of a single church organ student preparing a particular work for a concert performance'. *Psychology of Music*, 27 (pp. 218–229).

Nielsen, S.G. (2001) 'Self-regulating learning strategies in instrumental music practice'. *Music Education Research*, 3 (pp. 155–167).

Nilsson, B. (2002) *Jag kan gora hundra latar. Barns musikskapande med digitala verktyg* (*I can make a Hundred Songs. Children's creative music making with digital tools*). Malmo: Malmo Academy of Music.

North, A.C. and Hargreaves, D.J. (1996) 'The effects of music on responses to a dining area'. *Journal of Environmental Psychology*, 16 (pp. 55–64).

North, A.C. and Hargreaves, D.J. (1997) 'Experimental aesthetics and everyday music listening'. In D.J. Hargreaves and A.C. North (eds) *The Social Psychology of Music*. Oxford: Oxford University Press (pp. 84–106).

North, A.C. and Hargreaves, D.J. (1998) 'The effect of music on atmosphere and purchasing intentions in a cafeteria'. *Journal of Applied Social Psychology*, 28(24) (pp. 2254–2273).

North, A.C. and MacKenzie, L.C. (2000) *Musical Tempo, Productivity and Morale*. Report for the Performing Rights Society. London: PRS.

North, A.C., Hargreaves, D.J. and McKendrick, J. (1999) 'The influence of in-store music on wine selections'. *Journal of Applied Psychology*, 84(2) (pp. 271–276).

North, A.C., Hargreaves, D.J. and O'Neill, S.A. (2000a) 'The importance of music to adolescents'. *British Journal of Educational Psychology*, 70 (pp. 255–272).

North, A.C., Hargreaves, D.J. and MacKenzie, L.C. (2000b) *Music and Morale in the Workplace*. Preliminary Report for the Performing Rights Society. London: PRS.

Nuki, M. (1984) 'Memorization of piano music'. *Psychologia*, 27 (pp. 157–163).

Oblad, C. (2000) 'On using music – about the car as a concert hall'. *Proceedings of the 6th International Conference on Music Perception and Cognition*, 5–10 August, Keele, UK: Keele University.

Odam, G. (2000) 'The creative dream; teaching composing in secondary schools'. *British Journal of Music Education*, 17 (pp. 109–128).

O'Donnell, P.J., MacDonald, R.A.R and Davies, J.B. (1999) 'Video analysis of the effects of structured music workshops for individuals with leading difficulties'. In D. Erdonmez and R.R. Pratt (eds) *Music Therapy and Music Medicine: Expanding horizons*. St Louis, MO: MMB Music (pp. 219–228).

Ogata, S. (1995) 'Human EEG responses to classical music and simulated white noise: effects of a musical loudness component on consciousness'. *Perceptual and Motor Skills*, 80 (pp. 779–790).

O'Neill, S.A. (1996) Factors influencing children's motivation and achievement during the first year of instrumental tuition. Unpublished doctoral thesis, Keele University.

O'Neill, S.A. (1997) 'The role of practice in children's early musical performance achievement'. In H. Jorgensen and A.C. Lehmann (eds) *Does Practice Make Perfect? Current theory and research on instrumental music practice*. Oslo, Norway: Norges Musikkhgskole (Norwegian Academy of Music) (pp. 53–70).

O'Neill, S.A. (2002) 'The self-identity of young musicians'. In R.A.R. MacDonald, D.J. Hargreaves and D.E. Miell (eds) *Musical Identities*. Oxford: Oxford University Press (pp. 79–96).

O'Neill, S.A. and McPherson, G.E. (2002) 'Motivation'. In R. Parncutt and G.E. McPherson (eds) *The Science and Psychology of Musical Performance: Creative strategies for teaching and learning*. Oxford: Oxford University Press (pp. 31–46).

Orman, E.K. (1998) 'Effect of interactive multimedia computing on young saxophonists achievement'. *Journal of Research in Music Education*, 46(1) (pp. 62–74).

Ostwald, P.F. (1973) 'Musical behaviour in early childhood'. *Developmental Medicine and Child Neurology*, 15 (pp. 367–375).

Ott, D. (1996) 'Effects of musical context on the improvisations of children as a function of age, training and exposure to music'. Doctoral dissertation, University of Alabama. *Dissertation Abstracts International*, 57(2) (1469B).

Overy, K. (2000) 'Dyslexia, temporal processing and music: the potential of music as an early learning aid for dyslexic children'. *Psychology of Music*, 28(2) (pp. 218–229).

Owen, J.E. (1988) Improving practice techniques through use of a motor schema theory of learning. Unpublished doctoral dissertation, Ohio State University.

Ozeas, N.L. (1992) The effect of the use of a computer assisted drill program on the aural skill development of students in beginning solfege. Unpublished doctoral dissertation, University of Pittsburgh, Pennsylvania.

Pacey, F. (1993) 'Schema theory and the effect of variable practice in string teaching'. *British Journal of Music Education*, 10(2) (pp. 91–102).

Panneton, R.K. (1985) Prenatal auditory experience with melodies: effects on postnatal auditory preferences in human newborns. Unpublished doctoral thesis, North Carolina, University of North Carolina at Greensboro.

Pantev, C., Oostenveld, R., Engellen, A., Ross, B., Roberts, L.E. and Hoke, M. (1998) 'Increased auditory cortical representation in musicians'. *Nature*, 392 (6678) (pp. 811–814).

Pantev, C., Wollbrink, A., Roberts, L.E. *et al.* (1999) 'Short-term plasticity of the human auditory cortex'. *Brain Research*, 842 (pp. 192–199).

Pantev, C., Engelien, A., Candia, V. and Elbert, T. (2003) 'Representational cortex in Musicians'. In I. Peretz and R.J.A. Zatorre (eds) *The Cognitive Neuroscience of Music*, Oxford: Oxford University Press (pp. 382–395).

Papich, G. and Rainbow, E. (1974) 'A pilot study of performance practices of twentieth century musicians.' *Journal of Research in Music Education*, 22(1) (pp. 24–34).

Papousek, M. (1996) 'Intuitive parenting: a hidden source of musical stimulation in infancy'. In I. Deliege and J.A. Sloboda (eds) *Musical Beginnings: Origins and development of musical competence*, Oxford: Oxford University Press (pp. 82–112).

Parncutt, R. and McPherson, G.E. (2002) *The Science and Psychology of Music Performance: Creative strategies for teaching and learning*. Oxford: Oxford University Press.

Parr, S.M. (1985) 'The effects of graduated exercise at the piano on the pianist's cardiac output, forearm blood flow, heart rate, and blood pressure'. *Dissertation Abstracts International*, 46(6) (1436A) (University Microfilms No. AAT85–18673).

Parrish, R.T. (1997) 'Development and testing of a computer-assisted instructional program to teach music to non-musicians'. *Journal of Research in Music Education*, 45(1) (pp. 90–102).

Pascoe, C.B. (1973) cited in J.T. Humphreys, W.V. May and D.J. Nelson (1992) 'Research on music ensembles'. In R. Colwell (ed.) *Handbook of*

Research on Music Teaching and Learning: Music Educators National Conference. New York: Schirmer Books (pp. 651–668).

Pascuel-Leone, A. (2003) 'The brain that makes music and is changed by it'. In I. Peretz and R.J.A. Zatorre (eds) *The Cognitive Neuroscience of Music.* Oxford: Oxford University Press (pp. 396–412).

Pascuel-Leone, A., Grafman, J. and Hallett, M. (1994) 'Modulation of cortical motor ouput maps during development of implicit and explicit knowledge'. *Science,* 263 (pp. 1287–1289).

Patterson, B. (1974) 'Musical dynamics', *Scientific American,* 233 (pp. 78–95).

Patton, J.E., Stinard, T.A. and Routh, D.K. (1983) 'Where do children study?' *Journal of Educational Research,* 76(5) (pp. 280–286).

Paynter, J. (1977) 'The role of creativity in the school music curriculum'. In M. Burnett (ed.) *Music Education Review.* London: Chappell (pp. 3–28).

Paynter, J. (1992) *Sound and Structure.* Cambridge: Cambridge University Press.

Peiterson, D.N. (1954) 'An experimental evaluation of the transfer effects of rhythm training in spaced notation on subsequent reading of commercially printed music'. Doctoral dissertation, University of Minnesota, Minneapolis.

Pembrook, R. and Craig, C. (2002) 'Teaching as a profession'. In R. Colwell and C. Richardson (eds) *The New Handbook of Research on Music Teaching and Learning.* Oxford: Oxford University Press (pp. 786–817).

Penhune, V.B., Zatorre, R.J.A. and Evans, A.C. (1998) 'Cerebellar contributions to motor timing: a PET study of auditory and visual rhythm reproduction'. *Journal of Cognitive Neuroscience,* 10 (pp. 752–765).

Peretz, I. (1990) 'Processing of local and global musicl information by unilateral brain-damaged patients'. *Brain,* 113 (pp. 1185–1205).

Peretz, I. (2003) 'Brain specialization for music: new evidence from congenital amusia'. In I. Peretz and R.J.A. Zatorre (eds) *The Cognitive Neuroscience of Music.* Oxford: Oxford University Press (pp. 192–203).

Peretz, I. and Morais, J. (1987) 'Analytic processing in the classification of melodies as same or different'. *Neuropsychologia,* 25 (pp. 645–652).

Peretz, I. and Zatorre, R.J.A. (eds) (2003) *The Cognitive Neuroscience of Music.* Oxford: Oxford University Press.

Peretz, I. and Zatorre, R.J.A. (2005) 'Brain organization for music processing'. *Annual Review of Psychology,* 56 (pp. 89–114).

Peretz, I., Morais, J. and Bertelson, P. (1987) 'Shifting ear differences in melody recognition through strategy inducement'. *Brain and Cognition,* 6 (pp. 202–215).

Peretz, I., Champod, A.S. and Hyde, K. (2003) 'Varieties of musical disorders. The Montreal Battery of Evalution of Amusia'. In G. Avanzini, C. Faienza, D. Minciacchi, L. Lopez and M. Majno (eds) *The Neurosciences and Music*. New York: New York Academy of Sciences (pp. 58–75).

Perry, W.G. (1970) *Intellectual and Ethical Development in the College Years: A scheme*. New York: Holt, Rinehart and Winston.

Persson, R.S. (1994) 'Control before shape – on mastering the clarinet: a case study on commonsense teaching'. *British Journal of Music Education*, 11 (pp. 223–238).

Pfenninger, R. (1991) 'The development and validation of three rating scales for the objective measurement of jazz improvisation achievement'. Doctoral dissertation, Temple University. *Dissertation Abstracts International*, 51(8) (2674A).

Pick, A.D., Palmer, C.F., Hennessy, B.L., Unze, M.G., Jones, R.K. and Richardson, R.M. (1988) 'Children's perception of certain musical properties: scale and contour'. *Journal of Experimental Child Psychology*, 45 (pp. 28–51).

Pierce, J.R. (1999) 'The nature of musical sound'. In D. Deutsch (ed.) *The Psychology of Music*. (2nd edition) London: Academic Press (pp. 1–24).

Pierce, M.A. (1992) 'The effects of learning procedure, tempo, and performance condition on transfer of rhythm skills in instrumental music'. *Journal of Research in Music Education*, 40 (pp. 295–315).

Pieters, J.M. (1996) 'Psychology of adult education'. In A.C. Tuijnman (ed.) *International Encyclopedia of Adult Education and Training*. (2nd edition) New York: Elsevier Science (pp. 150–158).

Pinker, S. (1997) *How the Mind Works*. New York: W.W. Norton.

Pintrich, P.R. and Garcia, T. (1994) 'Self-regulated learning in college students: knowledge, strategies and motivation'. In P.R. Pintrich, D.R. Brown, and C.E. Weinstein (eds) *Students' Motivation, Cognition and Learning: Essays in honor of Wilbert J. McKeachie*. Hillsdale, NJ: Erlbaum.

Pitt, M.A. (1994) 'Perception of pitch and timbre by musically trained and untrained listeners'. *Journal of Experimental Psychology: Human perception and performance*, 20 (pp. 876–986).

Pitts, S.E. (2004) 'Everybody wants to be Pavarotti: the experience of music for performers and audience at a Gilbert and Sullivan festival'. *Journal of the Royal Musical Association*, 129 (pp. 149–167).

Pitts, S.E., Davidson, J.W. and McPherson, G.E. (2000a) 'Developing effective practising strategies: case studies of three young instrumentalists'. *Music Education Research*, 2(1) (pp. 45–56).

Pitts, S.E., Davidson, J.W. and McPherson, G.E. (2000b) 'Models of success and failure in instrumental learning: case studies of young players in the first 20 months of learning'. *Bulletin of the Council for Research in Music Education*, 146 (pp. 51–69).

Placek, R.W. (1992) 'Design and trial of a computer-controlled programme of music appreciation'. In H. Lees (ed.) *Music Education: Sharing musics of the world. Proceedings of 20th World Conference of the International Society for Music Education*. Seoul, Korea (pp. 145–152).

Platel, H, Price, C., Baron, J.-C. *et al.* (1997) 'The structural components of music perception, a functional anatomic study'. *Brain*, 120 (pp. 229–243).

Plaut, E.A. (1990) 'Psychotherapy of performance anxiety'. *Medical Problems of Performing Artists*, 5(1) (pp. 58–63).

Pollack, N.J. and Namazi, K.H. (1992) 'The effect of music participation on the social behaviours of Alzheimer's Disease patients'. *Journal of Music Therapy*, 29(1) (pp. 54–67).

Pollard-Gott, L. (1983) 'Emergence of thematic concepts in repeated listening to music'. *Cognitive Psychology*, 15 (pp. 66–94).

Poulin, B., Bigand, E., Dowling, W.J. *et al.* (2001) Do musical experts take advantage of global musical coherence in a recognition test? Conference of the Society of Music Perception and Cognition, 9–11 August, Queens University, Kingston, Ontario, Canada.

Powell, T.J. and Enright, S.J. (1990) *Anxiety and Stress Management*. London: Routledge.

Prasso, N.M. (1997) An examination of the effect of writing melodies, using an computer-based song-writing program, on high-school students' individual learning of sight-singing skills. Unpublished doctoral dissertation, Columbia University Teachers College, New York.

Pratt, D. (1992) 'Conceptions of teaching'. *Adult Education Quarterly*, 42 (pp. 203–220).

Pressing, J. (1988) 'Improvisation, methods and models'. In J.A. Sloboda (ed.) *Generative Processes in Music: The psychology of performance, improvisation and composition*. Oxford: Clarendon Press (pp. 129–178).

Pressing, J. (1998) 'Psychological constraints on improvisational expertise and communication'. In B. Nettl and M. Russell (eds) *In the Course of Performance: Studies in the world of musical improvisation*. Chicago: University of Chicago Press (pp. 47–67).

Price, H.E (1989) 'An effective way to teach and rehearse: research supports using sequential patterns'. *Update*, 8 (pp. 42–46).

Price, H.E. (1990) Sequential patterns of music instruction and learning to use them. Paper presented at March meeting of Music Educators National Conference, Washington, DC.

Price, H.E. (1992) 'Sequential patterns of music instruction and learning to use them'. *Journal of Research in Music Education*, 40(1) (pp. 14–29).

Priest, T.L. (1997) Fostering creative and critical thinking in a beginning instrumental music class. Unpublished doctoral dissertation, University of Illinois at Urbana-Champaign.

Priest, T.L. (in press) 'Self-evaluation, creativity and musical achievement'. *Psychology of Music*.

Prince, V. (1994) Teachers' and pupils' conceptions of emotion in musical experience and their perceptions of the emphasis given to cognitive, technical and expressive aspects of instrumental lessons. Unpublished MA dissertation: Institute of Education, University of London.

Pujol, T.J. and Langefield, M.E. (1999) 'Influence of music on Wingate Anaerobic Test performance'. *Perceptual and Motor Skills*, 88 (pp. 292–296).

Puopolo, V. (1971) 'The development and experimental application of self-instructional practice materials for beginning instrumentalists'. Doctoral dissertation, Michigan State University, 1970. *Dissertation Abstracts International*, 31, 8A.

Radocy, R.E. and Boyle, J.D. (1988) *Psychological Foundations of Musical Behaviour*. (2nd edition) Springfield, IL: Charles C. Thomas.

Raffman, D. (1993) *Language, Music and Mind*. Cambridge MA: The MIT Press.

Rainbow, B. (1980) *John Curwen: A short critical biography*. London: Novello and Co..

Ramos, L.V. (1993) 'The effects of on-hold telephone music on the number of premature disconnections to a statewide protective services abuse hot line'. *Journal of Music Therapy*, 30(2) (pp. 119–129).

Rauschecker, J.P. (1995) 'Compensatory plasticity and sensory substitution in the cerebral cortex'. *Trends in Neuroscience*, 18 (pp. 36–43).

Rauschecker, J.P. (1998) 'Cortical processing of complex sounds'. *Current Opinion in Neurobiology*, 8 (pp. 516–521).

Rauschecker, J.P. (2003) 'Functional organisation and plasticity of auditory cortex'. In I. Peretz and R.J.A. Zatorre (eds) *The Cognitive Neuroscience of Music*. Oxford: Oxford University Press (pp. 357–365).

Rauscher, F.H., Shaw, G.L. and Ky, K.N. (1995) 'Listening to music enhances spatial-temporal reasoning: towards a neurophysiological basis'. *Neuroscience Letters*, 185 (pp. 44–47).

Reimer, B. (1970) *A Philosophy of Music Education.* Englewood Cliffs, NJ: Prentice-Hall.

Reimer, B. (1991) 'Characteristics of aesthetic education'. *Journal of Aesthetic Education*, 25(3) (pp. 193–214).

Reimer, B. (1992) 'An agenda for music teacher education: part II'. *Journal of Music Teacher Education*, 1(2) (pp. 5–11).

Reinhardt, D.A. (1990) 'Preschool children's use of rhythm in improvisation'. *Contributions to Music Education*, 17 (pp. 7–19).

Reitman, W.R. (1965) *Cognition and Thought.* New York: Wiley.

Repp, R. (1999) 'The feasibility of technology saturation for intermediate students of applied voice'. In S. Lipscomb (ed.) *Sixth International Conference on Technological Directions in Music Education.* San Antonio, TX: IMR Press (pp. 16–21).

Revesz, G. (1920) cited in R. Shuter-Dyson and C. Gabriel (1981) *The Psychology of Musical Ability.* London: Methuen.

Rexroad, E.F. (1985) Influential factors on the musical development of outstanding professional singers. Unpublished EdD thesis, University of Illinois at Urbana-Champaign.

Ribke, W. (1987) *Uben aus kognitionspsychologischerund handlungstheoretischer Sicht* (*Practising from a Cognitive and Action-oriented View*). Musikpsychologische forschung, Band 8: Ausserschulische Musikerziehung. Laaber: Laaber-Verlag.

Richardson, C.P. (1996) 'A theoretical model of the connoisseur's musical thought'. *Bulletin of the Council for Research in Music Education*, 128 (pp. 15–24).

Richardson, C.P. (1998) 'The roles of the critical thinker in the music classroom'. *Studies in Music from the University of Western Ontario*, 17 (pp. 107–120).

Rider, M.S. (1987) 'Treating chronic disease and pain with music-mediated imagery'. *The Arts in Psychotherapy*, 14 (pp. 113–120).

Rider, M.S. and Weldin, C. (1990) 'Imagery, improvisation and immunity'. *The Arts in Psychotherapy*, 17 (pp. 211–216).

Robazza, C., Macaluso, C. and D'Urso (1994) 'Emotional reactions to music by gender, age and expertise'. *Perceptual and Motor Skills*, 79 (pp. 939–944).

Robb, S.L. (2000) 'Music assisted progressive muscle relaxation, progressive music relaxation, music listening, and silence: a comparison of relaxation techniques'. *Journal of Music Therapy*, 37(1) (pp. 2–21).

Robb, S.L., Nichols, R.J., Rutan, R.L., Bishop, B.L. and Parker, J.C. (1995) 'The effects of music assisted relaxation on pre-operative anxiety'. *Journal of Music Therapy*, 32(1) (pp. 2–21).

Roberts, E. (1972) Poor pitch singing. A survey of its incidence in school children and its response to remedial training. Unpublished MA dissertation, Liverpool University.

Rock, A.M.L., Trainor, L.J. and Addison, T.L. (1999) 'Distinctive messages in infant-directed lullabies and plays songs'. *Developmental Psychology*, 35(2) (pp. 527–534).

Roederer, J. (1984) 'The search for a survival value of music'. *Music Perception*, 1 (pp. 350–356).

Rogers, C.R. (1961) *On becoming a Person*. Boston: Houghton Mifflin.

Rogers, K. (1997) 'Resourcing music technology in secondary schools'. *British Journal of Music Education*, 36(2) (pp. 129–136).

Rogers. R. (1995) *Guaranteeing an Entitlement to the Arts in Schools*. London: Royal Society of Arts.

Roland, D. (1994) 'How professional performers manage performance anxiety'. *Research Studies in Music Education*, 2 (pp. 25–35).

Rosenshine, B., Froehlich, H. and Fakhouri, I. (2002) 'Systematic instruction'. In R. Colwell and C. Richardson (eds) *The New Handbook of Research on Music Teaching and Learning*. Oxford: Oxford University Press (pp. 299–314).

Rosenthal, R.K. and Jacobsen, L. (1968) *Pygmalion in the Classroom: Teacher expectation and pupils' intellectual development*. New York: Holt, Rinehart and Winston.

Rosenthal, R.K. (1984) 'The relative effects of guided model, model only, guide only, and practice only treatments on the accuracy of advanced instrumentalists' musical performance'. *Journal of Research in Music Education*, 32 (pp. 265–273).

Rosenthal, R.K., Wilson, M., Evans, M. and Greenwalt, L. (1988) 'Effects of different practice conditions on advanced instrumentalists' performance accuracy'. *Journal of Research in Music Education*, 36(4) (pp. 250–257).

Ross, D.A., Olson, I.R. and Gore, J.C. (2003) 'Absolute pitch does not depend on early musical training'. In G. Avanzini, C. Faienza, D. Minciacchi, L. Lopez and M. Majno (eds) *The Neurosciences and Music*. New York: New York Academy of Sciences (pp. 522–526).

Ross, E. (1964) 'Improving facility in music memorization'. *Journal of Research in Music Education*, 12(4) (pp. 269–278).

Ross, M. (1980) *The Arts and Personal Growth.* London: Pergamon Press.

Ross, M. (1999) 'Teacher training in the arts: at the vanishing point'. *Journal of Art and Design in Education,* 18 (pp. 351–358).

Ross, M. and Kamba, M. (1997) *The State of the Arts in English Secondary Schools.* Exeter: University of Exeter.

Ross, S.L. (1985) 'The effectiveness of mental practice in improving the performance of college trombonists'. *Journal of Research in Music Education,* 33 (pp. 221–230).

Rotter, J.B. (1966) 'Generalised expectancies for internal versus external control of reinforcement'. *Psychological Monograph,* 80

Rubin-Rabson, G. (1937) 'The influence of analytic pre-study in memorising piano music'. *Archives of Psychology,* 31 (pp. 1–53).

Rubin-Rabson, G. (1939) 'Studies in the psychology of memorizing piano music: I. A comparison of the unilateral and the co-ordinated approach'. *Journal of Educational Psychology,* 30(5) (pp. 321–345).

Rubin-Rabson, G. (1940a) 'Studies in the psychology of memorizing piano music: II. A comparison of massed and distributed practice'. *Journal of Educational Psychology,* 31 (pp. 270–284).

Rubin-Rabson, G. (1940b) 'Studies in the psychology of memorizing piano music: III. A comparison of the whole and the part approach'. *Journal of Educational Psychology,* 31 (pp. 460–475).

Rubin-Rabson, G. (1941a) 'Studies in the psychology of memorising piano music: IV. The effect of incentive'. *Journal of Educational Psychology,* 32 (pp. 45–54).

Rubin-Rabson, G. (1941b) 'Studies in the psychology of memorising piano music: V. A comparison of pre-study periods of varied length'. *Journal of Educational Psychology,* 32 (pp. 101–112).

Rubin-Rabson, G. (1941c) 'Studies in the psychology of memorising piano music: VI. A comparison of two forms of mental rehearsal and keyboard over learning'. *Journal of Educational Psychology,* 32 (pp. 593–602)

Rubin-Rabson, G. (1941d) 'Studies in the psychology of memorising piano music: VII. A comparison of three degrees of over learning'. *Journal of Educational Psychology,* 32 (pp. 688–696).

Rush, M.A. (1989) 'An experimental investigation of the effectiveness of training on absolute pitch in adult musicians'. *Dissertation Abstracts International,* 50 (826–A).

Ruthsatz, J. and Detterman, D.K. (2003) 'An extraordinary memory: the case of a musical prodigy'. *Intelligence,* 31 (pp. 509–518).

Rutkowski, J. (1996) 'The effectiveness of individual/small group singing activities on kindergartners' use of singing voice and developmental music aptitude'. *Journal of Research in Music Education*, 44 (pp. 353–368).

Ryan, C. (2004) 'Gender differences in children's experience of musical performance anxiety'. *Psychology of Music*, 32(1) (pp. 89–104).

Rybak, C.A. (1996) 'Older adults and "flow": investigating optimal experience in selected music leisure activities'. Doctoral dissertation, Arizona State University. *Dissertation Abstracts International*, 56 (4695A).

Sabo, C.E. and Michael, S.R. (1996) 'The influence of personal message with music on anxiety and side effects associated with chemotherapy'. *Cancer Nurse*, 19(4) (pp. 283–289).

Saffran, J.R. (2003) 'Mechanisms of musical memory in infancy'. In I. Peretz and R.J.A. Zatorre (eds) *The Cognitive Neuroscience of Music*. Oxford: Oxford University Press (pp. 32–41).

Saffran, J.R. and Griepentrog, G.J. (2001) 'Absolute pitch in infant auditory learning: evidence for developmental reorganisation'. *Developmental Psychology*, 37(1) (pp. 74–85).

Sakai, K., Hikosaka, S. and Miyauchi, S. *et al.* (1999) 'Neural representation of a rhythm depends on its interval ration'. *Journal of Neuroscience*, 19 (pp. 10074–10081).

Salaman, W. (1994) 'The role of graded examinations in music'. *British Journal of Music Education*, 11(3) (pp. 209–211).

Salame, P. and Baddeley, A. (1989) 'Effects of background music on phonological short term memory'. *The Quarterly Journal of Experimental Psychology*, 41A(1) (pp. 107–122).

Salmon, P.G. (1991) 'A primer on performance anxiety for organists: part I'. *The American Organist*. May (pp. 55–59).

Salzberg, R.S. (1980) 'The effects of visual stimulus and instruction on intonation accuracy of string instrumentalists'. *Psychology of Music*, 8 (pp. 42–49).

Salzberg, R.S. and Salzberg, C.L. (1981) 'Praise and corrective feedback in the remediation of incorrect left-hand positions of elementary string players'. *Journal of Research in Music Education*, 29(2) (pp. 125–133).

Samson, S. (2003) 'Neuropsychological studies of musical timbre'. In G. Avanzini, C. Faienza, D. Minciacchi, L. Lopez and M. Majno (eds) *The Neurosciences and Music*. New York: New York Academy of Sciences (pp. 144–151).

Samson, S. and Ehrle, N. (2003) 'Cerebral substrates for musical temporal processes'. In I. Peretz and R.J.A. Zatorre (eds) *The Cognitive Neuroscience of Music*. Oxford: Oxford University Press (pp. 204–216).

Sang, R.C. (1987) 'A study of the relationship between instrumental teachers' modelling skills and pupils' performance behaviours'. *Bulletin of the Council for Research in Music Education*, 91 (pp. 155–159).

Santana, E.L. (1978) 'Time efficient skill acquisition in instrumental music study'. Doctoral dissertation, Florida State University. *Dissertation Abstracts International*, 40 (732–A).

Satt, B.J. (1984) An investigation into the acoustical induction of intra-uterine learning. Unpublished DPhil thesis, Californian School of Professional Psychologists.

Savan, A. (1999) 'The effect of background music on learning'. *Psychology of Music*, 27(2) (pp. 138–146).

Scartelli, J. (1992) 'Music therapy and psychoneuroimmunology'. In R. Spintge and R. Droh (eds) *Music Medicine*. St Louis, MO: MMB Music (pp. 137–141).

Schellenberg, E.G. (2004) 'Music lessons enhance IQ'. *Psychological Science*, 15 (pp. 511–514).

Schellenberg, E.G. and Trehub, S.E. (1994) 'Processing advantages for simple frequency ratios: evidence from young children'. In I. Deliege (ed.) *Proceedings of the 3rd International Conference on Music Perception and Cognition*. Liege, Belgium European Society for the Cognitive Sciences of Music (pp. 129–130).

Schellenberg, E.G. and Trehub, S.E. (1996a) 'Children's discrimination of melodic intervals'. *Developmental Psychology*, 32(6) (pp. 1039–1050).

Schellenberg, E.G. and Trehub, S.E. (1996b) 'Natural music intervals: evidence from infant listeners'. *Psychological Science*, 7(5) (pp. 272–277).

Schellenberg, E.G. and Trehub, S.E. (1999) 'Culture-general and culture-specific factors in the discrimination of melodies'. *Journal of Experimental Child Psychology*, 74 (pp. 107–127).

Schenck, R. (1989) 'Above all, learning an instrument must be fun'. *British Journal of Music Education*, 6(1) (pp. 3–35).

Schlacks, W. (1981) 'The effect of vocalization through an interval training program upon the pitch accuracy of high school band students'. Doctoral dissertation, University of Miami.

Schlaug, G. (2001) 'The brain of musicians: a model for functional and structural adaptation'. In R.J.A. Zatorre and I. Peretz (eds) *The Biological Foundations of Music, Vol. 930*. New York: Annals of the New York Academy of Sciences (pp. 281–299).

Schlaug, G. (2003) 'The brain of musicians'. In I. Peretz and R.J.A. Zatorre (eds) *The Cognitive Neuroscience of Music*. Oxford: Oxford University Press (pp. 366–381).

Schlaug, G., Jancke, L., Huang, Y. and Steinmetz, H. (1995a) 'In vivo evidence of structural brain asymmetry in musicians'. *Science*, 267 (pp. 699–701).

Schlaug, G., Jaencke, L., Huang, Y. and Steinmetz, H. (1995b) 'Increased corpus callosum size in musicians'. *Neuropsychologia*, 33 (pp. 1047–1055).

Schmahmann, J.D. (1997) *The Cerebellum and Cognition*. New York: Academic Press.

Schmidt, C.P. (1989a) 'Applied music teaching behaviour as a function of selected personality variables'. *Journal of Research in Music Education*, 37 (pp. 258–271).

Schmidt, C.P. (1989b) 'Individual differences in perception of applied music teaching feedback'. *Psychology of Music*, 17 (pp. 110–112).

Schmidt, C.P. and Stephans, R. (1991) 'Locus of control and field dependence as factors in students' evaluations of applied music instruction'. *Perceptual and Motor Skills*, 73 (pp. 131–136).

Schmidt, R.A. (1975) 'A schema theory of discrete motor skill learning'. *Psychological Review*, 82(4) (pp. 225–259).

Schmidt, R.A. (1976) 'The schema as a solution to some persistent problems in motor learning theory'. In G.E. Stelmach (ed.) *Motor Control: Issues and trends*. New York: Academic Press (pp. 41–65).

Schramowski, H. (1973) 'Schaffenpsychologische Untersuchungen zur instrumentalen Improvisation' ('Psychology of creative behaviour regarding instrumental improvisation') *Beitrage zur Musikwissenschaft*, 15 (pp. 235–251).

Schuppert, M., Munte, T.F, Wieringa, B.M. *et al.* (2000) 'Receptive amusia: evidence for cross-hemisphere neural networks underlying music processing strategies'. *Brain*, 123 (pp. 546–559).

Schwaegler, D.G. (1984) 'A computer-based trainer for music conducting: the effects of four feedback modes'. Doctoral dissertation, University of Iowa.

Searby, M. and Ewers, T. (1996) 'Peer assessing composition in higher education'. *British Journal of Music Education*, 13 (pp. 155–163).

Seashore, C.E., Lewis, L. and Saetveit, J.G. (1960) *Seashore Measures of Musical Talents*. New York: The Psychological Corporation.

Seddon, F.A. and O'Neill, S.A. (2001) 'An evaluation study of computer-based compositions by children with or without prior experience of formal instrumental tuition'. *Psychology of Music*, 29(1) (pp. 4–19).

Seddon, F.A. and O'Neill, S.A. (2003) 'Creative thinking processes in adolescent computer-based composition: an analysis of strategies adopted and the influence of instrumental music training'. *Music Education Research*, 5(2) (pp. 125–137).

Seddon, F.A. and O'Neill, S.A. (in press) 'How does formal instrumental music tuition (FIMT) impact on self and teacher evaluations of adolescents' computer-based compositions?' *Psychology of Music*.

Seibenaler, D.J. (1997) 'Analysis of teacher–student interactions in the piano lessons of adults and children'. *Journal of Research in Music Education*, 45(1) (pp. 6–20).

Sergeant, D. (1969) 'Experimental investigation of absolute pitch'. *Journal of Research in Music Education*, 17 (pp. 135–143).

Sergeant, D. and Roche, S. (1973) 'Perceptual shifts in the auditory information processing of young children'. *Psychology of Music*, 1 (pp. 39–48).

Shaffer, L.H. (1992) 'How to interpret music'. In M.R. Jones and S. Holleran (eds) *Cognitive Bases of Musical Communication*. Washington, DC: American Psychological Association (pp. 263–278).

Shahidullah, S. and Hepper, P.G. (1994) 'Frequency discrimination by the fetus'. *Early Human Development*, 36 (pp. 13–26).

Shea, J.B. and Morgan, R.L. (1979) 'Contextual interference effects on the acquisition, retention and transfer of a motor skill'. *Journal of Experimental Psychology: Human learning and memory*, 5 (pp. 179–187).

Sheldon, D., Reese, S. and Grashel, J. (1999) 'The effects of live accompaniment, intelligence digital accompaniment, and no accompaniment on musician's performance quality'. *Journal of Research in Music Education*, 47(3) (pp. 251–265).

Shelton, J.S. (1966) 'The influence of home musical environment upon the musical response of first-grade children'. *Dissertation Abstracts International*, 26 (6765–6766) (University Microfilms No. 66–4419).

Shenfield, T., Trehub, S.E. and Nakata, T. (2003) 'Maternal singing modulates infant arousal'. *Psychology of Music*, 31(4) (pp. 365–375).

Shuter-Dyson, R. (1999) 'Musical ability'. In D. Deutsch (ed.) *The Psychology of Music*. (2nd edition) London: Academic Press (pp. 627–651).

Shuter-Dyson, R. and Gabriel, C. (1981) *The Psychology of Musical Ability*. London: Methuen.

Simms, B. (1997) The effects of an educational computer game on motivation to learn basic musical skills: a qualitative study. Unpublished doctoral dissertation, University of North Colorado, Greeley.

Simonton, D.K. (1997) 'Products, persons and periods'. In D.J. Hargreaves and A.C. North (eds) *The Social Psychology of Music*. Oxford: Oxford University Press (pp. 107–122).

Simpson, E.H. (1996) The effects of technology-assisted visual/aural feedback upon pitch accuracy of senior high school choral singing. Unpublished doctoral dissertation, University of Hartford, Connecticut.

Singh, P. and Bregman, A. (1997) 'The influence of different timbre attributes on the perceptual segregation of complex-tone sequences'. *Journal of the Acoustical Society of America*, 102 (pp. 1943–1953).

Sink, P.E. (2002) 'Behavioural research on direct music instruction'. In R. Colwell and C. Richardson (eds) *The New Handbook of Research on Music Teaching and Learning*. Oxford: Oxford University Press (pp. 315–326).

Slack, J. (1977) 'Values and personalities of selected high school choral music educators'. *Journal of Research in Music Education*, 25 (pp. 243–255).

Sloboda, J.A. (1976) 'The effect of item position on the likelihood of identification by inference in prose reading and music reading'. *Canadian Journal of Psychology*, 30 (pp. 228–236).

Sloboda, J.A. (1983) 'The communication of musical metre in piano performance'. *Quarterly Journal of Experimental Psychology*, 35A (pp. 377–396).

Sloboda, J.A. (1984) 'Experimental studies of music reading: a review'. *Music Perception*, 2 (pp. 222–236).

Sloboda, J.A. (1985) *The Musical Mind: The cognitive psychology of music*. Oxford: Oxford University Press.

Sloboda, J.A. (1990) 'Music as a language'. In F. Wilson and F. Roehmann (eds) *Music and Child Development*, St Louis, MO: MMB Inc. (pp. 28–43).

Sloboda, J.A. (1991) 'Music structure and emotional response: some empirical findings'. *Psychology of Music*, 19(2) (pp. 110–120).

Sloboda, J. (1992) 'Empirical studies of emotional response to music'. In M.R. Jones and S. Holleran (eds) *Cognitive Bases of Musical Communication*. Washington, DC: American Psychological Association (pp. 3–50).

Sloboda, J.A. (1996) 'The acquisition of musical performance expertise: deconstructing the talent account of individual differences in musical expressivity'. In K.A. Anders (ed.) *The Road to Excellence: The acquisition of expert performance in the arts and sciences, sports and games*. Mahwah, NJ: Lawrence Erlbaum Associates (pp. 107–126).

Sloboda, J.A. and Davidson, J.W. (1996) 'The young performing musician'. In I. Deliege and J.A. Sloboda (eds) *Musical Beginnings: Origins and development of musical competence*, Oxford: Oxford University Press (pp. 171–190).

Sloboda, J.A. and Howe, M.J.A. (1991) 'Biographical precursors of musical excellence: an interview study'. *Psychology of Music*, 19 (pp. 3–21).

Sloboda, J.A. and O'Neill, S.A. (2002) 'Emotions in everyday listening to music'. In P.N. Juslin and J.A. Sloboda (eds) *Music and Emotion: Theory and research*. Oxford: Oxford University Press (pp. 415–430).

Sloboda, J.A., Hermelin, B. and O'Connor, N. (1985) 'An exceptional musical memory'. *Musical Perception*, 3 (pp. 155–170).

Sloboda, J.A., Davidson, J.W., Howe, M.J.A. and Moore, D.G. (1996) 'The role of practice in the development of performing musicians'. *British Journal of Psychology*, 87 (pp. 287–309).

Sloboda, J.A., O'Neill, S.A. and Ivaldi, A. (2001) 'Functions of music in everyday life: an exploratory study using the experience sampling method'. *Musicae Scientiae*, 5 (pp. 9–32).

Small, A.M. (1937) 'An objective analysis of artistic violin performance'. *Experimental Research in Music: Studies in the psychology of music*, 4 (pp. 172–231).

Smith, A. (1973) 'The efficacy of immediate knowledge of results for tracking musical form'. *The Alberta Journal of Educational Research*, 19(4) (pp. 321–333).

Smith, D.S. and Singh, N.H. (1984) 'Self-management of music practice'. *Human Learning*, 3 (pp. 165–172).

Smith, J.M. and Szathmary, E. (1995) *The Major Transitions in Evolution*. Oxford: Oxford University Press.

Smith, K.C. and Cuddy, L.L. (1986) 'The pleasingness of melodic sequences: contrasting effects of repetition and rule-familiarity'. *Psychology of Music*, 14 (pp. 17–32).

Smith-Marchese, K. (1994) 'The effects of participatory music on the reality orientation and sociability of Alzheimer's residents in a long-term care setting'. *Activities, Adaptation and Aging*, 18(2) (pp. 41–55).

Snow, R.E. (1990) 'New approaches to cognitive and conative assessment in education'. *International Journal of Educational Research*, 14 (pp. 455–474).

Snyder, B. (2000) *Music and Memory: An introduction*. Cambridge, MA: The MIT Press.

Soderman, J. and Folkestad, G. (2004) 'How hip-hop musicians learn: strategies in informal creative music making', *Music Education Research*, 6(3) (pp. 313–326).

Sorich, L. and Dweck, C.S. (2000) 'Mastery oriented thinking'. In C.R. Snyder (ed.) *Coping*. New York, Oxford University Press.

Sosniak, L.A. (1985) 'Learning to be a concert pianist'. In B.S. Bloom (ed.) *Developing Talent in Young People*. New York: Ballantine (pp. 19–67).

Sosniak, L.A. (1990) 'The tortoise and the hare and the development of talent'. In M.J.A. Howe (ed.) *Encouraging the Development of Exceptional Skills and Talents*. Leicester: British Psychological Society (pp. 149–164).

Sousa, M., Neto, F. and Mullet, E. (2005) 'Can music change ethnic attitudes among children?' *Psychology of Music*, 33(3) (pp. 304–316).

Sperber, D. (1996) *Explaining Culture*. Oxford: Blackwell.

Sperti, J. (1970) 'Adaptation of certain aspects of the Suzuki method to the teaching of the clarinet: an experimental investigation testing the comparative effectiveness of two different pedagogical methodologies'. *Bulletin of the Council for Research in Music Education*, 37 (pp. 46–48).

Spychiger, M., Patry, J., Lauper, G., Zimmerman, E. and Weber, E. (1993) 'Does more music teaching lead to a better social climate?' In R. Olechowski and G. Svik (eds) *Experimental Research in Teaching and Learning*. Bern: Peter Lang (pp. 322–336).

Stadler-Elmer, S. (1994) 'Children's acquisition and generation of songs'. In I. Deliege (ed.) *Proceedings of the 3rd International Conference on Music Perception and Cognition*. Liege: Belgium European Society for the Cognitive Sciences of Music (pp. 119–120).

Standley, J.M. (1986) 'Music research in medical/dental treatment: meta-analysis and clinical applications'. *Journal of Music Therapy*, 23(2) (pp. 56–122).

Standley, J.M. (1991) 'The effect of vibrotactile and auditory stimuli on perception of comfort, heart rate, and peripheral finger temperature'. *Journal of Music Therapy*, 18(3) (pp. 120–134).

Standley, J.M. (1998) 'Pre and perinatal growth and development: implications of music benefits for premature infants'. *International Journal of Music Education*, 31 (pp. 1–13).

Stephens, T., Braithwaite, R.L. and Taylor, S.E. (1998) 'Model for using hip-hop music for small group HIV/AIDS prevention counseling with African American adolescents and young adults'. *Patient Education and Counseling*, 35(2) (pp.127–137).

Steptoe, A. (1989) 'Stress, coping and stage fright in professional musicians'. *Psychology of Music*, 17 (pp. 3–11).

Steptoe, A. and Fidler, H. (1987) 'Stage fright in orchestral musicians: a study of cognitive and behavioural strategies in performance anxiety'. *British Journal of Psychology*, 78 (pp. 241–249).

Sternberg, R.J. (ed.) (1988) *The Nature of Creativity: Contemporary psychological perspectives*. Cambridge: Cambridge University Press.

Stipek, D.J. and Gralinski, H. (1996) 'Children's beliefs about intelligence and school performance'. *Journal of Educational Psychology*, 88 (pp. 397–407).

Strauser, J.M. (1997) 'The effects of music versus silence on measures of state anxiety, perceived relaxation, and physiological responses of patients receiving chiropractic interventions'. *Journal of Music Therapy*, 34(2) (pp. 88–105).

Stumpf, C. (1883) *Tonpsychologie*. Leipzig: Hirzel.

Sudnow, D. (1978) *Ways of the Hand: The organisation of improvised conduct*. London: Routledge and Kegan Paul.

Sullivan, H.S. (1964) *The Fusion of Psychiatry and Social Science*. New York: Norton.

Sullivan, Y. and Cantwell, R.H. (1999) 'The planning behaviours of musicians engaging traditional and non-traditional scores'. *Psychology of Music*, 27 (pp. 245–266).

Sundin, B. (1997) 'Musical creativity in childhood – a research project in retrospect'. *Research Studies in Music Education*, 9 (pp. 48–57).

Sundin, B. (1998) 'Musical creativity in the first six years: a research project in retrospect'. In B. Sundin, G.E. McPherson and G. Folkestad (eds) *Children Composing*. Malmo: Malmo Academy of Music.

Swanner, D.L. (1985) Relationships between musical creativity and selected factors, including personality, motivation, musical aptitude, and cognitive intelligence as measured in third grade children. Unpublished dissertation, Case Western Reserve University, Cleveland, Ohio.

Swanwick, K. (1988) *Music, Mind and Education*. London: Routledge.

Swanwick, K. (1994) *Musical Knowledge: Intuition, analysis and music education*. London: Routledge.

Swanwick, K. and Tillman, J. (1986) 'The sequence of musical development: a study of children's composition'. *British Journal of Music Education*, 3(3) (pp. 305–339).

Sweeney, G.A. and Horan, J.J. (1982) 'Separate and combined effects of cue-controlled relaxation and cognitive restructuring in the treatment of musical performance anxiety'. *Journal of Counselling Psychology*, 29(5) (pp. 486–497).

Szabo, H. (1969) *The Kodaly Concept of Music Education*. London: Boosey and Hawkes.

Szubertowska, E. (2005) 'Education and the music culture of Polish adolescence'. *Psychology of Music*, 33(3) (pp. 317–330).

Tait, M.J. (1992) 'Teaching strategies and styles'. In R. Colwell (ed.) *Handbook of Research in Music Teaching and Learning: Music Educators National Conference*. New York: Schirmer Books (pp. 525–534).

Takeuchi, A.H. and Hulse, S.H. (1993) 'Absolute pitch'. *Psychological Bulletin*, 113 (pp. 345–361).

Tarrant, M., North, A.C. and Hargreaves, D.J. (2000) 'English and American adolescents' reasons for listening to music'. *Psychology of Music*, 28 (pp. 166–173).

Taylor, O. (1997) 'Student interpretations of teacher verbal praise in selected seventh and eighth-grade choral classes'. *Journal of Research in Music Education*, 39 (pp. 1–15).

Teachout, D. (1997) 'The relationship between personality and the teaching effectiveness of music student teachers'. Doctoral dissertation, Kent State University, Kent, Ohio. *Dissertation Abstracts International*, 58(07) (2581A).

Terwogt, M.M. and Van Grinsven, F. (1991) 'Musical expression of mood states'. *Psychology of Music*, 19 (pp. 99–109).

Tervaniemi, M. (2003) 'Musical sound processing: EEG and MEG evidence'. In I. Peretz and R.J.A. Zatorre (eds) *The Cognitive Neuroscience of Music*. Oxford: Oxford University Press (pp. 294–309).

Thaut, M.H. (2003) 'Neural basis of rhythmic timing networks in the human brain'. In G. Avanzini, C. Faienza, D. Minciacchi, L. Lopez and M. Majno (eds) *The Neurosciences and Music*. New York: New York Academy of Sciences (pp. 364–373).

Thayer, R.E. (1996) *The Origins of Everyday Moods*. New York: Oxford University Press.

Thompson, W.F. (1984) 'The use of rules for expression in the performance of melodies'. *Psychology of Music*, 17(1) (pp. 63–82).

Thomson, M. (1993) 'Teaching the dyslexic child: some evaluation studies'. In G. Hales (ed.) *Meeting Points in Dyslexia: Proceedings of the 1st International Conference of the British Dyslexia Association*.

Thorpe, L.A. and Trehub, S.E. (1989) 'Duration illusion and auditory grouping in infancy'. *Developmental Psychology*, 25 (pp. 122–127).

Thorpe, L.A., Trehub, S.E., Morrongiello, B.A. and Bull, D. (1988) 'Perceptual grouping by infants and pre-school children'. *Developmental Psychology*, 24 (pp. 484–491).

Thurman, L. and Welch, G.F. (2000) *Bodymind and Voice: Foundations of voice education.* (2nd edition) Iowa City: National Center for Voice and Speech.

Tillman, B., Bigand, E. and Pineau, M. (1998a) 'Effects of global and local contexts on harmonic expectancy'. *Music Perception,* 16(1) (pp. 99–117).

Tillman, B., Bigand, E. and Madurell, F. (1998b) 'Influence of global and local structures on the solution of musical puzzles'. *Psychological Research,* 61 (pp. 157–174).

Tillman, B., Bharucha, J.J. and Bigand, E. (2000) 'Implicit learning of tonality: a self-organising approach'. *Psychological Review,* 107(4) (pp. 885–913).

Tobacyk, J.J. and Downs, A. (1986) 'Personal construct threat and irrational beliefs as cognitive predictors of increases in musical anxiety'. *Journal of Personality and Social Psychology,* 51 (pp. 779–782).

Trainor, L.J. (1996) 'Infant preferences for infant-directed versus non-infant-directed playsongs and lullabies'. *Infant Behavior and Development,* 19 (pp. 83–92).

Trainor, L.J. and Heinmiller, B.M. (1998) 'The development of evaluative responses to music: infants prefer to listen to consonance over dissonance'. *Infant Behavior and Development,* 21(1) (pp. 77–88).

Trainor, L.J. and Schmidt, L.A. (2003) 'Processing emotions in music'. In I. Peretz and R.J.A. Zatorre (eds) *The Cognitive Neuroscience of Music.* Oxford: Oxford University Press (pp. 311–324).

Trainor, L.J. and Trehub, S.E. (1992) 'A comparison of infants' and adults' sensitivity to Western musical structure'. *Journal of Experimental Psychology: Human perception and performance,* 18 (pp. 394–402).

Trainor, L.J., Clark, E.D., Huntley, A. and Adams, B. (1997) 'The acoustic basis of preferences for infant-directed singing'. *Infant Behavior and Development,* 20 (pp. 383–396).

Tramo, M.J. and Gazzanigga, M. (1989) 'Discrimination and recognition of complex tonal spectra by the cerebral hemispheres: differential lateralization of acoustic-discriminative and semantic associative functions in auditory pattern perception'. *Soc. Neuroscience,* 15 (pp. 421–422).

Tramo, M.J., Cariani, P.A., Delgutte, B. and Braida, L.D. (2003) 'Neurobiology of harmony perception'. In I. Peretz and R.J.A. Zatorre (eds) *The Cognitive Neuroscience of Music.* Oxford: Oxford University Press (pp. 127–151).

Trehub, S.E. (1990) 'The perception of musical patterns by human infants: the provision of similar patterns by their parents'. In M.A. Berkley and

W.C. Stebbins (eds) *Comparative Perception: Vol 1. Basic Mechanisms.* New York: Wiley (pp. 429–459).

Trehub, S.E. (2003) 'Musical predispositions in infancy: an update'. In I. Peretz and R.J.A. Zatorre (eds) *The Cognitive Neuroscience of Music.* Oxford: Oxford University Press (pp. 3–20).

Trehub, S.E. and Henderson, J. (1994) 'Caregivers songs and their effect on infant listeners'. In I. Deliege (ed.) *Proceedings of the 3rd International Conference on Music Perception and Cognition.* Liege: Belgium European Society for the Cognitive Sciences of Music (pp. 47–48).

Trehub, S.E. and Nakata, T. (2002) 'Emotion and music in infancy'. *Musicae Scientiae*, Special Issue (pp. 37–61).

Trehub, S.E. and Schellenberg, E.G. (1995) 'Music: its relevance to infants'. *Annals of Child Development*, 11 (pp. 1–24).

Trehub, S.E. and Thorpe, L.A. (1989) 'Infants' perceptions of rhythm. Categorisation of auditory sequences by temporal structure'. *Canadian Journal of Psychology*, 43 (pp. 217–229).

Trehub, S.E. and Trainor, L.J. (1990) 'Rules for listening in infancy'. In J. Enns (ed.) *The Development of Attention: Research and theory.* Amsterdam: Elsevier (pp. 87–119).

Trehub, S.E. and Trainor, L.J. (1998) 'Singing to infants: lullabies and play songs'. *Advances in Infancy Research*, 12 (pp. 43–77).

Trehub, S.E., Bull, D. and Thorpe, L.A. (1984) 'Infants' perceptions of melodies: the role of melodic contour'. *Child Development*, 55(3) (pp. 821–830).

Trehub, S.E., Thorpe, L.A. and Morrongiello, B.A. (1985) 'Infants' perceptions of melodies: changes in a single tone'. *Infant Behavior and Development*, 8 (pp. 213–223).

Trehub, S.E., Thorpe, L.A. and Morrongiello, B.A. (1987) 'Organizational processes in infants' perception of auditory patterns'. *Child Development*, 58 (pp. 741–749).

Trehub, S.E., Thorpe, L.A. and Trainor, L.J. (1990) 'Infants' perceptions of good and bad melodies'. *Psychomusicology*, 9 (pp. 5–15).

Trehub, S.E., Unyk, A.M. and Trainor, L.J. (1993a) 'Adults identify infant-directed music across cultures'. *Infant Behavior and Development*, 16 (pp. 193–211).

Trehub, S.E., Unyk, A.M. and Trainor, L.J. (1993b) 'Maternal singing in cross-cultural perspective'. *Infant Behavior and Development*, 16 (pp. 285–295).

Trehub, S.E., Unyk, A.M., Kamenetsky, S.B., Hill, D.S., Trainor, L.J., Henderson, J.L. and Saraza, M. (1997a) 'Mothers' and fathers' singing to infants'. *Developmental Psychology*, 33 (pp. 500–507).

Trehub, S.E., Schellenberg, E.G. and Hill, D. (1997b) 'The origins of music perception and cognition: a developmental perspective'. In I. Deliege and J. Sloboda (eds) *Perception and Cognition of Music*. Hove: Psychology Press (pp. 103–128).

Trehub, S.E., Hill, D.S. and Kamenetsky, S.B. (1997c) 'Parents' sung performances for infants'. *Canadian Journal of Experimental Psychology*, 51 (pp. 385–396).

Trehub, S.E., Schellenberg, E.G. and Kamenetsky, S.B. (1999) 'Infants' and adults' perception of scale structure'. *Journal of Experimental Psychology*, 25(4) (pp. 965–975).

Trevarthen, C. (1999) 'Musicality and the intrinsic motive pulse: evidence from human psychobiology and infant communication'. *Musicae Scientiae*, Special Issue (1999–2000) (pp. 155–215).

Tseng, S. (1996) Solo accompaniments in instrumental music education: the impact of the computer-controlled Vivance on flute student practice. Unpublished doctoral dissertation, University of Illinois at Urbana-Champaign.

Tubbs, S.L. (1984) *A Systems Approach to Small Group Interaction*. New York: Random House.

Tucker, W.H., Bates, R.H.T., Frykberg, S.D., Howarth, R.J., Kennedy, W.K., Lamb, M.R. and Vaughan, R.G. (1977) 'An interactive aid for musicians'. *International Journal of Man–Machine Studies*, 9 (pp. 653–651).

Turk, I. (1997) (ed.) *Mousterian 'Bone Flute' and other Finds from Divje Babe I Cave Site in Slovenia*. Ljubljana: Zalozba ZRC.

Turner, M.L., Fernandez, J.E. and Nelson, K. (1996) 'The effect of music amplitude on the reaction to unexpected visual events'. *Journal of General Psychology*, 123(1) (pp. 51–62).

Unyk, A.M., Trehub, S.E., Trainor, L.J. and Schellenberg, E.G. (1992) 'Lullabies and simplicity: a cross cultural perspective'. *Psychology of Music*, 20 (pp. 15–28).

Vacher, P. (1992) An investigation into piano practising techniques. Unpublished MA. dissertation. University of Reading.

Vanderark, S.D., Newman, I. and Bell, S. (1983) 'The effects of music participation on quality of life in the elderly'. *Music Therapy*, 3 (pp. 71–81).

Vanderark, S.D. and Ely, D. (1993) 'Cortisol, biochemical and galvanic skin responses to music stimuli of different preference values by college students in biology and music'. *Perceptual and Motor Skills*, 77 (pp. 227–234).

Van Ernst, B. (1993) 'A study of the learning and teaching processes of non-naïve music students engaged in composition'. *Research Studies in Music Education*, 1 (December) (pp. 22–39).

Van Kemanade, J.F., Van Son, M.J. and Van Heesch, N.C. (1995) 'Performance anxiety among professional musicians in a symphonic orchestra: a self-report study'. *Psychological Reports*, 77 (pp. 555–562).

Vaughan, M.M. (1977) 'Measuring creativity: its cultivation and measurement'. *Bulletin of the Council for Research in Music Education*, 50 (pp. 72–77).

Venn, M. (1990) An investigation of the applicability of recent advances in computer technology to the development of a computer-based, random access audio test of common criterion-referenced objectives in elementary music. Unpublished doctoral dissertation, University of Illinois at Urbana-Champaign.

Versterlund, L. (2001) '*Strovtag I komponerandets landskap. Tre studier av komponerande med hjalp av dator och musikteknolog*' (*Excursions in the Landscape of Composing*). Lulea University of Technology, School of Music in Pitea.

Vispoel, W.P. (1993) 'The development and evaluation of a computerized adaptive test of tonal memory'. *Journal of Research in Music Education*, 41 (pp. 111–136).

Vispoel, W.P. and Austin, J.R. (1993) 'Constructive response to failure in music: the role of attribution feedback and classroom goal structure'. *British Journal of Educational Psychology*, 63 (pp. 110–129).

Vispoel, W.P. and Austin, J.R. (1998) 'How American adolescents interpret success and failure in classroom music: relationships among attributional beliefs, self-concept and achievement'. *Psychology of Music*, 26(1) (pp. 26–45).

Vispoel, W.P. and Coffman, D.D. (1992) 'Computerized-adaptive and self-adapted tests of music listening skills: psychometric features and motivational benefits'. *Applied Measurement in Education*, 7 (pp. 25–51).

Wagner, C. (1988) 'The pianist's hand: anthropometry and biomechanics'. *Ergonomics*, 31 (pp. 97–131).

Wagner, M.J. (1975) 'The effect of a practice report on practice time and musical performance'. In C.K. Madsen, R.D. Greer and C.H. Madsen, Jr (eds) *Research in Music Behaviour*. New York: Teachers College Press (pp. 125–130).

Wagner, M.J. and Strul, E.P. (1979) 'Comparisons of beginning versus experienced elementary music educators in the use of teaching time'. *Journal of Research in Music Education*, 27 (pp. 113–125).

Wallas, G. (1926) *The Art of Thought*. London: Watts.

Wallin, N.L., Merker, B. and Brown, S. (eds) (2000) *The Origins of Music*. Cambridge, MA: The MIT Press.

Wapnik, J., Gilsig, M. and Hummel, T. (1982) 'Relative effects of psychomotor practice, mental rehearsal and guided mental rehearsal on performance of undergraduate brass and piano music majors'. Paper presented at the meeting of the Music Educators National Conference, San Antonio, Texas.

Ward, W.D. (1999) 'Absolute pitch'. In D. Deutsch (ed.) *The Psychology of Music*. (2nd edition) London: Academic Press (pp. 265–298).

Ward, W.D. and Burns, E.M. (1982) 'Absolute pitch'. In D. Deutsch (ed.) *The Psychology of Music*. (2nd edition) London: Academic Press (pp. 431–451).

Waters, A.J., Underwood, G. and Findlay, J.M. (1997) 'Studying expertise in music reading: use of a pattern-matching paradigm'. *Perception and Psychophysics*, 59 (pp. 477–488).

Watkins, J.G. and Farnum, S.E. (1954) *The Watkins-Farnum Performance Scale*. Winnona, MN: Hal Leonard Music.

Weaver, H. (1943) 'A study of visual processes in reading differently constructed musical selections'. *Psychological Monographs*, 55 (pp. 1–30).

Weber, M. (1958) *The Rational and Social Foundations of Music* (D. Martindale, J. Riedel and G. Neuwirth, trans. and ed.) Southern Illinois University Press.

Webster, P.R. (1988) 'New perspectives on music aptitude and achievement'. *Psychomusicology*, 7(2) (pp. 177–194).

Webster, P.R. (1991) 'Creativity as creative thinking'. In D. Hamann (ed.) *Creativity in the Classroom: The best of ME*. Reston, VA (pp. 25–34).

Webster, P.R. and Hickey, M. (1995) 'Rating scales and their use in assessing children's composition'. *The Quarterly Journal of Music Teaching and Learning*, 6(4) (pp. 28–44).

Weerts, R. (1992) 'Research on the teaching of instrumental music'. In R. Colwell (ed.) *Handbook of Research on Music Teaching and Learning: Music Educators National Conference*. New York: Schirmer Books (pp. 577–583).

Weiner, B. (1986) *An Attributional Theory of Motivation and Emotion*. New York: Springer-Verlag.

Weiser, H.G. (2003) 'Lessons from brain diseases and some reflections on the "emotional" brain'. In G. Avanzini, C. Faienza, D. Minciacchi, L. Lopez and M. Majno (eds) *The Neurosciences and Music*. New York: New York Academy of Sciences (pp. 76–94).

Welch, G.F. (1985a) 'A schema theory of how children learn to sing in tune'. *Psychology of Music*, 13 (pp. 3–18).

Welch, G.F. (1985b) 'Variability of practice and knowledge of results as factors in learning to sing in tune'. *Bulletin of the Council for Research in Music Education*, 85 (pp. 238–247).

Welch, G.F. (1988) 'Observations on the incidence of absolute pitch in the early blind'. *Psychology of Music*, 16(1) (pp. 77–80).

Welch, G.F. (2000) 'Voice management'. In A. Thody, B. Gray, D. Bowden and G.F. Welch (eds) *The Teacher's Survival Guide*. London: Continuum (pp. 45–60).

Welch, G.F. and McCurtain, F. (1986) 'The use of an objective measure in teaching singing: a case study with controls of counter tenor voice trauma and rehabilitation'. *International Society for Music Education. 1986 Yearbook*, 13 (pp. 192–199).

Welch, G.F., Howard, D.M. and Rush, C. (1989) 'Real-time visual feedback in the development of vocal pitch accuracy in singing'. *Psychology of Music*, 17(2) (pp. 146–157).

Wentworth, R. (1991) 'The effects of music and distracting noise on the productivity of workers with mental retardation'. *Journal of Music Therapy*, 28(1) (pp. 40–47).

Wermouth, R.F. (1971) Relationship of musical aptitude to family and student activity in music, student interest in music, socioeconomic status, and intelligence among Caucasian and Negro middle school students. Unpublished doctoral dissertation, Ohio State University, Columbus.

Werner, D. (1984) *Amazon Journey: An anthropologist's year among Brazil's Mekranoti Indians*. New York: Simon and Schuster.

Wesner, R.B., Noyes, R. and Davis, T.L (1990) 'The occurrence of performance anxiety among musicians'. *Journal of Affective Disorders*, 18 (pp. 177–185).

Wessinger, C.M., Van Meter, J., Tian, B., Van Lare, J., Pekar, J. and Rauschecker, J.P. (2001) 'Hierarchical organisation of human auditory cortex revealed by functional magnetic resonance imaging'. *Journal of Cognitive Neuroscience*, 13 (pp. 1–7).

Whitaker, N.L. (1996) 'A theoretical model of the problem solving and decision making of performers, arrangers, conductors and composers'. *Bulletin of the Council for Research in Music Education*, 128 (pp. 1–14).

White, D.J., Dale, P.S. and Carlsen, J.C. (1990) 'Discrimination and categorisation of pitch direction by young children'. *Psychomusicology*, 9(1) (pp. 39–58).

White, J. (1992) 'Music therapy: an intervention to reduce anxiety in the myocardial infarction patient'. *Clinical Nurse Special*, 6(2) (pp. 58–63).

Wicinski, A.A. (1950) 'Psichologiceskii analiz processa raboty pianista-ispolnitiela and muzykalnym proizviedieniem' ('Psychological analysis of piano performer's process of work on musical composition'), *Izviestia Akademii Piedagogiceskich Nauk Vyp*, 25 (pp. 171–215).

Wigram, T. (1995) 'A model assessment and differential diagnosis of handicap in children through the medium of music therapy'. In T. Wigram and B. Saperston (eds) *The Art and Science of Music Therapy: A handbook*. Langhorne, PA: Harwood Academic Publishers/ Gordon and Breach Science Publishers.

Wilder, J.F. and Plutchik, R. (1982) 'Preparing the professional: building prevention into training'. In W.S. Pain (ed.) *Job Stress and Burnout: Research theory and intervention perspective*. Beverly Hills, CA: Sage Publications (pp. 113–132).

Williamon, A. (1999) 'The value of performing from memory'. *Psychology of Music*, 27 (pp. 84–95).

Williamon, A. (ed.) (2004) *Musical Excellence: Strategies and techniques to enhance performance*. Oxford: Oxford University Press.

Williamon, A. and Davidson, J.W. (2002) 'Exploring co-performer communication'. *Musicae Scientiae*, 6 (pp. 53–72).

Williamon, A. and Valentine, E. (2000) 'Quantity and quality of musical practice as predictors of performance quality'. *British Journal of Psychology*, 91 (pp. 353–376).

Williamon, A. and Valentine, E. (2002) 'The role of retrieval structures in memorising music'. *Cognitive Psychology*, 44 (pp. 1–32).

Williamon, A, Valentine, E. and Valentine, J. (2002) 'Shifting the focus of attention between levels of musical structure'. *European Journal of Cognitive Psychology*, 14 (pp. 493–520).

Williamson, S.C. (1964) 'The effect of special instruction on speed, transfer and retention in memorizing songs'. Doctoral dissertation, University of Kansas, Lawrence.

Wilson, J. (1971) 'The effects of group improvisation on the musical growth of selected high school instrumentalists'. Doctoral dissertation,

New York University. *Dissertation Abstracts International*, 31(7) (3589A).

Wilson, J. (1982) 'An electronic instrument for conditioning the singing formant'. *Journal of Research in Singing*, 5 (pp. 18–32).

Wing, H.D. (1981) *Standardised Tests of Musical Intelligence*. Windsor, England: National Foundation for Educational Research.

Winold, H., Thelen, E. and Ulrich, B.D. (1994) 'Coordination and control in the bow arm movements of highly skilled cellists'. *Ecological Psychology*, 6(1) (pp. 1–31).

Winter, M.J., Paskin, S. and Baker, T. (1994) 'Music reduces stress and anxiety of patients in the surgical holding area'. *Journal of Post Anaesthesia Nursing*, 9(6) (pp. 340–343).

Wise, G.W., Hartmann, D.J., Fisher, B.J. (1992) 'Exploration of the relationship between choral singing and successful aging'. *Psychological Reports*, 70 (pp. 1175–1183).

Witt, A.C. (1986) 'Use of class time and student attentiveness in secondary instrumental music rehearsals'. *Journal of Research in Music Education*, 34 (pp. 34–42).

Wolfe, D.E. (1987) 'The use of behavioural contracts in music instruction'. In C.K. Madsen and C.A. Prickett (eds) *Applications of Research in Music Behaviour*. Tuscaloosa, AL: University of Alabama Press.

Wolfe, M.L. (1989) 'Correlates of adaptive and maladaptive musical performance anxiety'. *Medical Problems of Performing Artists*, 4(1) (pp. 49–56).

Wood, D.J., Bruner, J.S. and Ross, G. (1976) 'The role of tutoring in problem solving'. *Journal of Child Psychology and Psychiatry*, 17 (pp. 89–100).

Woodward, S.C. (1992) The transmission of music into the human uterus and the response of music of the human fetus and neonate. Unpublished PhD thesis, South Africa, University of Cape Town.

Wragg, D. (1974) 'An investigation into some factors affecting the carry-over of music interest and involvement during the transition period between primary and secondary education'. *Psychology of Music*, 2 (pp. 13–24).

Yarborough, C. (1975) 'Effect of magnitude of conductor behaviour on students in selected mixed choruses'. *Journal of Research in Music Education*, 23 (pp. 134–146).

Yarborough, C. (1987) 'The relationship of behavioural self-assessment to the achievement of basic conducting skills'. *Journal of Research in Music Education*, 35(3) (pp. 183–189).

Yarborough, C. and Price, H.E. (1989) 'Sequential patterns of instruction in music'. *Journal of Research in Music Education*, 37 (pp. 179–187).

Yarborough, C., Wapnick, J. and Kelly, R. (1979) 'The effect of videotape feedback on performance, verbalisation and attitude of beginning conductors'. *Journal of Research in Music Education*, 27(2) (pp. 103–112).

Young, L. and Nettelbeck, T. (1995) 'The abilities of a musical savant and his family'. *Journal of Autism and Developmental Disorders*, 25(3) (pp. 231–247).

Young, V.M. and Coleman, A.M. (1979) 'Some psychological processes in string quartets'. *Psychology of Music*, 7 (pp. 12–16).

Young, W.T. (1971) 'The role of musical aptitude, intelligence and academic achievement in predicting the musical attainment of elementary instrumental music students'. *Journal of Research in Music Education*, 14 (pp. 385–398).

Younker, B.A. and Smith, W.H. (1996) 'Comparing and modelling musical thought processes of expert and novice composers'. *Bulletin of the Council for Research in Music Education*, 128 (pp. 25–35).

Zajonc, R.B. (1968) 'Attitudinal effects of mere exposure'. *Journal of Personality and Social Psychology*, 9(2) (pp. 1–21).

Zatorre, R.J.A. (2003) 'Neural specializations for tonal processing'. In I. Peretz and R.J.A. Zatorre (eds) *The Cognitive Neuroscience of Music*. Oxford: Oxford University Press (pp. 231–246).

Zatorre, R.J.A. and Beckett, C. (1989) 'Multiple coding strategies in the retention of musical tones by possessors or absolute pitch'. *Memory and Cognition*, 17(5) (pp. 582–589).

Zatorre, R.J.A., Evans, C., Meyer, E. *et al.* (1992) 'Lateralization of phonetic and speech discrimination in speech processing'. *Science*, 256 (pp. 846–849).

Zatorre, R.J.A., Halpern, D.W., Perry, D.W. *et al.* (1996) 'Hearing in the mind's ear: a PET investigation of musical imagery and perception'. *Journal of Cognitive Neuroscience*, 8 (pp. 29–46).

Zatorre, R.J.A., Perry, D.W. and Beckett, C.A. (1998) 'Functional anatomy of musical processing in listeners with absolute pitch and relative pitch'. *Proceedings of the National Academy of the Sciences*, 95 (pp. 3172–3177).

Zdzinski, S.F. (1991) 'Relationships among parental involvement, music aptitude, and musical achievement of instrumental music students'. *Journal of Research in Music Education*, 40(2) (pp. 114–125).

Zentner, M.R. and Kagan, J. (1998) 'Infants' perceptions of consonance and dissonance in music'. *Infant Behavior and Development*, 21(3) (pp. 483–492).

Zhenxiong, G., Quingyi, Z. and Yuzhen, J. (1995) 'On the musical instruments of Chinese nationalities'. *Proceedings of the International Symposiun on Musical Acoustics, Le Normont, Dourdan, France*. Paris: IRCAM, Centres Georges Pompidou (pp. 546–550).

Zillman, D. and Gan, S. (1997) 'Musical taste in adolescence'. In D.J. Hargreaves and A.C. North (eds) *The Social Psychology of Music*. Oxford: Oxford University Press (pp. 161–187).

Zimny, G.H. and Weidenfeller, E.W. (1962) 'Effects of music upon GSR of children'. *Child Development*, 33 (pp. 891–896).

Zulauf, M. (1993) 'Three year experiment in extended music teaching in Switzerland: the different effects observed in a group of French speaking pupils'. *Bulletin of the Council for Research in Music Education*, 119, Winter (pp. 111–121).

Zurcher, W.Z. (1972) The effects of model-supportive practice on beginning brass instrumentalists. Unpublished EdD dissertation, Teachers College, Columbia University.

Zurcher, W.Z. (1975) 'The effect of model-supportive practice on beginning brass instrumentalists'. In C.K. Madsen, R.D. Greer and C.H. Madsen, Jr (eds) *Research in Music Behaviour*. New York: Teachers College Press.

Index

Note: page number in *italics* refer to figures or tables

absolute pitch
19–20, 35, 36–9,
42–3, 59
achievement 110,
111–12, 119–21, 145
adolescence: conducting
skills 119; family factors
111; identity
184–5; listening to
music 67, 179–80, 181;
moods 63–4, 181,
184–5; peer group 147
adult music making 185–8
advertising 192
affect 151–3
age factors 17, 26,
37–8, 48–9, 186–7
Alzheimer's disease 190–1
American Medical
Association 179
anxiety 63, 102–5, 107–8,
151–3, 189–90
appraisal 65; *see also*
evaluation
arousal 27, 61, 63, 102–4,
108
assessment 155, 156–7,
162–3; communication
161–2; composition
156–7; computers 158;
expectations 161;
improvisation
157–8; jazz 158;
musical ability 91;
performance 156,
159–61
atonal music 34, 59
audiation 46, 58, 68,
79–80
aural schemata 127

aural skills 18–19, 46, *50*
aural tests 44
autonomic nervous system
24–5, 102–3

backwash 155
banjo players 87
bassoon players
129–30
biochemical changes 190
biofeedback 129
blind people 37
brain damaged people
12–13
brain functions 17–23
brain research 15, 25–7
brain structures 10–11, 23,
52; amygdala 24,
25; anterior cingulated
cortex 22; auditory
cortex 13–14, 18–19;
cerebellum 18, 22;
cerebral cortex 17;
corpus callosum 18;
hemispheric lateralisa-
tion 10–11, 14–15, 20;
Heschl's gyrus 13;
hypothalamus 24;
neuronal networks 23;
planum temporale 19;
temporal gyrus 20;
thalamus 24

ceremonies 4, 7
chamber music groups
171, 188
children: composition
74–5, 157; creativity 74;
emotional and beha-
vioural difficulties 68;

improvisation 36, 81–2;
musical impact 181–2;
rhythm
33–4; *see also* infants
Chinese study 110–11
classroom observations
81–2, 166–71
cognition 4, 64, 77, 143,
144, 155
cognitive behavioural
therapy 104, 107
cognitive skills *50*
commitment 49, 83, 146–7
communication 3, 6–7;
assessment 161–2;
musical ability 48;
performance 101–2,
163; types of 170;
verbal/musical 87–8
competence 76–7, 145
composers 77, 83–4, 174
composition 70–5,
88–9; assessment
156–7; children
74–5, 157; commitment
83; group 87–8;
notation 77–8; teaching
of 172–3
computers 158, 173
conducting skills 119
conductors 19, 170–1
confidence 86, 149–50
conscious cognitive
strategies 133
coping strategies 107–8
creativity 46, 70, 72–4;
children 74; composi-
tion 74–5; environment
85–8; individuals 83–4;
music education 89;

problem solving 85–6;
teaching 172
criterion-referenced tests
155–6
cultural factors:
atonal music 34;
improvisation 82;
music making 185;
musical knowledge 28;
neurological responses
16; tonal imagery 59;
tonal scales 31–2;
values 147

deaf people 188
developmental handicaps
189
drop-outs 92–3, 121, 149
drummers 19
dyslexia 189

emerging systems
theory 73
emotion 6–7, 23–7, 39–40,
61, 63, 69, 152–3
emotional and beha-
vioural difficulties,
children with 68
endorphins 190
environmental factors
52–3, 66–7, 85–8,
109–13, 137–8
evaluation 65, 86, 171
evolutionary adaptation
2–5
expectancy-value models
144–5
expectations 55, 110,
149–50, 161
expertise 92, 118–19
experts: judgement 160–1;
metacognition 126–7,
134; practice 122–3,
125–7; *see also*
musicians, professional

exposure to music 54, 59
expressivity 101–2, 125,
161
eye–hand span 98

failure 145, 150, 152–3
family factors 42,
109–13, 115, 136–7,
147–8
feedback 79; effective use
127–8; motivation
143–4; musical
instrument playing 93,
116; musicians 129–30;
self-assessment 86
focal hand dystonia 21–2
foetus 181
friendships 82–3, 87–8
functions of music 5–8

gender stereotypes
91–2
genetic inheritance 20,
36–7, 47, 51–3
Gestalt theory 73, 74
graded examinations 159
group tuition 168
group work 3, 4, 6–7;
benefits 86–8; composi-
tion 87–8; improvisa-
tion 82; musical
instrument playing 116;
rehearsal 127, 139;
singing 116, 186–7
guitar playing 132–3

harmony 14, 34
health benefits 187, 189–90
hearing 57

identity 145–9, 180, 184–5
Igbo of Nigeria 1
improvisation 48,
71–2, 88–9; assessment
157–8; benefits 82–3;

children 36, 81–2;
classroom 81–2;
consensual technique
156–7; creativity 70;
culture 82; friendships
82–3; jazz 80–1, 174;
professional
musicians 78–82;
rhythm 81–2;
songs 76
individuals 5–6, 83–4
industrial use of music
191–2
infants 181; absolute pitch
35; babbling 35–6;
harmony 34; melody
31–2; mother's voice
28, 29; music/
emotion 39–40, 43;
musical memory 34–5;
pitch 31–2; rhythm
33–4; tempo 35;
timbre 34, 35; tonality
32–3
information processing
theory 73
intellectual development
162–3
intelligence 44, 49,
50–1, 150
interpretation 46, 70,
101–2, 124–5, 162–3
interval recognition 59
intonation 128–9, 171

jazz 80–1, 87, 89, 148, 158,
174

keyboard programmes
173
knowledge 78, 89,
94–5, 165; *see also*
musical knowledge
Kodaly music teaching
method 182

labelling 55, 148, 153
learning: age factors 26,
37; assessment 155;
brain function 17–23;
metacognition 95, 134;
performance 150;
practice 140;
reading music 98–9;
technology 173–4;
transfer of 131–2; *see
also* musical instrument
playing
learning, types: associative
93; by ear 57–8; infor-
mal 94; self-regulated
118; supported 169–70
learning biographies 23
learning difficulties 188,
189
learning outcomes 166–7
learning skills *51,* 113,
177–8
listening skills 57–60,
67–9, 87
listening to music 67,
179–80, 181, 190
lullabies 28, 29, 39

magnetic resonance
imaging 16
major/minor keys 40, 63
marching-bands 160
marginalised people 186–7
Mekranoti Indians 185
melody 13–14, 31–2, 35
memory 95, 96–7, 133; *see
also* musical memory
mental health problems
71–2
metacognition 95, 119,
126–7, 134, 140
metre 14–15
modelling 168–9
moods 27, 61, 63–4, 69,
180, 181, 184–5

mother–child relationship
3, 28, 29
motivation 49, 54, 94;
family background
147–8; feedback 143–4;
individual/
environmental
factors 142, *143,* 144;
model of
143–4; music education
153; music making
185–6; musical instru-
ment playing 92, 115;
needs 142, 144; person-
ality 84; practice 136–7;
self-esteem 151;
self-regulation 135–6
motivation, types: extrinsic 149; internal 153;
intrinsic 85–6, 88, 149;
sensual-aesthetic 145
motor skills 3, 21–2, 46
music 1, 2; benefits 192–3;
extra-curricular 113;
teaching practices
116–17; ubiquity 179,
192–3
music education 8–10,
40–3, 89, 140, 153
music making 10, 52, 88,
148, 185–8
music teachers: effectiveness 147; and families
112–13, *114;* modelling
168–9; on-task beha-
viour 167, 177; person-
ality factors 175–6;
philosophies 166;
pupils 176–7; specialist/
non-specialist 157;
verbal/nonverbal
behaviour 170–1
music teaching 165, 168;
absolute pitch 42–3;
assessment 161, 163;

brain structures 52;
composition 172–3;
creativity 172;
effectiveness 165,
166–71, 177–8; pupil
activity 167–8;
software 174
music therapy 188–9,
190–1
musical ability: assessment
91; challenged 47–8;
genetic inheritance
51–2; music making 52;
nature of 45–6; testing
44–5, 54–6
musical imagery 22, 26–7
musical instrument play-
ing 2, 91–4; age factors
17, 48–9, 92; benefits
183–4; chamber music
groups 171; choosing
91–2, 110, 115; family
factors 115; feedback
93, 116; gender stereo-
types 91–2; from mem-
ory 96–7; motivation
115; personal satisfac-
tion 153; pupil–teacher
relationship 176–7;
recognising sounds 27;
self-esteem 183;
technological help
174–5; *see also* group
work
musical knowledge 28,
41–2
musical memory 16, 34–5,
48, 94–5
musical skills 12–13, 173,
193
musicality 45–6
musicians: appraisal 65;
brain functions 17–22;
classical/jazz 80–1;
developmental stages

99–100; feedback
129–30; listening to
music 59–60; personality
84; professional
78–82, 97, 122–3, 134;
skills required 18–19,
21–2, 46, 49, *50*
Muzak 191–2

neural systems 10–11,
21–3
neurological responses
16, 26
neurotransmitters 25
non-musicians 17–22,
59–60
notation 77–8, 97

off-task behaviour 167
on-task behaviour 167,
177
overpractising 21–2, 26

pain reduction 190
parents 109–13; *see also*
family background
peer group 147, 160–2
peer teaching 171
performance 6, 48, *50,*
101–2; anxiety 102–5,
107; arousal 102–4, 108;
assessment 156, 159–61;
autonomic nervous
system 102–3; commu-
nication 101–2, 163;
expert/novice 75–7;
learning 150; memory
96–7; multi-dimen-
sional models 105, *106*;
practice 120–1; prep-
aration for 107–8
performance scales 160
personal satisfaction 153
personality 84, 124–5, 143,
144, 146–7, 175–6

physiological responses
5–6
piano playing 21, 120,
134–5, 187
pitch 13–14, 19–20, 31–2,
35, 174; *see also*
absolute pitch
playing by ear 48
Portuguese child study 183
practice: achievement
111–12, 119–21; brain
functions 19; environ-
ment 137–8; expertise
92, 118–19; experts
122–3, 125–7; expres-
sivity 125; family
factors 111–12, 136–7;
learning 140;
motivation 136–7;
organization 134–5;
performance 120–1;
personality 124–5;
processes 127–33;
rewards 153;
satisfaction 151; as self-
teaching 118; strategies
124; supervision
111–12; task require-
ments 133–4; teaching
about 137–8; time spent
on 47, 120, 121–2, 135
practice, types:
deliberate 118, 119;
distributed 130–1;
effective 140; formal/
informal 118; mental/
physical 132–3; model-
supported 132, 169;
part–whole 131;
variable 130–1
praise 171
prenatal experiences 28
problem solving 85–6
prodigies 53–4
production deficiency 126

psychiatric conditions 191
pulse 14–15
pupil–teacher relationship
176–7

reading music 97–9
Recording Industry Asso-
ciation of America 179
rehearsal 22, 26–7, 95,
132–3, 139
reinforcement, positive
171; *see also* feedback
responses 24–5, 60–1, 63–4
rewards 137, 153, 185
rhythm 13–15, 33–4, 48,
78, 81–2, 99
rhythm imagery 46
rock music 7–8
rote-learning 124,
185

savants 12, 27, 53–4, 58
scaffolding 169
self 146, 153, 160–1;
see also identity
self-assessment 86
self-awareness 84,
134
self-confidence 84
self-esteem 180–1; adult
music making 187–8;
affect 151–2, 153;
cognition 143, 144;
motivation 151;
musical instrument
playing 183
self-fulfilling prophecy 55
self-handicapping 151
self-reinforcement 135
sensory modalities 17
sexual selection 2, 3
sight reading 48, 99, 132
singing 185, 186–7; group
116, 186–7; improvised
71–2, 76; to infants 28,

29, 39; from memory 96–7; mother's voice 39; musical ability 45; in play 41; presentation 161; work accompaniment 191
singing in tune 128
skills: aural 18–19, 46, *50*: cognitive *50*: conducting 119; learning *51*, 113, 177–8; listening 57–60, 67–9, 87; motor 3, 21–2, 46; musical 12–13, 173, 193; supported learning 169–70; technical *50*, 130–1; time spent on practice 121–2; vocal 91, 93–4, 132; *see also* musicians
social cohesion 2, 3–4, 7–8, 139, 182–3
special educational needs, children with 27, 71–2
stage fright 104–5, 108
stress 103, 176
stress inoculation 107

string players 19, 21, 128–9
Suzuki method 58

talent 47, 109–10
TAP Pitch Master 128
task performance 133–4, 184–5
taste in music *62, 66*–7
teachers: *see* music teachers
teaching: *see* music teaching
technology 8, 88, 101, 173–5, 188
teenagers: *see* adolescents
tempo 35, 131–2
Test of Ability to Improvise 158
timbre 15, 26, 34, 35
tonal imagery 46, 59
tonal scales 31–2
tonality 32–3, 59
trance 7, 61
trial-and-error searches 73
trombonists 128
trumpet players 129

understanding 67–9
United States of America: adult music making 187–8; classroom observations 166–71; music teaching 167; performance scales 160
universality 1, 2

value components 145–9
violin players 127, 129
violists 129
vocal skills 91, 93–4, 132; *see also* singing

Western musical tradition 70–1, 100–1
Williams syndrome 38
wind players 129
woodwind players 124

Yerkes-Dodson law 103–4
youth culture 6; *see also* adolescence